Slipping on the Ice

A Collection of Stories From a Peace Corps Ukraine Volunteer

Robert Minton

D1707093

Table of Contents

*For the People of Ukraine, and For Those
Who Encouraged Me During this Process*

Foreward

Today is February 24th, 2022. It is five days after I published this novel, and less than twelve hours after Russia escalated their invasion of Ukraine by firing missiles all around the country and sending in ground forces. This is a monumental escalation, and it is a dark time in the country that I love so dearly. History is being written, and Ukraine once again finds herself being existentially threatened by an authoritarian regime. My heart is broken for Ukraine and her people.

I'm not sure if this is a good moment or the worst moment to be publishing this, but this is a story about my experience in Ukraine as a Peace Corps Volunteer from 2018 to 2020. It was a relatively peaceful time, and although Russia's war was of course raging on in the far east, for the most part this period in Ukraine's history was littered with a beautiful since of normalcy. I taught in a school. People hung out in coffee shops. For the majority of the country, war was a foreign and faraway thing, and people went about their lives.

I hope that this book will not only give you some insight into Ukrainian history and culture, but also into the beauty of the people in this country. They are kind, loving, hospitable, battle-tested, and want the same thing that you and I do: To live, work, and love in peace.

Much of the story is about my personal experience as a Peace Corps volunteer, but I hope that throughout the reading you will get a different perspective of Ukraine from what you see on the news, and that you will come to understand why I grew to love Ukraine so much over the years.

Glory to Ukraine, and glory to the heroes.

Chapter One

Arrival

We arrived at the hotel in the mid-afternoon, only a couple of hours after our third flight of the trip. It was hot, much hotter than I expected, although to be fair I didn't know what to expect. I knew that Ukraine was in Eastern Europe, and all the videos I watched over the summer portrayed Ukraine as a country covered in snow and ice, but it was August, about ninety-three degrees, and the bus had no air conditioning. It was the first of many times I realized that most expectations I had were going to be blown out of the water, no matter how much research I tried to do beforehand.

I couldn't get off of the bus soon enough. Along with the lack of air conditioning, each of us were only given half a liter of water. My bus buddy, Daniel, was kind enough to give me some of his water, but I was running on fumes after the long effort of making it to Ukraine from DC. My plan after graduation of working out and losing a ton of weight crumbled in the infant stages, and my untrained form wasn't quite ready for the arduous travel to Eastern Europe. I needed to sleep somewhere besides a chair, although the seats on the airplane were a lot more comfortable than how I imagined they'd be.

After a sweat-filled ride with seventy of my future colleagues, we finally made it to the the Irpin Conference hall, an unassuming beige building about three stories high. Trees engulfed most of our surroundings, with old Soviet cinder block buildings sandwiched in between. Too exhausted to do any more socializing with the hoard of other new volunteers, I got my bags and waited inside, where I was elated to finally feel sweet cold air blowing against my brow. Others soon packed the lobby, but I was wise enough to already have snagged a seat on the only couch available. I patiently waited for my room key as more and more of my cohort flooded the room, excited to start this new adventure but at the same time reeling too much from the jet lag to do anything other than unpack and collapse in my bed.

After getting my key and finding my roommate, a skinny blonde guy named Sam I had talked to a bit in the airport, we headed up to the second floor. With two twin beds, a TV, and a bathroom, there was nothing particularly exotic or strange about the room, although at that point I was more than happy to have some sense of normalcy. This whole experience was setting up to be as abnormal as it gets.

During my first night in the Irpin Conference Hall I wanted to take it easy. I felt like I'd have plenty of time to get to know the group over the next two years, and not wanting to feel overwhelmed with the excitement of meeting seventy of my new colleagues all at once, I stayed in my room and whipped out the Peace Corps orientation manual to see just what I was getting myself into. It was a bland twenty-five page document, littered with typical orientation stuff about Peace Corps policies, mission statements, what our training schedule would be, and other important yet extremely dull material. However, around page eleven I saw something a little strange. There were a few bolded lines, which ended up being the only bolded part of the manual, where the author explicitly stated that, "**The mission of Peace Corps Ukraine is not for Americans to spend foggy and drunken nights out on the town, partying their way through service.**"

Huh. It seemed a bit out of place, being sandwiched in between information about our living stipend and the weekend travel policy, and while I couldn't help but to laugh at the fact that one of our bosses had to explicitly tell people to not get smashed every weekend, I didn't pay too much attention to it, mainly because I wasn't planning on doing much or maybe even any partying in the Peace Corps. Thinking I had gotten all of those foggy nights out of my system in college, I joined this highly regarded and federally funded international aid organization in the name of helping others and promoting international peace. I assumed I would be living and working in a small village without the internet, I would hardly be doing any traveling, and I would be spending most of my time adapting and becoming accustomed to the language and culture. Partying at that point was the last thing on my mind, and secretly I viewed the Peace Corps as a way to avoid the not so optional happy hours and weekend festivities that I would surely be involved in with a normal nine to five job in the States.

After skimming through the last few pages, I decided it was time to start conquering jet lag. Before going to bed, I took a shower, wanting to wash off the stench of two plus days of international travel. After getting in the shower that was meant for someone five inches shorter than me, I waited for a couple seconds before water weakly came out of the shower head. It smelled like nickels, but at least it was warm. After three separate flights, hours in the airport, and that damn two hour bus ride, I had absolutely no problem with metal-ladened water. This was the Peace Corps, after all, and I couldn't be asking for too much.

I finished my shower and quickly fell asleep. A few hours later at 3:00 am, I woke up unable to move any part of my body. Right then and there I discovered one of the potential side effects of jet lag: Sleep paralysis. Sleep paralysis is when your mind is awake, but your body is completely paralyzed, and this lovely terror is how I spent part of my first night in Ukraine. After attempting to move my limbs unsuccessfully, I tried to scream. My mouth wouldn't open, and at that point not even my vocal cords had escaped the throes of paralyzation. In hindsight I was grateful that I couldn't let out a scream, because it saved me from being "that guy" in my new cohort. You know, that guy in every group who wakes up screaming as loud as he can? Above all else I was trying to avoid that, so I guess I had something to be grateful for in my state of paralysis.

Luckily this wasn't my first time around the block in the sleep paralysis neighborhood, so after I finally realized what was happening, I breathed slowly and deeply and was eventually able to wrestle back control of my motor abilities. I woke up gasping, and looked over to make sure I hadn't woken up Sam. Thankfully, at three in the morning during our first night in Ukraine, Sam hadn't been woken up by a semi-paralyzed blood curdling groan.

Not wanting to face the terror of sleep paralysis for the second time in one night, I decided to stay up the rest of the night looking at Facebook.

The next day, with bags under my eyes but an extraverted energy pulsing through me, I went down to the dining hall of the hotel and began looking for a table of friendly faces as if I were back in middle school. Luckily Peace Corps volunteers aren't exactly your typical middle school bully type, so I had no problem finding an extra seat with a few people who looked as young as I did. I mostly stayed quiet, too insecure about maybe talking too much, and began listening to some exciting stories about drunken shenanigans from the night before. I was silently taken aback and started to not so subtly judge these people, who had decided to get hammered on the first night of working for the federal government and living in a second world country. I guess that bolded part of the manual was put there for a reason.

After departing the breakfast buffet filled with boiled hot dogs, baked potatoes, hard boiled eggs and chicken noodle soup, we all met in the conference hall of the Irpin Conference Hall. There were about seventy of us teaching volunteers, which made up half of our group, Group 53. We learned that the other half - Youth Development and Community Development - had arrived the week before.

"Congratulations on making it to Ukraine," a tall woman said in the front of the room, "For all of you who have complimented my accent, I want to say thank you, although I should point out that I'm American."

Most of us laughed. It was hard to tell who was Ukrainian and who wasn't at times.

"My name is Victoria, and I'm the Director of Training for Peace Corps Ukraine. We are so happy to have all of you here, and we're so excited to get to know everyone during these next twenty-seven months. Before we get kick things off, though, Irina is going to give a brief announcement. We've gotten a lot of questions about phones and sim cards and stuff like that, so Irina is going to explain all the details."

"Ok everyone," Irina, a short gray-haired woman with deep Ukrainian accent announced, "Today you'll be receiving your sim cards. We planned on talking about this later in the day but I don't want to be answering this question any more than I already have."

By then we had all gone about twenty-four hours without data, which for a group of young millennials like us is something that most of us hadn't experienced since middle school. Withdrawals were kicking in. We were all prepared for Peace Corps, "The toughest job you'll ever love," but it looked like none of us were prepared to go without the internet for more than a day.

"You all have the same plan," Irina continued, "It will cost one hundred and ten hryven, about four dollars a month, and you will have twenty gigabytes per month."

The crowd began to murmur.

"Twenty gigabytes?" A volunteer asked from across the hall.

"Yes, twenty gigabytes."

"Twenty gigabytes total?"

"No," Irina said, wondering why people weren't understanding her, "Twenty gigabytes a month. And if you don't use all of the gigabytes in a month, they roll over into the next month. It's what you call a rollover plan. We thought that twenty gigabytes would be enough."

"Is that a lot?" I asked the guy sitting next to me, having never paid for my own phone plan before.

"That's more than you could ever possibly use in a month," he whispered back, "This would cost hundreds of dollars in America."

When I initially thought of the Peace Corps, I imagined how it probably was back in the sixties or seventies: Working in a small village, living vicariously off the land, and never seeing or talking to anyone in the outside world. Yet now we were being told that we would have twenty gigabytes a month, which would roll over to the next month if all twenty weren't used. By the end of our first year of service, many volunteers reached triple digit gigabytes on their phone plan, a far cry from Peace Corps services of the past to say the least.

So instead of living in isolation without the internet, we were being given more internet than a bunch of smartphone addicted twenty-two year olds could ever know what to do with. I again readjusted my expectations, but even with social media by my side, I was still under the impression that I'd be living in a small, quiet village for the majority of my service. The internet would probably make things a bit easier, but I still wasn't expecting any part of this to be a walk in the park.

Later on during the opening announcements, we learned that we weren't going to hear about our training sites until the end of orientation, but they did end up divulging the region we would be staying in for training: Zhytomyr, an area in central Ukraine just west of Kyiv.

"Afterwards," another one of the administrators said, "You all will be placed in sites all around the country, from the most westward regions all the way to the eastern regions of Kharkiv and Zaporyzhiya. Some new regions in the east have opened up this year, after previously being closed off due to the war."

Right, the war. Ukraine had been at war since 2014 after Russia invaded and annexed the port region of Crimea and Russian-funded forces started a war in two regions in the east. It resulted in Peace Corps Ukraine evacuating the country, and after returning a little more than a year later, PC had mostly stayed away from putting volunteers in the east. However, after some careful consideration, I arrived the same year year eastern sites would be opening up again. I personally had no desire to be in the east, seeing as my mom would freak out, but if that's where they wanted to put me, I wouldn't put up a fight. I was in Ukraine to serve without question, even if it meant living near a war zone.

With that said, we didn't need to worry about that for a while. We were months away from learning our permanent site, and first and foremost we all needed to get through orientation. I decided early on to be one of those volunteers who took orientation extremely seriously, and it wouldn't be entirely inaccurate to say that I was brown-nosing. I sat in the front, answered questions - but not too many - and tried my best to complete all the orientation activities in a timely and efficient manner. Even if I had known then that those five days of orientation, along with all other subsequent Peace Corps conferences, would have absolutely no influence on any evaluation of my service whatsoever, I probably still would have tried to suck up to the admin. At that point in my life that was just the kind of person I set out to be, and I was willing to suck up to anybody who looked older than me on the off chance that they had any sway within Peace Corps Ukraine. Unfortunately for my orientation self, Peace Corps isn't exactly the job you can breeze through by brown nosing and speaking up in meetings, although I hardly knew it at the time.

However, compared to some of the older and more jaded volunteers who had gone through some time-consuming and bureaucratic orientations earlier in life, being overly eager and brown-nosy wasn't the worst way to go about things. In fact, in a job as exotic, isolating, and difficult as the Peace Corps, that might be one of the few ways to get through some of the rougher parts of it. There's no way you can truly prepare yourself for living in a culture completely different from your own and in a country with vastly fewer resources than in the States, all while also being isolated from all other Americans and not being able to understand a word of the language.

While orientation turned out to be miles easier than any other experience over my time as a volunteer, the most difficult part was the massive FOMO that came while making friends during breakfast, lunch and dinner. During one of the lunches I once again heard about volunteers getting smashed and having a great time at a local bar. A new friend of mine, Liam, a long haired fellow who like me had also studied philosophy in college, told me that his roommate came into his room in the middle of the night blackout drunk. His roommate then got in the shower, turned it on, and fell asleep. They both woke up to a partially flooded room.

"That's like, pretty crazy, right?" Liam asked me, looking like a man who had gotten a lot of no's to that question.

"Yeah, that's not normal," I replied, trying to confirm he wasn't crazy, "Did you two get in trouble?"

"No, but I'm afraid that we will. Like, he flooded the bathroom, and maintenance had to come and fix things. I'm scared they're going to tell the admin."

"You should snitch on him," I suggested.

Liam paused, "...What? Hell no man, why would I do that?"

"I don't know. Seems like a bad guy."

"I'm not going to snitch on him."

"Ok, well, just an idea."

"Do you snitch on people?" He asked with a slightly more aggressive tone.

I forgot for a minute that snitching is frowned upon.

"What? No, I mean very rarely. Only when they deserve it. I mean that guy blacking out on the first night and destroying your room? I wouldn't snitch the first time, but I'd snitch if he did it again."

Liam didn't seem satisfied by my answer. "Yeah, well, ok man. Maybe."

While my snitching idea risked a new friendship and threatened to saddle me with the "snitch" reputation, at least that would be better than being the "screams in his sleep" guy. I stood by what I said, though. If that guy got smashed beyond comprehension the first night and put Liam at risk of getting in trouble with admin, in my eyes it didn't seem like too difficult of a decision.

I couldn't imagine why people were binge drinking during the first few days of our service. First of all, like I read in the manual, PC Ukraine had a zero tolerance alcohol policy at Peace Corps events. I later learned that the year before that policy wasn't a thing, but apparently Group 52 absolutely destroyed the hotel - much like Liam's roommate - which led to the strict drinking policy that followed our group throughout our service. If anyone got caught drinking at a PC event, we were running the risk of getting early terminated (ET'd), and I was not trying to make it all the way to Ukraine only to throw it all away for a night of blacking out.

Additionally, I couldn't think of a worse impression to make on our superiors than showing up hungover and smelling like alcohol on the second or third day of orientation. The admin had complete control over our two-year assignments, and they even warned us early on that not everyone was going to make it to the swearing in ceremony in October.

Lastly, getting belligerently drunk in Ukraine is, well, say that out loud: "Getting belligerently drunk in Ukraine." It's just a terrible idea. Blacking out in a second world country, where you don't know the language, the customs, or any of the people, seemed like a perfect way to get beaten up and to have your wallet stolen.

As someone who prides himself on risk-aversion, I wasn't going to take any chances. Not only did I not want to get beat up by big scary Ukrainian men, but also my standing would take a serious hit if I was anything less than one hundred percent enthusiastic and overbearing during those morning meetings. I ended up spending each night either in my room or playing ping pong with the more straight edge volunteers, and while the bar did seem pretty fun, I stuck to the plan, followed the manual, and focused on orientation.

It's a good thing I did, because there was quite a bit of good information during the ten hour days of presentations. We learned topics ranging from the Ukrainian education system to Ukrainian cultural norms, and presentations even went so far as to tell us how to properly decline food.

"Say no three times to extra food," one of the Ukrainian instructors told us, "In our culture, it's polite to say no the first time and then yes the second time, so if you don't want to be stuffed with dumplings and buckwheat every night, you need to say no three times."

Getting stuffed with dumplings didn't seem like the worst problem to have, but as someone who has issues saying no, it was useful info. I continued to be active and engaged throughout all of the meetings, and while the jet lag was still having a huge effect one me, I did my best to make sure that none of the instructors noticed. By the third and fourth day I felt like I had been crushing orientation, but I didn't make my grand impression until the penultimate night.

It was a Friday night, and after arriving almost a week earlier, on Saturday we would finally be learning our training sites. We had already gotten through most of orientation, and by then I was getting a little worn down by the hour and a half seminars on safety and security and how to fill out our work documentation forms. I had been a good volunteer for almost the entire time, and feeling confident and excited about the future to come, I was finally ready to kick back and meet some new people.

I remember hanging out on one of the benches outside of the hotel, when a few volunteers my age came up to me.

"Hey Bob!" Liam said, "Guys this is Bob, he's a great guy. Bob, we're going to go to a bar tonight, do you wanna come with?"

I looked up at Liam and the group, and was happy to see that his roommate wasn't there.

"Hmm," I replied, "I don't know man, it sort of feels like a bad idea."

"It's actually not too bad," Olivia, another volunteer, told me, "I thought that too at first but it's actually a pretty low-key place. The bar's just a few minutes away, and usually we are the only ones in there."

"Really?" I asked, slowly giving into the temptation. I was still weary about the opportunity, but I missed having friends.

"Yeah," Liam said, "We've gone there the past few nights. It's pretty chill, and after the whole room flooding debacle, I don't think any of us are really looking to party too hard anyway."

As much I wanted to fit into the Peace Corps mold that I had created for myself, right then and there I realized how badly I was craving something besides getting nine hours of sleep. Additionally at that point I was dealing with some pretty bad FOMO, and while I was holed up in my room, most of the other volunteers were having a good time and getting to know one another. After a week of listening to their conversations and laughter from afar, I began to wonder if I was missing out on something important.

I soon started to justify it.

A beer or two couldn't hurt. You've been pretty attentive at all of the lectures. Liam's pretty cool, and it'll probably help you to meet some new people. Why not man, you deserve it...

Wanting to take the edge off and deciding to reward myself after a long orientation and successfully getting over jet lag, I caved.

"Sure, I'm down."

"Alright, let's go!"

"Right now?"

"Yeah, we wanna get there a little early. That ok?"

I made sure I had my wallet, "Yeah, that's fine."

"Alright! First drink's on me!"

Like they said it was only a five minute walk, and before I processed my decision, the six of us had already made it to the bar. We opened the door to some wooden stairs, and walked down to find a pretty small room, with about three wooden tables across from the taps. Just like Liam promised, we were the only ones there, and my new friends greeted the lady at the bar like they had known her for ages.

"Marissa, pryvit (hello)!" Liam exclaimed, as we piled into one of the tables.

Marissa then exclaimed something back, and Liam and her began to chat in Ukrainian. Having no idea what anyone was saying, I sat down waiting to order.

"No man," Olivia said, nudging me, "You gotta go up there and order."

Oh, nice. Of course. I knew how to order at bars. At the bar, of course, not like some pampered Western prince who waits for drinks to come to him. I asked Liam what he was going to get, and he smiled and told me to watch.

"It's really cool," Liam said, "They fill it up in big water bottles!"

As the bartender began to pour, I saw a light brown and slightly dirty looking substance shoot out of the tap and into a huge plastic water bottle.

16

Unfiltered beer is pretty popular in Ukraine, and additionally it was the only beer that the pub served. I had no idea at the time what the difference was between filtered and unfiltered, but I figured I'd be finding out soon enough.

I ordered one next, saying "pivo," the Ukrainian word for beer. As she began to pour, I got a slight confidence boost for finally communicating in this mysterious Slavic language. I soon grabbed my beer filled water bottle and paid twenty seven hryven (about one dollar) and then sat down with the rest of the group.

I began by sipping slowly, as if I was getting away with some sort of highway robbery and needed to be as quiet and delicate as possible in order to not get caught. After an hour or so, I saw that I wasn't going to die or get fired on the spot, and things started to pick up.

As things began to get a little loose, I started to see that these people were more similar to me than I had previously imagined. Throughout orientation I experienced an underlying feeling of imposter syndrome because over the summer I read that the Peace Corps only had a twenty-five percent acceptance rate. With my seemingly average college resume, I almost couldn't believe it when I read my acceptance email just six months earlier. However, over the course of the night it became clear that while these people were extremely intelligent, they were extremely approachable, and we were able to kick back and unwind without too many barriers.

Feeling more open and comfortable with my new colleagues, I subsequently let my guard down. About an hour later, after finishing my second unfiltered beer, I had the bright idea of ordering vodka shots.

"We're in Ukraine," I shouted while banging my fist on the table, "Let's drink vodka!"

"Let's do it!" Liam hollered back.

I strolled up to the counter, saying "Dobry Den, Vodka?" (Hello, Vodka?)

The bartender replied by shaking her head.

"No vodka?" I asked.

"Ni," she said, which was one of the few words I actually did understand.

No vodka In Ukraine? I didn't expect to hear that.

"Visky?" She asked, pointing at the only bottle of whisky at the bar.

"Tak!" I said, reveling in the pleasure of getting through yet another conversation in Ukrainian.

She poured us six whisky shots from a Jack Daniels bottle, and soon afterwards Liam helped me bring them to the table. We toasted to the end of orientation, took the shots, and a few minutes later, my roommate Sam woke me up.

"Bob," he said, nudging me, "Get up man. We're starting in like twenty minutes."

"What?"

"The morning meeting is starting in twenty minutes."

It took me a couple seconds, but I soon regained consciousness and realized what happened.

"NO," I yelled as opened my eyes.

You blacked out. You blacked out during orientation.

I couldn't believe it. I let my guard down for *just one night* and I blacked out! I sprung out of the bed, still drunk and wearing the same clothes from the night before. A wave of anxiety hit me, as it tends to do when you have no memory of how you got home or anything you said along the way. I was lucky that I didn't have a phone plan yet, but that only made my emotional state slightly better. What the hell happened, and how did I get home?

I'd have to think about all that later. With only twenty minutes until the start of the most important day of orientation, I had to quickly pull myself together.

My first move was to do anything to alleviate the inevitable mid-day hangover that was slowly but surely on its way. I didn't have enough time for breakfast, so I found a half of a sausage I bought the day before and quickly devoured it, not considering that eating half of a sausage might be worse for my stomach than eating nothing at all.

I then scrambled to find my water bottle, which was almost empty. Great. After quickly drinking all that was left, a massive thirst came over me. I rushed to the bathroom, only to be reminded that the sink water, metals and all, is undrinkable in Ukraine. I spit out my first gulp of metal water, and asked Sam if he had any.

"Sorry man."

With an untucked collared shirt and some janky pants from the night before, I rushed to the main conference room, where they kept that precious miracle liquid. In a matter of seconds I found the treasure trove of water bottles, which was being guarded by one of the admin, who was enforcing the "one bottle a day" policy that was undoubtedly caused by PC's shoestring budget. I grabbed my government issued liter of water, doing my best to avoid any and all contact with the administrator, and ran back to my room. I chugged half of it and then rushed to the bathroom to brush my teeth, hoping to reduce the smell of beer and whisky that was bound to alert my superiors that I broke the rules the night before.

As I finished brushing I checked my laptop. It was 8:55, just minutes before the announcements were set up to start. I bypassed showering, believing that being late would look worse than showing up unshowered after a long night of drinking, and instead took the time to make sure I was presentable.

I looked in the mirror, only to realize that I wasn't wearing my glasses. I did a quick search of the room, and immediately realized that they weren't there. In the process I also discovered that my room key was missing.

"Yeah," Sam said, calmly fastening his belt, "I had to let you in last night around two in the morning. You said you had lost your keys...you doing alright man?"

"Yeah, yeah, I just, man, I really messed up."

"Haha," Sam laughed, "No shit. Good luck today - let me know if you need to get into the room or anything."

I thanked Sam and checked the time. 8:58. It was time to go.

I speed-walked as smoothly as I could, and I arrived right before things got under way. *A small victory,* I thought, during what was inevitably going to be an awful day. I decided to sit in the back, looking to breeze through those thirty or so minutes unnoticed. Afterwards I could go to my room, shower, pull myself together, and hopefully find some of my belongings.

However, I wouldn't need to spend any effort at all finding my stuff that morning. Towards the end of morning announcements, the short Ukrainian woman from the first day, Irina, began speaking.

"Hello everyone. Before we get started with the final day, we need to discuss a few quick things. First, we need to go through the lost and found. We had a few lost items that we are looking to return, and then we can get things rolling."

One of the admin handed Irina something that I couldn't see from the back row.

"First, did anyone lose a pair of glasses?"

She raised them in the air: A black pair of specs, which of course were mine. I raised my hand, and to my dismay, I was beckoned to come up and take them from Irina.

Well, like a normal person who does normal people things, I stood up and made my way to retrieve them. Because I chose to sit in the back, I had to walk all the way to the front of the room to get them from Irina. I did my best once again to avoid all eye contact, as I tried to hide my unruly and drunken disposition. Some of the gang from the night before quietly snickered, but other than that I thankfully wasn't ridiculed.

Right as I sat down, one of the admin handed Irina something else that I couldn't see.

"Okay, is anyone missing keys? These keys are for room three twenty-seven, who is staying in room three twenty-seven?"

That again was me. I raised my hand, stood back up, put my head down, and dragged myself to the front of the room. This time my friends from the night before started heckling, and even people I didn't know began laughing. I tried to focus on the bright side - my room keys and glasses had been found, and at least they weren't lurking somewhere in a Ukrainian sewer.

I took my keys from Irina, and scurried all the way back to my seat in the last row. I sat back down, took a deep breath, and focused again on the announcements. I told myself that everything was going to be fine, not to sweat it, and now I just have to - wait, where is my-

"And lastly," Irina said, taking a nice long look at the black wallet in front of her, "Someone left their wallet in one of the conference rooms last night. Whose wallet is this?"

Sure enough, that was my wallet. The entire lost and found, which I had undoubtedly catapulted out of my pockets the night before in a drunken rage/excitement, belonged to me. I knew what was to come if I claimed my wallet, and fearing the reaction of both my new colleagues and superiors, this time I didn't want to say anything. After spending four days trying to look as competent and stable as possible, I just couldn't bring myself to face the shame of walking all the way to the front once again with my head down.

Unfortunately, things didn't work out that way. Irina, being the wise older Ukrainian that she is, merely opened the wallet to find an ID.

"Is Robert Minton here?"

That's when the entire crowd of seventy volunteers erupted in laughter. I raised my hand and for a third time walked to the front of the room, pretty much admitting to my new colleagues and to my superiors that I was Dr. Blackout M.D. the night before. It didn't take a genius to put two and two together, especially by looking at my frizzled hair and wrinkled collared shirt.

I snagged my wallet from Irina and darted to the back of the room, as the shame started to cloud in my stomach. Right before I sat down, William, the Country Director, walked towards me. As if the public embarrassment wasn't enough, now the head of PC Ukraine was coming to chastise my drunken and irresponsible behavior. Expecting the worst, I waited with bated breath, which still likely had the stench of beer and whisky from the night before.

"Hey man," William said with a smile, patting me on my back, "Don't worry about it. Happens to everyone." He then put out his fist, which I bumped, and he walked away. Either William, a former Peace Corps volunteer himself, didn't figure out what was going on, or he was super chill about the whole situation and gave me a break. I didn't put too much thought into it: I was just glad I wasn't getting fired.

While I was relieved to not be on the Country Director's naughty list, I was still reeling. Before the announcements ended, I left the meeting room and headed for the hallway. I took a left, which led me to a dead end with a window. I pushed it wide open, began to breathe deeply, and took a good look at the view from the third floor of the Conference Hall, which mostly consisted of rugged and chipped cinder block buildings with wet clothes hanging off the balconies.

"You're going to be ok," I said to myself, "You're going to be ok. You can do this. That's over. Take a deep breath. You can do this."

After the pep talk, I decided to forgo the final part of announcements. I used my newfound keys to get in my room, wiped the smudges off my glasses, and started up the shower, hoping to put my first big screw-up behind me forever.

Chapter Two

Hryshkivtsi

The next day, less than a week after arriving in Ukraine, we all packed our bags and checked out of our mostly in-tact hotel rooms, ready to finally start our journey with the Peace Corps. The week in Irpin had been pretty intensive, but we all knew that it was nothing compared to what our experience was actually going to entail. We didn't know exactly what was waiting for us, but I think most of us had enough intuition to understand that it wouldn't involve a group full of seventy young Americans partying together on the dime of the American government.

That morning we said our goodbyes to the only people in the country we could come close to calling friends, knowing that within a few hours we would be completely separated. Some training sites had multiple groups of Americans, but in the small village of Hryshkivtsi, it was just going to be me and four others. Hryshkivtsi. Hrish-kiv-tsee. I couldn't even pronounce it, so whenever anyone asked me about my training site, I just said it's the one with the H. This was less due to Hryshkivtsi's exotic name and more due to my inability to speak Ukrainian, but I hoped I'd be able to pronounce it soon, along with some of the other common words and phrases we had learned throughout orientation.

After learning my training site during one of the worst hangovers of my life, I tried finding any sort of information on the place I'd call home for the next three months. I first looked up the one with the H on Wikipedia, but I was disappointed to find that there weren't any submissions. I then tried searching for it on Google Maps, but it was just a tiny dot with nothing else around it. At first I thought that maybe Google Maps wasn't well developed in Ukraine, but since the other volunteers had no problem finding all sorts of cool places around their respective sites, it just looked like Hryshkivtsi was going to be a pretty small place.

That morning, the seventy of us got on two separate busses and began the trip to our new homes. After finding a seat near the back, I spent some time getting to know a volunteer named Andrea, who already knew a couple other languages and seemed a whole lot smarter than me. I then dozed off, still feeling a bit groggy from the massive hangover the day before. When I woke up about an hour later, I looked out the window, and saw something that made me wonder if I was still dreaming.

Tanks. Lots of tanks. We were on the highway at that point, but to our right was a band of tanks rolling by us. Our bus wasn't going that fast in the first place, but I was still a little surprised how fast those big green killing machines were moving.

"Are those-"

"Yes," Andrea said, "Those are tanks. They've been passing us for a few minutes now, but no, I have no idea what they're doing here."

I knew the country was at war, but thought it was only in the east. Would I have to worry about tanks at my training site?

"Oh, don't worry too much," a voice said from behind. Another volunteer, Aiden, had plopped his head between Andrea's headrest and mine, "Today's Independence Day. Those tanks are probably just for a parade, or something. I wouldn't think too much about it."

"That's good," I said, "It's not everyday you see tanks on the highway."

"Yeah, kinda weird, but it makes sense. Anyway, Bob, right? Where you headed for training?"

"I'm going to a village, but I have no idea how to pronounce it. There's an H in the beginning."

"Hryshkivtsi?" Aiden said perfectly.

"Yeah, that one. How do you say it?"

"Hrish-kiv-tsee," he said slowly.

"Hri, Hrivkit, Hreevkitsee?"

"Close. Hrish-kiv-tsee."

"Hrivkkishee?"

"Yeah, well, not quite."

After a couple more minutes of trying, I still wasn't able to get the pronunciation down. I thanked Aiden, who did his best, but the whole interaction only made me more nervous for training. If I couldn't even pronounce the name of my site, getting anywhere with Ukrainian was going to be nearly impossible.

I once again fell asleep, and when I woke up the second time, the bus had already stopped. Most of the other volunteers were already gone, and I only woke up because Andrea needed to squeeze by me and get her bags.

"See ya later Bob," she said while grabbing all of her possessions, "Good luck out there."

"Thanks Andrea, you too."

Aiden soon followed her off of the bus, "I'll see you around Bob. Remember: Hrish-kiv-tsee."

"Thanks Aiden, hopefully I'll be able to pronounce it next time I see you. Good luck!"

"You too man."

Andrea and Aiden, along with the rest of their training group, were greeted outside the bus by a bunch of school children, who were waiting for them with signs and balloons. It looked like a pretty nice welcome party, and I secretly hoped that we'd experience something similar.

After they departed, the only stragglers left were me and my sitemates:

- Chloe, who was in her mid twenties and engaged to another volunteer named Ron.

- Olivia, one of my twenty two year old drinking buddies from a couple nights before.

- Noah, a twenty nine year old who helped me with my bags in the airport.

- And Sam, my orientation roommate and fellow philosophy major.

I hadn't gotten to know any of them very well except for Sam, and aside from waking him up at two in the morning when I was blackout drunk, we generally got along pretty well. As for the rest of the group, after only brief interactions with most of them throughout orientation I didn't notice any immediate red flags, which is all I could have asked for before the start of training. I was going to be spending a lot of time with these people over the next three months, and as long as no one was noticeably toxic, then I knew it couldn't go too poorly. I could only hope that I wasn't the toxic one.

We travelled a bit through Andrea's and Aiden's city, Berdychiv, which like many things in Ukraine caught me by surprise. I was expecting all of us to be plopped down in rural villages like Hryshkivtsi, but Berdychiv was looking way more developed than anywhere I thought any of us were going. There were cafes, restaurants, flower shops, but also various old women with fruit and flower stands on the sidewalk. There were a lot of concrete block apartment complexes, like I had seen in various documentaries, but we also passed a whole host of churches with spiral domes, a couple modern looking malls, and tons of metropolitan looking people walking to and from the city center. Aiden was also right about the parade; while driving past a park we saw hundreds of people gathering and celebrating, although we didn't catch any tanks. It looked like a lot of fun, and compared to where I thought most PC volunteers were going, this place looked like a paradise.

I wasn't far off in that assumption. After making our way out of the city and passing through a few miles of wheat fields, the bus finally started to slow down for the last time.

"We're here," Natalia, our language instructor told us. Finally, Hryshkivtsi.

I took my first good look at the place out the bus window: All I could see ahead of me was a two lane road. On each side of the road were various one story houses, all of which were guarded by green gates. There was a walking path in between the road and the houses, which was mostly covered in gravel, dirt and dust. The bus driver didn't have anywhere to park, so he parked on the side of the road, where some people were hanging out on a wooden bench.

Those people ended up being our host families. As the bus rolled up to the stop, the five women sitting on the bench, most of whom looked to be about in their fifties or sixties, stood up. They all had short hair cuts, which I was starting to notice often amongst the older women in the country, and a couple were wearing leopard printed pants. There were a couple of older men a few feet away smoking cigarettes, and for the most part, everyone was looking around, as if waiting for someone to tell them what to do.

At least I'm not the only one, I thought. I grabbed my bags from under my seat, made sure I wasn't forgetting anything, and followed my sitemates off the bus.

"Welcome to Hryshkivtsi!" Natalia told our group as the bus drove off into the distance. "These ladies are your host mothers, who you'll be living with for the next three months."

She then turned to our host mothers, and in Ukrainian Natalia said the same thing. After a few seconds of discussion with our new guardians, Natalia once again turned back to the group of culture shocked and nervous Americans.

"Robert?" Natalia called. I went by Robert in Ukraine, because "Bob" means bean in Ukrainian, and I did not want to be, "bean boy."

"Yes?"

"You'll be staying with Larysa and Valik. Do you have all of our stuff?"

I checked my bags one more time, even though the bus had already left. You can never be 100% sure.

"Yes, I have everything."

"Ok, follow them!"

One of the men smoking cigarettes, Valik, hastily walked up to me and grabbed my bags. He had grey hair and a tan face full of wrinkles, but before I even could say hi, he was already walking away. Just as hastily, Larysa, who was one of the women wearing leopard pants, walked up to me, grabbed my hand, and led me to my new home. They were both quite a bit shorter than me, but were moving really well for people who looked to be in their sixties.

"Bye everyone!" I said while being pulled away by Larysa.

27

"Bye Bob!" They all yelled back to me. It all happened so fast, but I assumed I'd be seeing them frequently throughout our three months of training together. Now the training wheels were off, and it was time to start the whole Peace Corps thing.

Soon we caught up with Valik, who was standing in front of one of the numerous green gates in the village. Larysa, who had already said a few things I couldn't understand, grabbed a key out of her pocket and unlocked the huge bolt on the front of the gate. Later on in training we learned that the closest police station to Hryshkivtsi is over ten miles away, so the bolted up gate and the aggressive dog that greeted us made all the sense in the world.

The dog, who was chained to a metal poll, barked ferociously as I walked onto the front lawn for the first time. It ran around in circles, doing whatever he could to break free and attack the new scent. It wasn't exactly what I was imagining when Natalia said I would be able to spend some time playing with a dog, but I probably should have known better.

After the lovely greeting by my new furry friend, I soon noticed a decently-sized garden and backyard next to the house. Throughout the area they were growing what looked to be potatoes, cucumbers, and other sorts of vegetables I had trouble identifying. I also saw a wooden outhouse, which I hoped I wouldn't be using, and a few wooden shacks next to the garden where I heard some chickens singing the songs of their gods. There were also a few apple trees, but before I got a chance to walk up and snag one, Larysa hurried me into the one story brick house.

As I walked inside, Larysa stopped me and pointed to my house slippers. She said something I couldn't understand, so I replied back, "Ya ne rozumiyu," which means, well, "I don't understand." She said something else, and once again I repeated that beautiful phrase and looked at her blankly. She then took her shoes off, motioned me to take my shoes off, and watched me as I put on the slippers. First task in Hryshkivtsi achieved!

After slipping them on she took me to my room, which turned out to be much bigger than mine back in America. When I stepped inside my eyes were immediately drawn to the walls, which were covered in brown and red carpets, all of which matched the one I was standing on. To my left was a massive wooden dresser, and to my right was a light brown couch, which folded out into a bed. At the end of the room was a TV which I never planned on turning on, and next to the TV was a brown wooden desk where I was going to toss all of my possessions instead of organizing them neatly. After not knowing what the facilities were going to be like in the small village, I was pleased to see such a nice living area.

"Thank you," I said in Ukrainian.

"You're welcome," she replied, and motioned me to put my stuff down.

After letting me collect myself, Larysa told me to follow her, and led me across the home to the bathroom, which consisted of a sink, a small washing machine and a shower without a curtain. For some reason, maybe due to my view of the stereotypical Peace Corps experience, I imagined I'd be taking bucket baths, so seeing a full blown shower and sink was quite a welcomed site. Additionally, after walking through the living room and kitchen, which didn't look too different than a typical living room and kitchen back home, it became clear that there were going to be more than enough modern amenities to get by.

Larysa pointed at the shower, and mimicked washing her hair.

"Ok," I said, shooting a thumbs up. I felt pretty grimy after a few hours of travel and was more than ready to wash up. The shower looked completely normal too, so I didn't think I'd have any problem figuring it out.

The water was hot, and even though I had to hold the shower head while washing myself, things began without a hitch. However, as soon as I started to wash my hair, something went terribly wrong.

A loud and jarring noise shocked me to my core. After gasping and dropping the shower head, I located the noise, which was coming from something that looked like a radiator in the corner of the bathroom. If I wasn't startled enough, seconds later Larysa barged in while I was butt naked. She turned off the water, pointed at the generator, imitated the noise it just made, and then mimicked a turning off the water motion.

"What???" I said in English.

She tried explaining in Ukrainian, but no luck. I didn't know a lick of the language and standing wet and vulnerable like that in front of my new host mother wasn't making it any easier to process her hand gestures. She then turned on the water, waited a minute for the noise to start, and once it did, she turned off the water.

"Oh," I said, finally understanding, "Ok."

"Good," she said in Ukrainian, and left. I continued washing myself, hoping that I wouldn't encounter any other surprises during my first shower in Hryshk-itvsti.

As I later exited the bathroom into the kitchen, Larysa had already whipped up some tea and cookies. I sat down, feeling fresh, and attempted to taste the tea. It was scolding hot.

Larysa looked at me, "Hariachi?" She asked.

That word I knew: Hot.

"Yes," I replied.

Larysa got up, grabbed another mug, and poured the tea in the new mug. She then told me to try it again. It was much cooler.

Ahh, a Ukrainian tea trick, I thought.

"Better?" She asked.

"Yes," I repeated, proud of my first Ukrainian communication success with my new host family.

After enjoying tea in silence, I remembered the presents. PC told us to bring presents from America to give to our host families in order to start things off right. We all went to the living room, where the yellow walls were also covered in carpets. I started by giving them some American coins, along with some souvenirs I had gotten from DC that summer.

"Who is he?" Valik wrote into Google Translate while pointing at the penny.

"Abraham Lincoln," I wrote back, "He freed the slaves. We had slaves in the United States until 1865."

"Ah, Lincoln," Valik replied knowingly as he took my phone. Once he finished typing he handed it back to me.

"That's what we were like in the Soviet Union. Slaves."

Valik then went to a closet and he pulled out photos of when he was in the army, pointing at his various comrades.

"He was from Kazakhstan, and he was from Russia. Our nation wasn't important. We were all on the same team," he wrote again, "But it was far from freedom."

Looking through those black and white pictures of Valik and the other soldiers, who were wearing fur hats, sporting Communist logos, and were standing in the snow with rifles, it was the first moment when I began to truly process just where the hell I was.

This is Ukraine, I am in Ukraine, and less than thirty years ago this was the Soviet Union. And now I'm living here with a couple of the locals, one of whom was a Soviet soldier. Months ago I was graduating from a college in a tiny town in North Carolina, and now I'm here.

....

Later on in the day, after I had time to set up my room, I used hand gestures to ask Larysa if we could go out to the garden. Larysa nodded, and took me outside. That's when I made my first mistake: I shut the door, and directly afterwards Larysa looked at me as if I had just broken a window.

"Uhhh, good?" I asked in Ukrainian.

"No, not good," she replied.

She went up to the door, pulled the handle, and showed me that I had just locked us out of the house. Valik was off somewhere else, and I became immediately concerned that I had locked us out for the night.

Being entirely helpless, I simply shrugged and gave a "what should we do" type of movement. Larysa, looking a whole lot less concerned than I was, laughed and walked to the garden, where she pulled out a thin sharp piece of metal. I'm not sure exactly why that was in the garden or it's intended function, but with that sharp metal square, in a matter of minutes Larysa picked her own lock and let me in the house. I walked in slightly ashamed, deciding to go to my room in order to avoid any other potential mess ups.

On the second or third day, after taking a bit of time to adjust to my rural surroundings, I decided to go on a run. Running is one of the only de-stressing activities that I genuinely enjoy, and the Peace Corps, after decades of sweeping mental health problems under the rug, strongly emphasized at orientation the importance of healthy coping mechanisms.

When I told and mimicked my plans to Larysa, she once again looked at me as if I had broken a window.

"Why?" She asked.

This reaction wasn't surprising. A few years back when I studied in Prague, I got a lot of strange looks whenever I went running. I heard from someone that jogging hadn't really gotten popular in Eastern Europe until the twenty-first century, and if I got the occasional weird glance in a capitol city like Prague, I'd have bet half of my crummy Peace Corps salary that the people in Hryshkivtsi would react the same way.

While explaining to Larysa why I wanted to run I tried not using Google Translate, seeing it as a crutch that would only deter me from learning the language. So in preparation, before this whole interaction I wrote down my reasons for running, and was ready to read them off the notecard I had brought from the States.

"It helps me think, it helps me relax, and it helps me not be fat."

Larysa laughed and said, "You're not fat. But what about the dogs?"

"The dogs?"

Oh, the dogs. I hadn't thought of that. Even though I had only been in Ukraine for about a week, I noticed something that's impossible to miss if you spend more than a few days there: There are a lot of stray dogs. A lot. I was initially very hesitant to go near any of them, and would sometimes even cross the street if they were ever on my side of the walking path. However, as I gained experience in Ukraine, I learned that the vast majority of these furry nomads are nicer than most dogs you'll see on a leash in the States. I don't know why that is - maybe all the aggressive ones were killed by people throughout the years, but from my perspective, the ones that remain have only been extremely calm and dare I say polite in our many interactions. The locals regularly pass stray dogs without even paying them any attention, because it'd be a huge shock if any of the furry street friends bit or so much as barked at anyone.

However, during my first couple of weeks, I had no idea about this phenomenon, and I wasn't trying to risk getting chased by a pack of rabid and vicious strays. Luckily, the Peace Corps had also gone over this during orientation, and my safety and security manager's words still ring in my head:

"If a dog ever comes up to you and starts snarling and barking, you must pick up a rock and act like you are going to throw it at the dog. The dog by then will usually run away, but if it doesn't, then you'll need to throw the rock at the dog. This will work in most situations."

It sounded ridiculous, but this came from the Peace Corps Ukraine head of safety and security, so from then on, most of us always made sure to have a couple rocks in our pocket.

After considering the potential danger of the dogs, I bit the bullet and began my jog because I really needed to run. Culture shock, frustration with communication and the feeling of being trapped were beginning to set in, and without many other methods to cool my mind down, I thought that it'd be a bigger risk to stay in my room and develop a mild panic attack than go on a run and confront a dog or two. After Larysa urged me a couple more times to not go, she pulled out her phone to translate an important message.

"If you see a dog, walk until it's gone. Call me if there are problems."

I had little doubt that I was probably one of the only people to ever go on a jog in the village's history, but other than a few strange looks from some of the people at the bus stop, I didn't have many issues. I ran past a ton of different houses, all of which seemed to have trees and gardens just like Larysa's, and jogged past a couple of wide fields full of various crops and animals roaming the land. Every now and then I had to slow down after seeing the occasional dog, but they didn't pay me much attention.

After running far enough down the road, I made it to the bridge that connects Hryshkivtsi to an outlying town. I wondered if I should keep going, but in the middle of my daydream I caught something in the corner of my eye. As soon as I turned, sure enough a huge and aggressive dog jumped out of the bushes and was inches away from biting me. I quickly jumped back, and luckily the dog didn't pursue me any further. My heart began beating rapidly, and I wisely I took it as a video-game-like message.

"Turn around traveller," the dog beckoned, "You have not unlocked this part of the map yet." I happily conceded and made my way back to the village.

Instead of going straight back to Larysa's house, I took a right on one of the side streets and started exploring. Everything pretty much looked the same, but after a few minutes I once again encountered a dog at the top of a hill. Standing on its hind-legs, the mere physical presence of the dog made me stop in my tracks. The white beast was leaning up against a fence, a fence that was at least as tall as I was, which it used to prop itself up in order to eat leaves off of a tree. I had never seen a dog do something like that in my life, which after a little investigating, made a lot of sense.

As I got closer and closer I realized that it wasn't a dog at all: It was a goat, who, at my realization, stopped eating, turned its head, and began staring at me. At that point we were only about twenty feet apart, and while I didn't know how aggressive goats are, the head of safety and security sure as hell didn't give us any advice in a situation like that, so I made the easy decision to turn around and let the goat continue destroying someone else's apple tree.

I decided to slow down and start walking, tired of all of the surprises from my run, and I couldn't help but to notice how just about every tree I passed grew some sort of fruit. I thought that just Larysa and some other people around had planted some sort of special fruit tree, but here on the sidewalk I was finding out that these weren't just a part of someone's backyard - they were everywhere. I picked some grapes and apricots on my walk home, and devoured them under the hot Ukrainian sun.

This is all to say that I was in a rural site. From fruit trees growing near the sidewalk to the vast green fields to a goat gnawing on leaves in front of someone's house, what Hryshkivtsi lacked in infrastructure it made up for in natural beauty.

On our first weekend, a couple days before our training actually started, my new sitemates and I decided to explore our new home and all that came with it. We met up by a bodega near the middle of the village, which out of the four or five non residential buildings was the easiest to find. We began walking down the road that cut through Hryshkivtsi, talking about our host mothers and their individual intricacies, and after about fifteen minutes we went down some side street at the end of the village. It was a dusty gravel pathway in between rows of buildings, all of which had subsequent farmland and gardens to survive, well, anything.

The road led to a field, and soon all we could see was a wide flat field with miscellaneous farmland. I was a bit hesitant, thinking some angry farmer was going to chastise us for walking on his bread and butter, but Noah walked confidentially ahead. The farmers, who were tending to their fields, didn't seem to mind. The only danger we had to watch out for were the free roaming cattle, horses, and geese, the latter of which were by far the most aggressive.

"You know," Noah said as we skirted past those long-necked terror birds, "Two weeks ago we were in DC, and now we're in Hryshkivtsi." He reached in his pocket and pulled out a flask, "I've been taking some polls on the other sites, and it looks like we got one of the tough ones. Lucas is in the capitol city and his host sister is in college, and he's been having the time of his life."

"Yeah," Chloe chimed in, "Ron, my fiancé, is in Berdychiv, and he said it's a full blown city. They can pretty much do whatever they want and have already gone on a few tours already."

"Well," I replied, "There's something to be said about being in a village though. I mean, this is the real deal. This is what the Peace Corps is all about, right?"

"Ehh, I don't know about that," Noah rebuffed, "I think that sort of mindset is a bit of a trap. You romanticize the toughness and hardship that comes from living in a village like this, only in an attempt to make yourself feel better when your colleagues are living in the thick of a downtown city center. We got a bit of a raw deal, but that's just how it is."

Silently disagreeing, we continued our walk into farmland, soon muddying up our shoes and the bottom of our pants. I took a swig of the whisky, and then thanked Noah for the smooth adult-person move of nabbing some Jack Daniels ahead of time. Although the village life wasn't going to be a cake walk, I thought that living in a rural area in the middle of Ukraine could have a lot of advantages. The fruit trees and free roaming animals were right out of any sort of Peace Corps propaganda video, and going into the Peace Corps, this type of situation was exactly what I wanted.

I was excited, truly excited, to be in this village of three thousand with little infrastructure, thinking that I'd find it hell of a lot more fulfilling being in a place like this than partying with Ukrainian undergrads in a big city.

Chapter Three

Struggling

Boy was I wrong. After a couple of weeks the honeymoon period wore off, and a feeling of dread set in after we realized just how hard this training was going to be.

Each week was an absolute grind. Our days consisted of four hour Ukrainian lessons, followed by four to five hours of technical training. The technical training consisted of learning about different teaching methods, student learning styles, how to properly lesson-plan, and doing real-life teaching with a Ukrainian counterpart at the school in the village. We did this five days a week, and every day we did not go a single minute under time. We heard from other groups that their language instructors gave them some slack by maybe shedding off an hour or two during the more difficult days, so week after week we hoped that we would eventually get that same treatment.

We didn't. Standing no higher than five feet tall, our language instructor Natalia didn't let up the entire time. She was a former track athlete, and unlike some of the more laid back language instructors, we were expected to start at 8:00 am sharp and not go a single minute under the four hours Peace Corps allotted for language practice, even if dinner was cold by the time we made it home. I don't know if you've ever tried to learn anything for four hours straight, but it sucks. Natalia, wanting to get the best out of her students, didn't even subtract the breaks from the overall time, so every break was a negotiation between how long we wanted to relax and how early we wanted to get home.

Having such a stringent instructor, as one can imagine, had its pros and cons, the latter of which were magnified due to all of the other stressors going on in our lives. While there is no way that I could've been any more prepared language-wise by the time swearing in rolled around, the mental toll of four hours of language a day, four hours of teacher training, and doing everything in our power to simply get by in an environment like Hryshkivtsi without having an emotional breakdown really put our group in a bind.

At least we could be thankful that Natalia, to her credit, is a wonderful teacher. She constantly varied the activities and put them in a well thought out and precise order: Things began with lighthearted warmup, which led to some grammar instruction, which was then followed by a song or something easily digestible, which then led to partner work, and you get the picture. She made sure to have activities for all different types of learners, and made sure to give the best students a little extra work if she ever had to re-explain some grammar rules to a student or two who was falling behind. In hindsight, I'm extremely lucky I had a teacher like Natalia instead of another teacher I heard about, who mainly turned on Ukrainian TV shows and let his students out an hour early every day. However, hindsight didn't make the days any easier, and by the time we walked home we were completely gassed.

It also didn't help that, out of all of the groups nearby, we were definitely in the least stimulating area. After a week of exploring, we found out that the road that passes through the village was the only significant road around. Most of the village was just houses on both sides of the road, and the majority of the cars that drove by us were simply passing through in order to get to somewhere else. The only buildings besides houses were the school, a library we never found, a cafe and two bodegas. There were busses that regularly travelled to the closest city, Berdychiv, but unfortunately for us, the Peace Corps forbade travel to neighboring cities for the first five weeks of training. This means that, along with not being able to get the out of the village, we couldn't even buy groceries for ourselves, due to the fact that there were no grocery stores in Hryshkivtsi. As far as food was concerned, we were bound to whatever our host families wanted to feed us.

I was lucky that Larysa's cooking was pretty fantastic. She generally made the same three meals everyday, which consisted of potato dumplings, some sort of mixture with diced eggplant and olive oil, buckwheat, and a delicious meat I never bothered to ask about. However, after the first few weeks the lack of variety and well as things to do started to take a toll. We began to look for any sort of change, and the only way we could spice up our pallet was by walking over to one of the two bodegas to find whatever they had fixed up that day. Besides a selection of frozen dumplings and vegetables, all the bodega offered was candy, sausages, fresh bread, cigarettes, water bottles, soda, an ATM that didn't work, and pre-made pizza which sat on the counter by the clerk. We ate a lot of pizza.

Out of the available infrastructure, only a cafe a few minutes away from the central bodega caught the collective eye of our cluster. We had seen Instagram stories of other volunteers exploring various malls, restaurants, and even a museum here and there, so the cafe in our town seemed like our one chance at shedding away some of the FOMO that had gripped us early on in our training experience.

One day Chloe brought up the cafe with Liudmyla, our technical training instructor, during one of our breaks.

"Hey Liudmyla, what's the deal with that coffee shop?"

"What?"

Filtering out slang and idioms soon became a consciousness process that all volunteers had to learn.

"Oh, um, we've seen a coffee shop near Bob's host mother's place. It says it's a cafe, and we want to go there."

"You...want to go to the cafe?"

"Umm," Chloe said, looking around, "Yeah, we think it'd be nice to go to the cafe."

Natalia raised her head and spoke up, "Chloe, why do you want to go to the cafe? What would you possibly do in the cafe?"

"I, uh, I think we'd go there and drink coffee. It'd be a nice place to relax after a long day of lessons."

We all nodded, although both Natalia and Liudmyla looked uneasy. I had no clue what was going on, and neither did most of our training group. Luckily

Noah, the only real adult in our group, somehow had the cross cultural wisdom to get us out of this mess.

"In America," he said, "Cafes are pretty popular. People go there and drink coffee, relax, get some work done, and maybe meet new people. Does that happen in Ukraine?"

Our instructors looked at one another, took a sigh of relief, and afterwards changed their tone.

"Oh, haha, well," Natalia replied on, "We have some of those, but this cafe is where the mob spends time. It's mostly just mob men getting drunk and fighting each other, so we don't think it's a good idea for any of you to go there."

Noted. We all nodded and became devastated that our one potential refuge turned out to be a place for mobsters beating the crap of each other.

At least we got lucky with water. In a great deal of Ukraine, as I learned in the Irpin Conference Hall, tap water is undrinkable and in some regions it's not even optimal for bathing. While the Berdychiv cluster seemed to have all they could ever ask for, their honeymoon period ended after some time with a tainted water supply. After a few weeks they soon started experiencing fierce acne breakouts, and one girl's hair changed color because the water was eroding her hair dye.

In contrast, the village was rife with well water, which is not only safe to bathe in but also safe to drink. That was a huge relief, because our water stipend - yes, we had a water stipend - was close to twenty five hryven a day, which at the time was less than one dollar. Even for Ukraine that was pretty low, and it became apparent that when Peace Corps Ukraine was crunching the numbers, they severely underestimated how much water we needed.

I don't know how the other volunteers did it. As a bit of a tubster, I would regularly sweat merely from walking to training, so much so that in the beginning of Peace Corps I had to borrow one of my friend's undershirts. I'm a cold weather guy, and I even considered heat and sunburn as factors while applying to different Peace Corps countries. I expected that some of my excess chunkiness would serve as a bit of a useful buffer during the harsh Ukrainian winter, but alas, here I was sweating bullets on my daily walk to training.

I would regularly return home after those long training sessions parched, but thankfully I could enjoy as much sink water as I desired. I don't know what I would've done with only a dollar of water a day, so while I wasn't living it up in the Berdychivs of the world, at least once a day I could be grateful that I was plopped down in a village of three thousand people in central Ukraine.

While the non-toxic water helped sweeten the experience a bit, by the end of the first month life turned into nothing less than a drag. I'd regularly wake up at 6:30, eat a breakfast of porridge or dumplings whipped up by Larysa, and make it out of the house by 7:15. There I'd wait for Sam, who lived the farthest away, and around 7:30 we'd be on our way to training. We'd make it just before 8:00, but then wait for a couple of our sitemates while Natalia fumed about our tardiness. Then, ten to eleven hours later, more often than not we would still be there silently begging Natalia to let us go.

This often concerned our host mothers, who over the weeks became quite overbearing. The long days, which inevitably ended after sunset, routinely had them terribly worried about their host children walking home as the sun began setting. They would often wonder why on earth we hadn't arrived home before sundown and ended up calling us on a daily basis while we were still at training at Natalia's.

"I'm at training," I would always say after Larysa called for the third time.

"When are you coming home?"

"I'm not sure, maybe in an hour."

"Ok. I'm waiting for you. Call me when you're done."

Dinner was always waiting before we got home, and no matter how many times we told them we wouldn't be back before seven, as each minute passed their anxieties and loving yet overbearing nature ate away at them until we finally walked through those doors. This meant that after our lengthy days when we were desperate for some time to relax or decompress, we had to rush as quickly as we could back home in order to subdue our host mothers.

Then, after finally making it home and eating dinner, we had a choice: Hang out with the host family or take the break we'd been waiting for since 8:00 am. If we chose the latter, we'd inevitably feel guilty for not keeping our host parents company, not practicing the language, and not squeezing the most out of the PC experience. Often I went against my bodily desires and hung out with them, trying my best to use some new words and phrases I learned earlier that day. However, more often than not I was too tired to utilize the language and would hardly be able to use it. We mostly watched TV together in silence.

Finally, around 9:30 pm, after tea and cookies I got to experience my first period of relaxation of the day. However I'd quickly fall asleep due to the physical and mental exhaustion from adapting to a new country, language, and culture, on top of the long and stringent lessons that were immeasurably more intensive than anything I experienced during my four years in undergrad.

This cycle repeated five times a week for ten weeks, and since we weren't allowed to leave Hryshkivtsi for the first half of training, the weekends either revolved around decompressing with our cluster, who were the same four people we had been surrounded with for ten hours a day five days a week, or spending time alone and trying not to think too hard about how difficult things were.

About six weeks in, after a tough round of lessons one day, we all finally had enough.

"Screw it," Olivia said, "Let's get drinks after this."

No one opposed, although it was sure to be risky. In order to pull this off and spend just one hour getting drinks after work, we needed to coordinate a conspiracy. This was because we already knew by then that our host families were NOT chill with us drinking, and through some sort of "lost in translation" moment with Peace Corps, our host families thought that we would be kicked out of Peace Corps if we ever drink alcohol.

Olivia came up with the idea of telling our host families that the lesson would be going late and we'd be arriving home later than expected. During our lunch break, we all texted them at the same time during the first step of our plan. Our respective host mothers all bought it, and the first step of the conspiracy went on without a hitch. Now just came the drinking part.

For any volunteer outside of a village, having a drink or two after work didn't require a second thought. However, us five Americans stuck out like a sore thumb in Hryshkivtsi due to our look, volume, and exotic accent. Everyone in the village knew who we were and what we were doing there, and we were heavily encouraged to never let anyone catch us drinking. This would've been fine if there was some sort of shelter to drink in, but the only place to drink was on a porch outside one of the bodegas. We decided to risk it and walked over to the second bodega, which was closer to the outskirts of Hryshkivtsi than the one we usually went to.

So on a grey and depressing Friday, with nine hours of training behind us, the five of us used our water stipend to get beers together for the first time in Hryshkivtsi. I tried my best to enjoy my one-liter beer with my tired and miserable sitemates, but my paranoia of kids seeing us and telling their teachers/parents kept me from enjoying myself too much.

"We're allowed to have a beer after work," Chloe implored, "I mean, this isn't illegal. We are adults, and we are having a beer after work. There's nothing wrong with that."

"My host mother said that the Peace Corps told them any and all drinking is against the rules," I replied, trying to hide my beer behind my leg while a couple kids walked by.

"That's not true!" Chloe barked back, "That's only at Peace Corps events. They can't control us like this!" On the verge of a nervous breakdown, Chloe looked at her phone, which only accelerated her distraught mood. Her fiancé, Ron, had been one of the volunteers living it up in Berdychiv. The only reason he wasn't with Chloe in Hryshkivtsi is because he had studied Russian for six years, and the Berdychiv language group was specifically learning Russian. We later learned that couples were more likely to be placed in the east, where Russian is the dominant language, since they were seen as more responsible and could handle living in a more dangerous part of the country.

It made sense, but what didn't make sense was why Chloe was learning Ukrainian with us in Hryshkivtsi, which subsequently led her to a front row seat to all the fun the Berdychiv cluster was having. That cluster, unlike us, was having the time of their life, playing guitar together after language lessons, going on various tours of the city and even exploring a botanical garden that we only got to see online. They regularly hung out at a local bar after lessons, of course after being let out a little bit early by their instructor. They all seemed to be having a jolly ole time together, and on that dreary Friday, Chloe got the news that sent her over the edge.

"They are touring a brewery right now," Chloe cried, looking up from her phone. "Ron's host family owns a brewery, and they've spent half the day there."

Chloe's eye began to twitch, "I don't know why I wasn't placed there. Why am I here why am I not there Ron's my goddamn fiancé I should be there I'm not even going to use Ukrainian I know I shouldn't be here WHY am I not there why am I separated from my fiancé WHY AM I STUCK IN HRYSHKIVTSI??"

None of us had the emotional energy or ability to show her the bright sides of being in the village. As we hid our beers and dreaded inevitably going back to our host mothers, no one had a good answer.

"I don't really know why you're here either," Noah replied.

Chloe finished her beer as I tried to remind her that at least our water doesn't smell like nickels.

"That's true," Chloe considered, "I've heard people have been losing their hair after showering in Berdychiv. But still."

Our shared misery at times was the only thing that gave us a pick me up, but Chloe was going through a special kind of misery, being away from her fiancé who was having just a bright and dandy time in Berdychiv.

The only thing that kept us from going insane was that during the second half of our training, we were finally able to travel outside of Hryshkivtsi. The moment we had the chance, we of course trekked over to Berdychiv every weekend to finally spend time with other Americans, have a few beers without feeling anxious, and get away from all the stresses of village life. But, without fail, we'd always have to return and stare down another week of stress, ten hour work days, and a by the book instructor who didn't take too kindly to tardiness.

There was one particular day when the village life got the best of me. It was about a week before our final evaluations, and things had started to get really tough. First of all, we had the LPI on our minds. The Language Placement Interview, a twenty minute language exam which determined whether or not we would become official volunteers, was about a week away. Everyone was rightfully freaking out because if we didn't reach a certain level of Ukrainian (upper beginner), we could kiss being a volunteer goodbye. Yup, if we didn't reach that level, we'd have to go back to America, after experiencing all the misery of training.

Second of all, during the same week we were also going to be evaluated on our teaching. Natalia told us that various administrators from Kyiv were coming to sit in on our classes to see if we had what it took to be teachers. This resulted in a few (almost) sleepless nights, because the class they would evaluate would be just the eighth time I had ever taught in a classroom before, and in my eyes the other seven times weren't exactly up to snuff.

However, before all of this, we also needed to complete various assignments on our own. They were mostly online modules about the different aspects of Peace Corps that without a doubt were made for every Peace Corps trainee around the globe. The assignments were on a wide range of topics, including safety and security protocols in the event of an evacuation, the ten core tenets of the Peace Corps, situational awareness essays, and other papers that seemed extremely important at the time but ultimately turned out to be meaningless. We got them about halfway through training and we had more than enough time to complete them, but of course I waited until the last couple of days to get started.

The day before my assignments were due and less than a week before the LPI and teacher assessments, I had only completed about twenty percent of the online modules. We had just come from another tough day of training around 6:30 pm, and my plan was to eat some dinner and then immediately start working on my assignments. I scarfed down potato dumplings for the second time that day, and afterwards I raced to my room and dove into the burdensome modules, looking to finish these assignments once and for all. I estimated that all in all it would take me three to four hours to complete them in an adequate manner, so since by then it was only around 7:00 pm, I didn't worry too much about finishing them before getting to bed at a reasonable hour.

Then, Larysa entered my bedroom.

"Robert, we need to wash clothes."

"Ok, sure," I said, being able to understand that much after eight weeks of training, "I'll go get my clothes now."

"I've already set it up for you," she said, calling me towards the bathroom. She had never asked me to wash clothes before, and I had no idea how to work the Ukrainian washing machine next to the bathtub. However, I didn't think much of it, that is until I entered the bathroom.

The tub was halfway full of water, covered in bubbles with a pile of my clothes lying next to it. Larysa said something to me that I didn't understand, so we once again used google to figure things out.

"Natalia sent me a list of things you need to do to become a volunteer. It says you need to wash your clothes by hand."

"What?" I said, feeling the first of the five stages of grief.

Larysa shrugged and said, "Natalia said you must."

Larysa then turned to the tub, where she showed me how to properly wash my clothes by hand. Soak it in the soap water, squeeze it, soak it again in clean water, and then wring it until the water stops dripping. If I was forced to do this during my first week, maybe I would've had the ole "up for anything" Peace Corps attitude that I came to Ukraine with. However, two months in, all the shine had worn off.

Almost all other volunteers were undergoing a surreal wallflower experience, having kumbaya guitar time before and after their tours of various breweries and beer gardens, while my group and I were stuck with ten-hour work days, nowhere to have fun, and almost no chance to relax. And now, during the worst possible time, I had to hand wash all of my clothes in order to check some bureaucratic box in order to become a volunteer? Surely we could skip this part, right?

Wrong. By the time I had finished fuming, Larysa had already gone back to watching television. I got on my knees, picked my clothes out of the hamper, and started washing. And man, hand washing clothes is no walk in the park. My weak and pasty forearms were no match for hand washing a week's worth of clothes, which included heavy sweaters, my sheets, and almost every pair of pants I owned. Within ten minutes my forearms were burning like crazy, but I hadn't even covered a fifth of the hamper. I had no luck trying to half-ass it, either - Larysa periodically came in the bathroom to make sure I was doing it right, and any clothes that had soap on them in the finished pile had to be redone. It took me a little over an hour to do a sufficient enough job, and I was cursing under my breath the entire time.

After finally finishing, I checked my phone. It was only around 8:00 pm, so at least I could get back to my modules and make it to bed by midnight.

Once again, wrong. After the enriching and necessary cultural experience of hand washing my clothes right next to a washing machine, Larysa took me outside to the garden. She pulled out a big bucket of potatoes, and with a knife, showed me how to peel them.

"We need to peel potatoes," she said, "Natalia said so."

She looked sorry for me, but I had already succumbed to the fact that I would probably be up until two in the morning finishing the assignments. Once again cursing under my breath, I took the knife from Larysa, trying to do my best but unsurprisingly failing to peel the potatoes in an efficient or timely manner. I am so much more appreciative of peelers now, because peeling something with a knife is a horrible combination of tedious, time consuming, and dangerous. You have to be graceful enough to chop the skin off without getting too deep into the potato, but at the same time must be forceful enough to get the skin off in the first place. I continued with neither the dexterity, strength nor the grace to get the job done. I had no clue how I would be evaluated on this, but at that point, just a couple months after being a mega try-hard at orientation, I couldn't care less.

Thirty minutes later, after watching me through the window, Larysa came back outside. I thought she was going to correct me and show me again how I was screwing up the potato peeling, but instead she just chuckled to herself and joined me. I was happy for her help, and not even slightly depressed or insecure after seeing how easily she peeled those bad boys.

In a matter of minutes she had out-peeled me, and all of her potatoes were almost flawlessly round. It was another one of the many moments (and many more to come) where I felt like an absolute idiot. In the first few months, that's mostly what the Peace Corps experience is - looking like an idiot, unable to do the most seemingly simple things, and needing a nice older woman to help you properly feed and take care of yourself.

By the time I was sitting and watching Larysa go to town, I had already felt stupid so many times that I was numb to it, and I simply appreciated her help. At that point my pride had been thrown out the window a long, long time ago.

Larysa, after taking pity on this sad incompetent child she had taken in, finished up her half and led me back inside, even though there were still some potatoes left to go.

"The sun is setting," she said, "We can't peel in the dark."

After some tea time, capped off with cookies and honey, I made it into my room a little after 9:30 pm, almost three hours after I started working on the assignments. I sat in my bed, exhausted from my work day, hand washing clothes, and peeling potatoes, yet still facing the monotonous mountain of modules I had put off up until that point. My night was just beginning.

Chapter Four

Placement

I thankfully finished the assignments on time, so I was able to go into the site placement interview without needing an excuse for turning them in late. The site placement interview was more hoops to jump through, but unlike the various essays I had written detailing the importance of cross cultural awareness and my favorite Peace Corps commandment, this is when things actually started to count. While training felt excruciatingly long, it was no comparison to two years of actually serving/living tens to hundreds of miles away from all other volunteers. The interview and the eventual reveal of our permanent site was the part we had all been anticipating during training, so you can imagine the group-wide anxiety that came with such a determination process.

Seemingly every other day I heard all sorts of tips and advice of what and what not to say in the interview:

Don't ask for a city, that'll only rub them the wrong way. Don't tell them you want to go to the east and speak Russian, especially after they've been teaching you Ukrainian for the past two months. Talk about teaching. Tell them if you have any medical conditions that would be easier to tend to in a more developed area. Discuss what makes you happy. Ask for a gym, because nicer sites have gyms. Don't be too nervous, they already know where they're going to put you anyway. They have no idea where to put you, so really try to be strong in your preferences.

The advice was all over the place, so I decided to go with the gym idea. I didn't need to go to a huge site or anything, but by then Hryshkivtsi was talking a huge toll on me. If my permanent site had a gym, I theorized, the town would probably be developed enough to include at least some other places to hang out and relax. I could bet on there being at least a few restaurants or cafes (the ones where mobsters aren't beating people up), and after almost three months living the village lifestyle, a couple places to hang out were all I was looking for.

Three of the administrators, including the head of the TEFL program, a former English teacher named Khrystyna, drove down to Hryshkivtsi on a blue and sunny day during one of the last few weeks of training. When they showed up at Natalia's house we fixed them all tea and cookies like Natalia had taught us the day before, hoping that a kind yet mandatory gesture would put us in a decent light.

"Ready to get started?" Khrystyna, asked. "Who's first?"

"I'll go first," Sam blurted out. He was even more of a wreck than I was, and he asked us if he could go first in order to get this "nerve-wracking anxiety death trap" of an interview out of the way.

We waited in the kitchen while Sam sat down with the god-like figures who would decide what the next two years of his life would look like. While standing in the cramped kitchen with the rest of my cluster, I decided to fix myself some coffee. No one was in the mood to talk, so although I had already had a couple cups earlier that morning, I wanted to do something to take my mind off of things.

Instant coffee was the only thing we had, so after warming some water up in the noisy kettle, I poured a packet of the brown gravel in my cup and added as much sugar as possible in order to make it bearable. As I started to gulp it down my mind began to wander, and for whatever reason my lips and hands stopped communicating. I ended up pouring some of the coffee on my pressed white button down, with only about sixty percent of the contents of the cup reaching my lips.

"Oh God Robert," Natalia said while slapping her forehead.

Naturally I began to panic.

"Is it noticeable?" I asked Olivia.

"Well," Olivia said, cranking her head to the left, "Well, yes, it's all over your shirt. It's very noticeable. I'm sorry."

"It's ok," I replied.

50

It wasn't ok. A coffee stained white button down was the last impression I wanted to give the people who would decide my future in Ukraine.

"Ooh, a coffee stain?" I imagined Khrystyna saying, "Another village for you!"

I couldn't let that happen, although as far as solutions were concerned, I was pretty low on options. Luckily Natalia had some wipes on her, and wiped enough of it off of my shirt to make it look like an older stain instead of one that happened five minutes before. I once again showed my shirt to Olivia, who once again confirmed it was still extremely noticeable, "But this time a little less damp."

With that second honest rebuke I ran to the closet to put on my brown jacket, a heavy and beat up work jacket with the phrase "Foreman's Plumbing," on the front.

Better wearing an old brown jacket than to strut in with a coffee stained shirt, I thought while zipping it up high enough to cover up my mistake. It would have to do.

After Sam finished, he walked in the kitchen solemnly.

"Bob, you're up."

I walked in the living room after making sure one more time that the coffee stain was nowhere to be seen. I was greeted by three smiling middle aged Ukrainian women with clipboards, who were sitting in front of the language posters that Natalia had created over our time training together.

"Welcome Robert!" Khrystyna announced, "So nice to finally talk to you. Please, sit down. How is Larysa?"

"Oh, she's good. Very helpful, very caring."

"That's great to hear. I remember coming here and talking to her back in the summer. She is such a nice lady. She has a son, you know. He's already working for a news station in Kyiv. Anyway, how's training going?"

"It's good," I replied, "Long days, but learning a lot. It's been a great process."

"I totally understand. We know Natalia is really getting the best out of you all. Tell us, how is the language coming along?"

Once it clicked that the interview had started, I began to try to look as impressive as possible. "Well," I said while pushing my glasses up, "It's a bit similar to Czech, which I learned for a bit while studying in Prague. Some of the words are similar, so that's made the transition a lot easier." Yes, the four words in Czech I knew after dicking around in Prague with twenty other Americans made the language a lot easier. Quite helpful during my four hour Ukrainian classes. I was begging that they didn't know any Czech.

"That's great to hear, Robert, that's great to hear."

The interview only lasted ten or so minutes. Khrystyna mostly asked me various questions about how training was going, how I was taking care of myself, and what I had learned about teaching. A few of the questions, however, threw me off.

"Would you be ok working with people who speak multiple languages or who maybe don't speak Ukrainian at all?" Khrystyna asked after a routine teaching question. "Some of our sites are on the border of Romania and Hungary, so some of the towns there have their own specific dialect. Would you be ok with, for example, learning Romanian?"

Two months of Ukrainian, just to go to a site where I wouldn't need it at all? It sounded terrible.

"Sure, of course," I said, trying not to wince, "Whatever you need, I think that'd be interesting."

"That's the spirit."

I tried to give standard answers, attempting not to say anything that would make me seem entitled. During the mental health question I made sure to mention the gym, and was pleased to see Khrystyna nod and write it down.

As the interview concluded, Khrystyna looked up from her clipboard after taking notes on one of my final answers.

"So Robert, this has all been very informative. Thank you for taking the time to talk with us. Before we go, I just want to ask, is there anything else you'd like to tell us, anything you'd prefer, before we figure out your site?"

For some reason I didn't expect to hear that question. I froze, and subsequently went to my standard reaction, which was brown nosing and saying exactly what my superiors wanted to hear.

"Honestly, you can put me wherever you need me. Coming in I expected to be put in a village, one like Hryshkivtsi. I'm here to do hardcore Peace Corps, so I'm willing to go wherever and I'll be flexible with anything. Put me wherever you need me."

Khrystyna paused, put her pen down, and smiled, "You're mother raised you well. Thank you Robert."

I made it back to the kitchen feeling like I had crushed it. However, almost immediately afterwards the terror of my final answer quickly began to dawn upon me.

I just told them to put me in the toughest site possible, I thought as the caffeine-infused anxiety began to pick up.

With my brown nosing answer I put up little to no fight against finding myself in another one-road village, but if that was going to be my Peace Corps experience, well, I couldn't say that it wasn't something I signed up for.

The day of reckoning was set to come a couple weeks later, but beforehand it was time for evaluations. A couple weeks before swear-in the Language Placement Interview arrived, and my cohort was on the verge of having a group wide panic attack. Going off of late night Facebook messages, seemingly everyone in our group was spending multiple all-nighters reviewing vocabulary, going through grammar rules, and doing research trying to figure out what an LPI even is. We thought it would make or break our chance to become volunteers, and when the day of reckoning came, just like during the site-placement interview, my cohort and I waited in a kitchen filled with an atmosphere of nerves and despair.

Well, it turned out that all we had to do to succeed was talk in Ukrainian for a few minutes with an instructor. The questions progressively got harder, but if we made it that far in the LPI then we had nothing to worry about. Soon enough we learned that everyone we knew of passed, even a couple of my sitemates who hadn't managed to learn much of the language to that point. All in all, it was a lot more laid-back than we had anticipated.

"Oh," Noah said, "So that's how the LPI goes. Got it... Wish I knew that before losing sleep over it."

I lost sleep over it too, but overall I was just happy to lose another potential barrier to service. About a week later we finished our last few language classes (thank god), and all that was left was the teaching evaluation. Just like with the LPI, I stayed up late the night before, going over every possible problematic situation that could happen in forty-five minutes in front of a group of twenty-five seventh graders.

However, after a tense final lesson with my Hryshkivtsi co-teacher, where we had problems with the projector and didn't get through every step of our lesson in time, a few days later I found out that I was all cleared to swear in. It kind of seemed like this whole evaluation process was a little bit... loose, like Noah had said, but I didn't mind that one bit. After a few months of intense and grueling training in Hryshkivtsi, my desire to get it all over and done with had really chipped away at my rule following inclinations.

After making it through what turned out to be fool-proof evaluations, we finally saw the light at the end of the tunnel. All we had in front of us before swearing in was learning our sites and tying up some loose ends. It was all but guaranteed we'd officially become Peace Corps volunteers.

....

A few days later, our entire TEFL cohort had the rare opportunity to meet up, but the circumstances were far more serious than orientation. Before swearing in, we all travelled to Kyiv to get our residency cards.

"Meaning you'll learn your permanent sites," Natalia said, after the majority of us didn't put two and two together.

Oh. We'd be learning our sites. We'd be learning our sites!!!

I woke up at 6:00 in the morning, and at 6:10 a van packed with volunteers rolled up in front of my gate. I hopped in the old beat up van, which barely had enough room for me to spread my legs. Once again, the under-budgeted Peace Corps really knew how to make every kopek count.

During our three hour ride to Kyiv, most of us didn't say a word in the claustrophobic van. Within hours we'd all learn our sites, ranging from small villages like Hryshkivtsi to region capitals of over a million people. We were literally about to learn our fate, one that would heavily influence whether many of us would make it to the end of the twenty-seven months.

Personally I don't know how I'd get through another two years of Hryshkivtsi. Maybe I'd get used to it, and maybe without the stress of training it would be a much easier experience. Or maybe I'd quit after fourteen months, being unable to take another Ukrainian winter in the village. I heard that twenty percent of the previous cohort had quit for various reasons, and while that number seemed unexpectedly large, I was determined not to be one of them. However, living in another Hryshkivtsi might really test how badly I wanted to do Peace Corps after all.

After a long drive that was delayed by an hour of bumper to bumper traffic on the highway, we finally made it into Kyiv. I had spent most of the ride trying to catch up on sleep, but after rolling into the capital city of about three million people, I was in awe of how different this country can look after merely a couple hours of driving.

We began driving in between roads filled with twenty story apartment buildings, all beige yet tall and modern enough to encompass me with extreme culture shock after coming from the village. The roads were wide and full of cars, which is something I wouldn't have batted an eye at a couple months ago, but after only seeing one road, the only road, over the course of my time in Hryshkivtsi, I began to feel uneasy. We drove past various churches, all of which had the patented Eastern European spiral dome and were all easily four times the size of the only church in the village. Of course there were restaurants, high end department stores, and giant buildings that said "Android," "Rolex," and "Huawei" at the top. Naturally, the people were of a different stature: They were metropolitan looking types with colorful overcoats, extravagant dresses, well-fitted suits, the occasional pair of leather pants, and high heels. Lots and lots of high heels.

I was also drawn in by the sheer amount of statues, many of which screamed "Soviet-Era," although other than the general sadness emitting from the frowning stone facades, I couldn't quite put my finger on why they felt so Soviet. Many of the them were taller than any house in Hryshkivtsi, with the pinnacle being the golden sixty foot victory monument in the middle of the city center with some sort of bronze goddess at the top.

I recognized the city center, Maidan, from the documentary about the revolution I watched from the summer before. Just four years earlier, tens of thousands of Ukrainians were protesting here, setting tires on fire in the middle of winter in an attempt to fight against brutal police forces and a pro-Russian government that was trying to push Ukraine back into the dark ages. It resulted in the overthrow of the government and the installation of a new pro-European direction for Ukraine, but over one hundred people died in the struggle, all of whom are commemorated in the Maiden square and throughout the country. Even my training school had a poster of each of the fallen revolutionaries, and my teachers reminded me weekly about their sacrifices for the good of the country. Soon after the revolution, in retaliation Russian funded and trained forces started a war in the east as Russia illegally annexed the Ukrainian territory of Crimea. Ukraine has been at war ever since (much more on this in Chapter six).

With all of this in mind, Ukraine's icy relations with Russia makes it even crazier, at least from the outside, that most people in Kyiv primarily speak Russian. Yes, in the capital of Ukraine, a country that is currently at war with Russia and is fighting for an autonomous, democratic future, Russian is the one of the most popular spoken language.

Why is Russian the most used language in Kyiv, and so many other parts of Ukraine? It all comes from Russia's colonial history and totalitarian rule of Ukraine during the 20th century. During Soviet rule, language mandates throughout the union made Russia the official (and only) language of the Soviet

Union. Ukrainian was outlawed, and just like that Russian was the only language spoken in all aspects of society for the better part of six decades. Even as Ukraine gained independence in the early 90s, the country couldn't simply rid itself of the Soviet influences with a new constitution.

While some western regions mostly use Ukrainian, the majority of Ukrainians still use Russian as their primary language. With all this said it's important to note that while Russian and Ukrainian might seem similar because they are both slavic languages, they're different enough to where if you have no knowledge of the other language, you simply won't be able to understand it. The accents are pretty far apart, many of the words are different, and a few differences in grammar make Russian almost incomprehensible for a Ukrainian speaker like myself. As someone who understands the majority of Ukrainian that I hear, I still can barely understand any Russian at all. All in all, they are two unique languages.

With all of this in mind, I knew I wouldn't be getting to practice any Ukrainian in Kyiv, even if I tried. Not that I wanted to, seeing as I was too nervous to be saying much of anything that day, but it was frustrating as all get out to not understand a single word in the capital of Ukraine after studying the national language for the previous ten weeks.

A few minutes after passing through Maidan, we eventually pulled up to another humongous beige building, the Kyiv mall, where the passport office operated on the third floor. I burst out of the van, hoping to finally get some fresh air, only to end up gasping and air-like substance that tasted like a mix of gas and smoke. Kyiv, I learned later, has the worst air quality in Ukraine and has close to the worst air quality in Europe. I wish someone had told me that before I jumped out of the van and filled my lungs with the stuff.

Our group quickly entered the mall, and while the long ride lulled many of us into a sense of boredom, being so close to learning our permanent site jolted us up the stairs and kept us from noticing the nearby elevator ready and available. We climbed to the third floor and found the passport office, a sizable white room with ten different kiosks and a huge map of Ukraine by the entrance. To the left of the entrance was a cafe inside of the office, where some volunteers were already huddled up drinking coffee and having animated discussions.

Most of them were holding sheets of paper, filled with what I could only assume was information about their permanent sites. FOMO once again hit me like a brick: Everyone knew their site except for me, and anxiety soon swelled.

After bouncing around a few groups, trying to get as much information as possible, I found that most volunteers had their hands in their pockets, hunching over and showing signs of grief. It didn't take too long to figure out why: After spending two plus months of training in big cities like the region capital of Zhytomyr, the vast majority were experiencing what my group went through when we were first assigned Hryshkivtsi: Staring down the barrel of a tiny village in the countryside with at the very most ten thousand people, and at the very least (for one volunteer I heard about) a population of five hundred.

"Well, at least my site is close to Lviv," one volunteer mentioned, "I'll be able to find a change of scenery whenever I need to."

"Mine doesn't have a Wikipedia page either," I overheard from another, "So yeah we're going to get real rural real quickly."

"Andrea," I asked, approaching my bus mate from a couple months earlier, "Where did you end up?"

She looked deflated. "In a village." She, unlike most of the other volunteers, had heard about the troubles and hardship that me and my group went through after only two months in Hryshkivtsi. She knew what was coming.

The possibility of that happening to me started to weigh heavily. While lots of my friends were a little bummed about going from a well developed Ukrainian city to the countryside, most were trying to look forward in a positive light, hoping to enjoy the more simple and natural lifestyle I had experienced in the Hryv. However, while many went to their villages and did their best over the course of their service, sooner or later they all started to experience what I went through during training. It's a draining and frustrating lifestyle, one with constant failure and hardship that nobody coming out of college in a first world country like the

U.S. is ready for. We all tried our best, but this "thing we signed up for" became by far one of the greatest challenges any of us ever had to go through.

Throughout our time in Ukraine, I didn't blame anyone for quitting. You sign up to do Peace Corps and to serve communities in need. You don't sign up for the misery that comes along with it, and I was extremely afraid of that misery continuing for another twenty-four months.

"Screw it, let's get this over with," I said to no one in particular while turning to find one of the admin. I walked up to someone holding a folder, hoping he was working with the Peace Corps instead of just a random guy in the passport office. I was in luck.

"What's your name?" the plump bald man said, picking up a thin manilla folder off of one of the benches.

"Robert Minton."

"Where is your training site?"

"Hryshkivtsi."

"Ok," he said, shuffling through some of the folders, "Here you go."

And just like that, I had my site. It was that quick, that easy. After almost three months of waiting and hundreds of conversations about our sites, it was finally in my hand, given to me unceremoniously by an administrator who had woken up too early and had been waiting too long.

"Thank you," I said while immediately looking down. It was all in Ukrainian. My eyes darted to every inch of the page to see if there was a single sentence I could understand. There wasn't. I didn't even see the word for city, region, or anything like that. Parts of it were bolded, but that didn't give me any clue of where I'd be moving to. This is how they announced one of the biggest decisions of our lives? With a single piece of paper I couldn't comprehend in the slightest?

I found one of the language instructors, Dima, who had taught one of the Berdychiv clusters.

"Dima," I said with a stressed excitement, "Where am I going?"

"Where are you going? What do you -"

"Where is my site? Where is my site?"

I handed him the piece of paper, and he examined it for roughly as long as I did. I started to wonder if my site was on the paper at all-

"Mukachevo," he said as his eyes widened, "You're going to be living in Mukachevo."

"Is that…" I muttered, "Is that good?"

Dima looked at me and smiled. "It's a ski resort in the Carpathian mountains. Do you like to ski? Also, do you mind if I stay at your place sometime in the future?"

Ski resort? I was left speechless.

"This is one of the nicest towns in Ukraine," he added, "So, can I stay-"

"Yes, Dima," I replied as my lips began to widen, "You can stay whenever you want."

"Thanks! Congrats Robert, you lucked out."

I took a deep breath and tried to absorb what Dima just said. Mukachevo. Carpathians. Nicest city in Ukraine. Ski resort.

After pulling myself together, I googled Mukachevo, not quite believing what Dima told me. I immediately saw a Wikipedia page, and the most important number on it: 100,000. A ski resort with a population of 100,000 in the Carpathian mountains.

Hell yeah.

Chapter Five

Teaching

I suppose there should be a section on teaching. Right, teaching. That thing that I was supposed to do for two years. While not as entertaining as me getting my butt kicked by culture shock, I came to Ukraine first and foremost as a teacher, although I hardly thought about it before actually arriving in Kyiv.

I applied to join the Peace Corps for a lot of reasons, none of which had anything to do with teaching. I wanted to do something service-oriented, see a different part of the world, and finally have a response to those terrible, "What are you doing after college" questions that everyone and their mother ask graduating seniors. The Peace Corps seemed like it would more than just fit the bill, but with all of that said, I hadn't thought for one minute about what I would actually be doing in Ukraine.

While applying I barely even skimmed the job description of being a TEFL (Teaching English as a Foreign Language) instructor because I was solely obsessed with the idea of becoming a "Peace Corps Volunteer," whatever that means. I was planning on applying a year after graduation after bolstering up my resume, but in late December 2017, I got an email from the Peace Corps that looked a little bit different from what usually showed up in my spam folder.

Prioritized Listing

TEFL Volunteer Ukraine

Application Due December 31st.

That got me thinking: *A prioritized listing telling me to apply a few days before the application is due? That must mean they're short on applicants.*

The only other prioritized listing I had seen to that point was in Mozambique, which I was thinking about applying to, but the idea of living in Ukraine after a semester studying in the Czech Republic was much more enticing, especially considering my risk of sunburn and sweaty nature. That night I quickly reconstructed my resume, rushed through the application, and within an hour I had applied to PC Ukraine.

I was a little concerned about my chances of getting accepted due to my lack of teaching experience, but after arriving with my cohort, I soon learned that I was the rule instead of the exception. Peace Corps Ukraine was a mixed bag, but in that bag was a surprising lack of teachers. You had your classic international relations type people who had dreams of working in the foreign service, the straight out of college kids like myself looking for some direction and to do something good, a few actual adults who were disillusioned with corporate life, some people looking to solely party abroad, a few outliers, and finally a couple actual teachers sprinkled in. In a group of seventy teaching volunteers, I only knew three or four people who were a teacher by trade.

It felt problematic because PC was sending the majority of volunteers to sink or swim in a foreign workplace after less than three months of professional training. I doubt that was by design, though, and I assume that I got that prioritized listing email a few days before the application deadline for a reason. For whatever the cause, there simply weren't enough qualified teachers applying to do Peace Corps Ukraine. This was great for me because I wandered my way into the opportunity of a lifetime, but bad for the Ukrainian schools who inevitably needed to baby us through growing pains throughout the first few months on the job.

There wasn't even a training program over the summer to get us ready. There were cultural and language modules, but when it came to teaching, it very much felt like a, "We'll figure it out when we get there" type of deal. At no point did I come around to the idea that some sort of knowledge of English grammar, pronunciation, student learning styles, or educational psychology would be beneficial in the slightest. All I could focus on was that I was going to be a volunteer, and the teaching stuff would come later.

That teaching stuff came in November of 2018. After swearing in as Peace Corps volunteers, we were lucky enough to arrive during the first week of fall break, so most of us got a bit of a buffer period to get settled in with our new host families. However, just a couple days after touching down, my new counterpart Myroslava, who I had met the week before at the swearing in ceremony, called me.

"Hello Robert, I hope you're doing well. Are you on your way?"

"What?"

"Are you on your way to school? What, fall break is for the students, not just for the teachers you know!"

"Oh my gosh Myra, I didn't know, I'm so-"

"Oh Robert, I'm kidding!"

Ah, I thought, *a classic Ukrainian rouse. Maybe Ukrainians love sarcasm. Noted.*

"Oh, haha," I remarked after getting swindled.

"You can have a rest today. How is your host family, everything good so far?"

"Yes, things are great over here."

"Do you need anything? You can always ask me for anything."

Myra, like every single other Ukrainian woman I had met, always made sure that I was feeling comfortable and that I was well fed. While she was in her late 20s and a little more modern than some of the other people who had taken care of me thus far, that part of Ukrainian culture seems to spread across generations.

"Thanks Myra. Nothing right now but I will let you know."

"Wonderful. I do want to ask you something, though. I know it's fall break and you just made it to Mukachevo, but later this week some of the high-schoolers will be coming to school to practice for the Olympiad. Do you know what the Olympiad is? It's like a competition where the kids demonstrate their English abilities. Would you mind coming and seeing what level they are? It should be super simple and should only take-"

"Of course," I replied. I was feeling rejuvenated after basically having a week off before the swearing in ceremony, and helping some high-schoolers prepare for an English competition seemed like a pretty easy landing spot. And what was I going to do, say no to the first time my school needed my help just because it was fall break?

"Oh Robert that's amazing. Great, you can also get a good look at the school too before we come back into session. The Olympiad students are coming in on Wednesday, so let's meet then at the school around 9:00 am. Do you need directions?"

"Oh, I think I'll be ok!"

"Great, see you then!"

The next morning I was out the door at 7:30 am. Google Maps told me that I only needed forty-five minutes to get to the school, but using public transportation in a foreign country is always a circus, so I wanted to give myself as much room for error as possible.

That room for error came when I tried getting on the first bus. It was a modern looking bus, with digital monitors that told riders the next stop, as well as a television on the inside advertising various businesses around town. It was far from the old timey marshutka (bus) that I used when I was in Central Ukraine, and when I tried to give the bus driver some money, he shook his head and said something incomprehensible. I had no idea what to say, but then he pointed at a ticket scanner that I somehow had overlooked. Because he wasn't grabbing the blue bill out of my hand, I used my educational prowess to determine that I needed a ticket in order to get on.

Dang.

While I appreciated many of the luxuries in Mukachevo, such as the cobblestone roads that define the walkable center, the various lovely neoclassical townhouses, a park that hosts a variety of beer and wine festivals throughout the year, cherry blossoms that bloom in the spring, eye-catching mountains that surround the city, a movie theater, a plethora of coffee shops, a few malls, a couple of croissant sandwich shops, countless pizza parlors and even a place to kick back and play videos games, I wasn't expecting one of those perks to be a hindrance. But there I was, staring at a high-tech futuristic bus that wouldn't take my simple-person paper money. I had no chance of getting on.

Luckily, a woman walked up to the entrance of the bus, pressed her pass up to the ticket scanner and mercifully let me on. She sat back down without saying a word.

"Thank you," I said in Ukrainian. She still didn't say anything, so I just walked to the back of the bus and sat down.

After intensely watching Google Maps for the next forty minutes, I was blessed that the bus didn't take any random turns like they sometimes did in Hryshkivtsi, and I got off at the closest stop to School 16. I had to walk for a few more minutes to find my new workplace, and while the maps weren't being incredibly clear about the school's exact location, I caught a glimpse of a big yellow building in the distance in the general area of where I was supposed to go.

Must be it, I thought.

I was right. School 16, the specialized english school I was set to teach in for the next two years, was three stories high and light yellow. None of the paint was chipping, unlike many of the surrounding buildings, and there were two big Ukrainian flags hanging from the facade. It was on a bit of an island at the end of the block, surrounded by cobblestone roads which divided suburban neighborhoods on adjacent streets. Behind the premises was a mostly paved backyard, with a few net-less basketball hoops and soccer goals as well as a couple dogs who were sun-bathing in some patches of grass.

I made it to the front of the school, which had a yard of trees as a buffer in front of the street. I decided to wait for Myra in front of the main entrance, where I was greeted by another harmless stray dog and some graffiti saying "lil pump" and "XXX Tentacion." Everything was about what I expected.

Just a few minutes later, Myra came outside. She was about my height, with long black hair and green eyes, and welcomed me to School 16 with a hug.

"Robert! What are you doing outside? Aren't you cold?"

"No," I replied, "I feel fine. Just waiting for you!"

"I'm already here. The doors are unlocked, you know."

I did not know that. The lights were turned off, so I assumed I was the first one there.

"Are you nervous?" she asked as she ushered me into the school.

"Definitely," I said. The training wheels were off, the Peace Corps safety net was gone, and I was finally ready to get started.

We walked into the virtually empty school, where we were greeted by a painting of a smiling sun on the floor. To my left I saw a huge board with pictures of students dressed in traditional Ukrainian clothing called Vishivankas. There were plants - lots of plants, and a Ukrainian flag flung around a wooden column in the middle of the hallway. There were also various posters that covered some of the walls, advertising karate classes and various other things that I couldn't decipher.

"That's the principal's room," Myra said while pointing at a huge wooden door next to the board of smiling children. "We'll go on a full tour next week, but for now the students are already waiting. They're so excited to meet you!"

Myra led me up a few flights of concrete stairs to the third floor. We took a right and then walked to a room that had the number 26 on the door.

"This is it!" She said, leading me into the small classroom. It was thin room, almost like a closet, with hardly enough space to hold two rows of desks. As she opened the door, I was greeted by four students and a teacher, all sitting and waiting patiently.

"Robert," Myra said, bringing me over to the teacher, "This is Yana. You two will be working together today. Is it ok if I leave you with her? I have a lot of paperwork."

"No problem," I said.

Right after Myra closed the door, an awkward silence ensued, as if none of us had any idea of what to do next. I looked to my left, where I saw a blackboard and chalk, and subtly pumped my fist. Working with a classic black board was something that I had only seen in TV shows, and purely for aesthetics I was elated to be greeted by the large black square on the wall.

"Hello Mr. Robert," Yana said, breaking my focus from the blackboard, "I'm Yana. Surely Myra has told you about the Olympiad, which is just a week away, so we'd really love your help listening to our participants."

"Of course," I said while turning to the terrified teenagers. At that point I wasn't quite used to getting scared looks from youth, although after my first few weeks it was something I quickly got used to. I assumed that these teens, like the students in Hryshkivtsi, had never met an American before and were extremely intimidated. With this in mind I didn't want to be too critical of their work, because the last thing I wanted to do was destroy their confidence just one week away from the competition.

I sat down, greeted them, and pulled out my notebook to write down their names: Nastia, Alexandra, Anastasia, and Maria. They ranged from ninth to eleventh grade, and none of them were participating in their first Olympiad.

"Ok," I said after quick intros, "I think we're ready to get started."

"Girls," Yana said, "Who would like to go first?"

"I would," Nastia, the tenth grader said.

The first Olympiad question: Why is pain sometimes funny?

I don't remember what I was expecting, but within a couple of minutes I realized that these kids were freaking geniuses.

"I've noticed," Nastia began after standing up, "That many people find fail videos very entertaining. They are very quick, so you don't get to see what happens to the person afterwards. To be honest I'm not sure exactly why they are funny, but in this case, pain is only able to be funny because the screen separates the viewer from reality."

I was in awe.

"Seeing something like that in real life wouldn't be as funny. It might not be funny at all, once you see that the person is really hurt. However it's always funny online."

"Except," she emphasized after taking a couple of seconds to think, "Except when there's blood. It's never funny when there is blood, even online. When there is blood, you always know it's real. Even blood takes away the barrier from reality that your computer screen provides."

"Robert," Yana said, "Do you have any follow up questions?"

At that point I could barely believe what I just heard. I went into this not knowing if they could even speak English for two minutes straight, let alone spit off some genius rhetoric about a screen separating ourselves from reality. I looked up at Yana, who was smiling with pride, and turned back to Nastia.

"Well," I said, "Why does blood make it real?"

For the next forty-five minutes, I listened to those four impeccable students recite various two to three minute responses to the Olympiad practice questions. I went in wanting to go really easy on them, but after learning their level I began overtly looking for any little mistake in grammar or vocabulary that I could find. There were hardly any. Each response was just as impressive as the previous, even from the lone ninth grader in the room. I understood that these were probably the best students in the school, and my cynical side pushed me to believe that they didn't actually need any help, and the English Department just wanted to show off their amazing students to their new volunteer. Either way, it didn't matter. Compared to teaching a class of thirty fourth graders in Hryshkivtsi, those forty five minutes of listening to such well developed thoughts and ideas were heaven on earth. If this was what teaching was going to be like at School 16, then these two years were going to fly by.

Of course, things didn't work out that way. Within a week I'd be back in the classroom with loud and restless ten year olds. But just like I thought, working with the Olympiaders during my first day was a welcomed landing spot for the next year or two to come.

The next week, after spending the weekend walking around Mukachevo with my host family, I walked into a much brighter and more crowded school. It was loud. Very loud. Younger children were going absolutely ballistic in the hallways playing tag and tackling each other while some overworked teachers halfheartedly told them to stop. As I waited for Myra in the lobby like a lost toddler, all the kids who ran passed me began to not so subtly stare. This was much more akin to what I imagined my first day would be, although I was pleasantly surprised that at least ten percent of the stares were more curious and not as fear-ladened as the week before. Earlier I saw various Instagram stories of some volunteers being given gifts and making speeches, so while there wasn't a parade for my arrival, there were at least a few students who ran up to me, shook my hand, and then ran away laughing after I said something to them in English. I can't count the amount of kids I either talked to or hugged that week, but it must have been well into the hundreds.

However, I had a job to do. A scary one, and the reality of my upcoming work dawned on me that first day.

"Robert!" Myra said after finding me in the lobby, "Let's go to class."

As I followed Myra, likely more scared than the students who were waiting for me in her classroom. As we walked down the hall, students lined up against the walls clutching their books as if I were going to walk up to them and evaluate them on the spot. Although the vibe was generally off-putting, I could easily understand where they were coming from. I was nervous enough speaking Ukrainian after three months of intense training, so I could sympathize with these tiny humans' fears of talking with a native English speaker. However, my primary purpose was to show them that speaking English doesn't have to be scary, so although I had been feeling butterflies since leaving home that morning, I did my best to wear a smile.

We made it to her room in no time, and I soon began staring down twenty eighth graders who had nowhere to hide. Unfortunately I didn't either, as much as I wanted to during that first lesson.

"Hello class," Myra announced after the second bell, "This is Mr. Robert. As you may know, he will be working with us for the next two years. Everyone say hello!"

"Hello," they all said monotoned and in unison.

"Hi everyone," I said, terrified. My face soon became red, or so I assumed.

"Does anyone have any questions?"

After a few crickets, Myra looked around, apparently not surprised.

"No questions for Mr. Robert?"

More crickets.

"They're a little bit shy," Myra said, "You might be the first American they've ever met."

"I understand," I said. I wouldn't know what to say either.

"We'll have plenty of time for questions throughout the year. Class, Robert is going to help us with conversational English. So if he asks you a question, try to answer the best you can. But before all of that, he'll watch us while we go through our lesson, so be on your best behavior."

And with that, I sat in the corner while Myra effortlessly and energetically taught some sort of English grammar. After an overwhelming training experience, I was extremely thankful that us teaching volunteers would always be working with a Ukrainian counterpart, who would generally be leading the class. Our counterparts knew that they would be the ones typically teaching the more technical parts of the language, while the most useful thing volunteers could provide was speaking practice. Assimilating into the school system was hard enough, but needing to teach non native speakers English grammar felt like an impossible task, so I was more than happy early on to simply lead discussion activities.

Right as I started to daydream, I heard Myra say my name. I looked up, and she motioned me over to center stage in front of the chalkboard.

"Now, Robert has a little activity for us. Robert, are you ready?"

"Alright everyone," I said, trying to feign confidence and remember the plan Myra and I came up with the night before, "We have a project today. We will be working in groups and discussing our future dream house. Please get into groups of four, and then we can get started."

They all proceeded to stare at me wide-eyed. I assumed they just didn't understand me, so I spoke slower.

"We - are - doing - a -"

"They understand you, Robert," Myra said, jumping in, "Kids!" she exclaimed as they all suddenly perked up, "Get into groups of four!" However, they continued to look frozen. She then translated the instructions in Ukrainian, but to no avail. They seemed absolutely perplexed.

"Sorry, Robert," Myra said, "They aren't usually asked to do that."

"To do what?" I asked, wondering what sort of cultural rule I had defiled on my first day.

"To get into groups. We always assign them into groups."

I remembered this being true in Hryshkivtsi, too: The kids had no idea how to get into groups. At the time I had no idea why, but after a few months of experience and exposure in School 16, I started to gain a little more insight on what specifically was going on.

All I have to go on are the anecdotal experiences of myself and other volunteers, but after a while it became apparent to all of us that the Ukrainian teaching method is extremely instructor-centered. The instructor stands in front of the class, and throughout every step of the lesson kids are told what to do and how to do it properly. Many lessons in Ukraine are lecture and worksheet based, where students end up writing down everything the teacher says, and then wait for the teacher to ask them a question. There are always very clear right and wrong answers, and the lessons often follow a very rigid structure.

Such a significant part of our training was about making things more student-centered, and while during orientation it was just some sort of theoretical idea, it became an extremely apparent need during that first month. It didn't take me too long to notice that there wasn't much student choice or direction involved in the educational process, and the kids rarely had the space to do anything outside of the box. After a couple months of being exposed to this, it made sense why something as simple as telling kids to get into groups left my students perplexed.

However, all that future knowledge didn't help during the first lesson. Myra and I spent about five minutes trying to get the students to choose their groups, but we soon gave up and assigned each individual student to a group. This formality took almost half of my portion of the lesson, so after speeding through short group discussions of different types of houses, we barely had enough time for students to present to the class. No one seemed confident in their answers, so no one dared to speak up. That's another thing I noticed throughout my time in Ukraine: A lot of the students were perfectionists, due to an intense fear of being scolded after saying a wrong answer. And trust me, there was a lot of scolding and public humiliation after a few too many wrong answers.

The authoritarian classroom and lack of grey area screams Soviet Soviet Soviet. Back in the Soviet era, if you didn't think a certain way or behave a certain way, you were bound for trouble. Intellectual purges in the 1950s and 60s made it clear that any form of free thinking in the Soviet Union would be a one way track to being exiled, and while it's far from that sort of intensity nowadays in the school system, many of the remnants still remain. Back then it simply wasn't safe to have a way of thinking that strayed away from what the government wanted you to believe, and nowhere was that more significant than in the classroom. Curriculum throughout the entire region in the USSR was state curated and mandated, and I heard stories that if teachers were ever found deviating from the curriculum, they could be arrested.

Imagine that: A teacher being arrested by government authorities for going off track a little bit. It's no wonder why the current classroom experience is so rigid and by the book. It doesn't make the effect on the students any less troubling, but it's easier to go about trying to fix a problem when you know some of the causes.

For someone in their 20s like me, the Soviet era seems like an imaginary time and a far cry from the fake-Gucci belt wearing teenagers who walked through the halls of School 16. However, for many Ukrainians the Soviet Union is an unforgettable period in the not too distant past. Anyone over the age of forty will have a clear memory of what life was like back then, and the teachers in Ukraine are no exception.

Throughout my first month, I saw this time and time again. A strict structure, little creative thinking, students afraid of being wrong, and subsequently afraid to speak to me. *So that's why they're all terrified of me,* I thought, slightly relieved I wasn't freaking out because of my general vibe.

After a few weeks of getting my sea legs and taking some time to sort out what was going on, I decided that student choice/confidence was the main area that I wanted to initially focus on. I tried to help students think a little bit more for themselves and to be less afraid of mistakes, and I started making activities and lesson plans intentionally focused on giving the students more choices and autonomy.

Maybe fifteen to twenty minutes of conversation practice per class isn't going to make any of these kids fluent English speakers, I brainstormed at a coffee shop after scarfing down my second croissant sandwich of the day, But maybe I can help them start thinking outside of the box a little bit. After discussing this with my counterparts, I later initiated this by giving students choices during our various discussion activities.

For example, during one of my classes with seventh graders, we were studying technology vocabulary. I divided the students into three groups and said that we would be writing a dialogue. I told each group to use four terms that we learned during the lesson and gave each of them a vague topic, such as "weekends," or "surprises." Without hesitation, the questions flooded in.

"What about weekends do you want us to write about?"

"How many sentences?"

"Which words should we use?"

My response tended to be the same each time.

"I don't know, that's up to you. Write something about weekends, use at least four words, and make sure that everyone has a part of the dialogue."

The more vague the better, I thought, and Myra agreed. While the activities took much more time and caused a lot more student anguish than if we had spoon fed them the instructions, after a few months the kids started getting used to working without clear and defined rules. It was a small step that I was very proud of early on in my service.

I was a little afraid of trying to change things up too much, because as a twenty-two year old with no prior teaching experience, I wasn't exactly comfortable telling these seasoned professionals how to do their job, especially while in some aspects of teaching they were more capable than I could have dreamed of. However, to their credit, they applied for a Peace Corps volunteer and wanted to look for ways to improve. It was very easy to work with my counterparts Myra, Marina, Yana, and Diana, and when it came to my ideas they didn't need much convincing. So, within a relatively short amount of time, we made a small difference in some of the learning methods at the school with something as small as instructions.

In my first few months of teaching, although some lessons were a bit rough around the edges and I was reeling daily from some of the draconian teaching practices, I began to find a bit of a niche in the classroom. There were immense struggles, though. I had no idea how to manage the students and their behavior, sometimes my activities were either way too easy or way too difficult, and every now and then I'd be in over my head if my co-teacher ever had to take a call and left me alone with the kids. However, with all of that said, on a daily basis I had no trouble finding something that made me feel good about the work I was doing. At the core of my job I was working with children and trying to help them develop, which felt really good. Thank goodness there were redeeming qualities, because again, I didn't think of teaching English for one second when I was preparing for Peace Corps. Giving fist bumps in the hallways to eleventh graders and shaking the tiny hands of first graders made my heart melt on a daily basis, and throughout my time in School 16 there was no shortage of fulfilling and meaningful moments.

Here are some of those moments from School 16:

At the end of the first semester, students were taking exams. For the listening portion of the exam, my co-teachers had me read a text out loud that students would need to decipher. After reading it the first time, my co-teacher Yana politely nudged me and asked, "Mr. Robert, here we focus a little more on British English, and for the state exams there will be a British person speaking. Would you mind using a British accent?" I had no clue of how to do a British accent, but in order to not undermine Yana in front of her ninth graders, I gave my best 'tally ho' and read the text three times in my best London accent. No one laughed at the butchered British accent, but I highly doubt it was good enough to prepare in the slightest for the state exam.

....

One night, one of my co-teachers, Marina, messaged me saying that eleventh grade wanted to know how the president gets elected in the United States, "And specifically how a president with fewer votes becomes elected." Oh boy. That next day, laptop in hand, I gave a watered down lecture on the Electoral College, trying to sound as apolitical as possible. A lot of the students liked that the little states had a lot more of a voice, but when I showed them that only eight or so states actually decide the election, they changed their tune a little bit. All in all it was a smooth lesson, where most of the kids were able to understand me because of their advanced English level.

Then Alexandra, one of the Olympiaders, raised her hand and asked, "Is it true that Russian President Vladimir Putin helped Donald Trump win because Hilary Clinton is in favor of Ukraine?"

Oh jeez. I was blatantly told by the Peace Corps over and over again not to discuss anything political with anyone, but after doing a quick mental calculation, I thought, "screw it," and told them the deal.

"Yes, it's been shown that Putin helped Trump become President by manipulating the American people using Facebook advertisements. We don't know if Trump worked with Putin or not. I also don't know if Trump hates Ukraine, but Hilary Clinton definitely would have been better for Ukraine."

"Are there any other reasons that Putin likes Trump?" Another one asked.

"Well," I said, grinding my teeth, "Well, Putin hates," and I pointed to the word "Democracy," I had written on the board. "And Trump, well, as you can see, has been pretty bad for...uh, well..."

"We understand," Alexandra said, as the rest of the students nodded their heads.

There I was, a member of the federal government, telling Ukrainian teenagers that the President of the United States was a threat to Democracy.

"Yeah, uh, if you guys could not tell anyone that I said this,"

"Don't worry!" Another student said, as she gave the "my lips are sealed" sign with her hands. The rest of the students followed, putting their index fingers and thumbs on their lips and sewing them shut.

Almost on cue, the bell rang and the students left.

....

During a lesson with tenth grade, we went around talking about our plans for the winter holidays. My co-teacher Diana had left to take a call or do some other work or something, so I was left alone with them. I was a little nervous, but since they were in tenth grade and knew English pretty well, I was confident that I could handle them for a few minutes while Diana was out.

"Try to use the grammar from class," I said, not really knowing what grammar we had gone over, "And tell me about your plans for New Years. Anastasia, what will you be doing over the winter holidays?"

"Buhaty," Anastasia said. The class laughed, and to Anastasia's horror, so did I. I had only been in Ukraine for a few months to that point, but by then I knew that buhaty meant, "To get super drunk." The class looked at me, some in shock and others in wild amusement.

"Do you know what that means?:" Anastasia asked.

"Of course I do!" I said as pure terror clouded Anastasia's expression. I moved on to the next student, and when Diana came back in I made the easy decision of not snitching and subsequently becoming the lamest teacher in the entire planet. After staring at me and trying to read if I was going to rat her out, Anastasia breathed a little easier towards the end of class, when she knew the coast was clear.

....

"Mr. Robert," one of my sixth graders asked me during one of our first classes, "What is your favorite Ukrainian dish?"

A layup of a question, I thought. What easier way to worm into the good graces of my class than to talk about my favorite Ukrainian meal? Feeling confident, I gave my best shot at Ukrainian. The only problem was that my Ukrainian sucked.

Holoptsi is a delicious Ukrainian dish, which is a cabbage roll filled with rice and meat and covered in oil. However, hloptsi is plural for boys.

"Well Ihor," I said, "My favorite Ukrainian dish is boys. I love to eat boys. Thanks for the question."

No one corrected me, and I continued on the class with a pep in my step, until afterwards my co-teacher told me what I said. Ah, what better way to become less intimidating than telling a sixth grader that I eat his kind.

....

While I can't say that every day or week was perfect, I was elated to find a few months into the job that I actually liked it. It was a total toss up, especially because I hadn't given English teaching one second of thought while preparing for PC, but in hindsight I understand that if I absolutely hated teaching, there is no way I could've made it past a year in the Peace Corps. By the end of my service I couldn't say that I completely revolutionized the Ukrainian education system or eliminated outdated Soviet teaching principles, but I was able to leave knowing that I had at least some sort of positive impact on a whole host of students. And after hearing some horror stories of other Peace Corps volunteers, that's something I'm eternally grateful for.

Chapter Six

The Kerch Strait

By the end of my first month in Mukachevo, I finally felt like I had actually started the whole Peace Corps thing. After a grueling training process, in which I wasn't helping anyone other than myself, I felt a newfound pride actually going to work everyday and contributing to society. While things in the classroom had been far from smooth, I was at least leaving school everyday feeling like I had accomplished something and being thankful that I was not only loving the beautiful town I was placed in, but also the work that came along with it.

This is why the events of November 25th, 2018 were all the more distressing.

That night, I was laying in bed in my new home after having dinner with my host family. As I scrolled through stories on the Instagram I had created a few weeks earlier (which is obligatory if you want to make friends in Ukraine), I came across a post saying something along the lines of "Russian Navy Attacks Ukrainian Vessels at the Kerch Strait" That... was concerning. What was more concerning was the email I got the next morning from our safety and security director:

Security Message to ALL PCVs - ALERT status declared!

Hello Volunteers,

Tension between Russia and Ukraine escalated yesterday and last night due to Russia's aggressive actions towards 4 Ukrainian Navy ships that took place near the Kerch strait in the Azov Sea.

As of now, we do not anticipate a threat to PCVs. The issue was brought to the attention of the international community by Ukraine and the Government of Ukraine is working on actions in response. One possible scenario is the introduction of Martial Law, which would limit ability for mass gatherings, require additional checkpoints on roads, limit movement in the conflict area, etc...

Tension between Russian and Ukraine? Alert Status? Martial Law?

Uh oh, I thought while getting ready to sing songs with some ten year olds. This could only mean one thing: We're going to be evacuated, just one month after I had made it past training.

Crap.

To give some context, I should explain some of the details about the current conflict between Ukraine and Russia. In 2014, Ukrainian citizens overthrew their government. Protests began on November 21 2013, when the sitting president, Viktor Yanukovych, refused to sign an economic pact with the European Union, and instead chose to pursue a similar agreement with Russia. This was all after Yanukovych promised in 2011 to do the opposite. This sudden change of course did not sit well with the majority of the country, who saw the move as a major step away from the democratic and western trajectory of Ukraine to the oppressive times of Soviet rule.

That night, protests erupted in the central square in Kyiv, as thousands of Ukrainians started to make their voices heard. About a week later on November 30th, tensions flared as the "Berkut," an oppressive semi-autonomous militia that was commonly known for attacking and torturing protesters, ruthlessly beat a group of student protesters and non-protesting civilians with batons. This further inflamed protests, and by December over one million people were gathering at the the central square every day.

Soon, what started out as pro-European protests quickly turned into a full scale revolution, which is now known famously as "Euromaidan," "The Maidan Revolution," and the "Revolution of Dignity." After months of tension, lethal violence erupted in February, when the Berkut began shooting live rounds at protesters between February 18th-20th, which resulted in over one hundred casualties. The capital city of Ukraine turned into a war-zone, as protesters used DIY shields and literal fire to protect themselves (I highly recommend the documentary "Winter on Fire" on Netflix. It does more justice telling the story of the revolution than I ever could).

On February 22nd, as protests continued and intensified, the sitting president fled to Russia in the middle of the night, confirming his true allegiance that most Ukrainians knew all along. Soon afterwards snap elections were held, a new government was formed, the European Association Agreement was signed, and the Ukrainian people successfully protected their independence from Russian influence and intervention. The Ukrainian people had won, for the moment.

The revolution that ousted Putin's man and completely changed Ukraine's ideological course from being a Russian pseudo-state to a Western ally came with swift retaliation from the east. Not less than a month later, Russian-backed forces started an armed conflict the eastern regions of Luhansk and Donetsk, which began a war between the two parties that has killed over 14,000 Ukrainians. This has led to hundreds of thousands of IDPs (internally displaced people) fleeing their homes in the east, civilian deaths, immeasurable trauma and billions of dollars in infrastructure damage. And now, in February 2022, Russia has *escalated* the invasion and and started shelling cities all throughout Ukraine.

At the same time conflict began escalating in the east, unmarked Russian forces invaded and subsequently annexed the profitable tourist port region of Crimea in the southeast, which on the international stage has been condemned as illegal and has drawn world-wide criticism and sanctions against Russia. The Berkut, having been dissolved by the Ukrainian government after the revolution, defected to Russia and now has a sizable presence maintaining "order" in Crimea.

Here enters the Kerch Strait. The Kerch Strait, a sort of passageway that connects the Black Sea and the Sea of Azov, is directly in between Crimea and Western Russia. Basically, this slim body of water is the only thing separating Crimea and greater Russia. This strait leads to the Azov Sea, which as you can see in the map below directly borders Crimea in the east, the active war zone of Donetsk in the north, and Western Russia. The sea is a strategic region for both Ukraine and Russia, and in 2003 they signed a treaty stating that both countries could peacefully operate and co-exist there. However, a lot has happened since 2003, and to say that this is a hotly contested and sensitive region is like saying fish enjoy water.

(Mother Jones, 2018).

On that November evening in 2018, this potential hotbed is where the Russian Navy attacked Ukrainian vessels, captured them, and took the Ukrainian crew as hostages. Although I tend to be on the more neurotic and paranoid side, it wasn't a far jump to think that an attack and capture of Ukrainian vessels by Russian forces in an incredibly sensitive region could have been a tipping point to a full scale escalation of war.

With all of this impressed into my mind, an email from the safety and security manager that morning talking about Russian aggression and the implementation of martial law set off an atomic bomb of nerves at seven in the morning.

"What is wrong, Robert?" My host brother Zhenya asked me at breakfast, as I aimlessly stared into my soup.

"Oh nothing, just a lot of work today," I replied while going through worst-case scenarios in my head.

I looked up at my host family, who was acting completely normal.

I guess they haven't heard the news, I thought while slurping down the remains of breakfast. I left the table as soon as I could, not knowing how well I'd be able to continue to hide my "end of the world" type disposition.

Reading the "Alert" part of the email left me the most distraught. During our various safety and security meetings during training, we learned that the Alert Stage is the first of three stages that occur when there is a heightened security risk in the country. The third stage is evacuation of all volunteers, and merely one month into our service we were one third of the way towards evacuating. This wouldn't be a new experience for PC Ukraine, which successfully evacuated volunteers in February of 2014 due to the Maidan Revolution, so evacuation was far from out of the realm of possibilities.

The stars of me being traumatized were beautifully aligning, and all I could do was scream internally as I ironed a white button down. Our prospects of continuing service weren't looking good, especially for the paranoid type like myself, and if the Peace Corps could evacuate volunteers for geopolitical problems with Russia before, they could do it again.

However, just like the rest of the country, I still had to go to work that day and fulfill my societal duties. I don't know how I or any of my colleagues could be asked to do that, because it's hard to put on a happy face and sing songs about farm animals when we could be in a full scale war in less than a week. How could I shove this news in the back of my mind? How could I look my optimistic eleventh graders in the eye, wondering if half of them could be drafted by graduation?

My second shot of an espresso on the bus simply made matters worse, and my fervent anxiety catalyzed into a hyper caffeinated tailspin.

"Yup, we are totally going to get evacuated," I mumbled to myself on the bus, "We are going to get evacuated, just like in 2014, and four months after leaving my American life behind for my coming of age wallflower international adventure, I will be back in Nashville living with my mom." While earlier that morning I initially worried about the welfare of the country and its citizens, during the bus ride only selfish waves of anxiety flooded my mind.

This is going to screw me professionally, I thought, *How could I put four months of Peace Corps on a resume? What did I learn here, besides how to peel potatoes with a knife and say "I don't understand" in Ukrainian? I've barely even began to work, and it would totally suck if I went through two and a half months of training and living in Hryshkivtsi only to pack up and leave when it started getting good. Not to mention it's gonna be a pain adapting back to life in the States. Culture shock here was hard enough, but I just now started getting used to to the cold stares and lack of smiles from strangers. I'm not ready to go back to Tennessee and say to on the sidewalk and make small talk with cashiers. Oh, the humanity.*

Of course, I thought while putting all of my pressure into my jaw, *I could reinstate and go to a new country, but I picked Ukraine for a reason! I can't live in Africa or South America! I burn too easily, and there are (probably) no croissant sandwich shops there. Two absolute dealbreakers.*

Yet it might be either that or leaving the Peace Corps altogether. How much of the past year did I dream about Peace Corps, the freaking Peace Corps, only to say goodbye just when things started to get good.

That was a bad bus ride.

Halfway through convincing myself that getting placed in West Africa wouldn't be too big of a leap from my comfortable croissant ladened town in Western Ukraine, I arrived at my school, thankful for something that could take my mind off the geo-political situation at hand. I didn't know how my colleagues were going to react to a huge escalation of Russian aggression in the east, but I expected the worst.

I entered the school, and much like the cloudy and grey atmosphere that accompanied my bus ride, the entire school was dim. In fact, I noticed that there were no lights on at all. I wondered if it was a holiday or something, but I heard teachers working in various classrooms.

Maybe the power's out, I thought. Fitting on a day like this.

I sulked up to the teachers' room, not knowing if it would be appropriate to bring up the situation, but luckily I didn't face that choice because no one was there. It felt a little odd, being in a dark and deserted teachers room, but I had arrived about twenty minutes into the second period of the day, so I assumed everyone was teaching.

I took a seat at the wooden oval table in the center and sprawled my things. While waiting for the third period to start, I began writing the pros and cons of getting evacuated.

"Ok, pro," I said quietly enough so no one could hear I was talking myself, "I've made six hundred and fifty bucks during my stay in Ukraine. After coming home I will get a nice chunk of change in my bank account. Not bad." Alright, not bad. One pro for evacuation.

"Con: My dreams will be destroyed." Ok, one con for evacuation.

I tried to make as many pros as I could, but they were mostly reaches. The other pros of getting to say I lived in Eastern Europe for four months and that I had lost some weight after being slightly underfed during training were all I had to justify why getting evacuated wasn't going to be the worst thing to ever happen to me. My anxiety was far from subsiding, and checking group chats where other volunteers were texting in all caps didn't make things better. The enraged caffeine frenzy wasn't helping either, but even then I debated grabbing a third espresso in a desperate attempt to feel something different than existential terror.

Before I could make such an unwise decision, my counterpart Myroslava came into the teacher's room with a solemn look on her face. We greeted each other, and I could tell that something was wrong.

"Robert, do you mind if we speak in my room?" she asked.

"Of course, is everything ok?"

"Yes, but we need to talk in my room."

Not a good sign. We walked through the dark hallway and down two flights of stairs without saying a word. When we finally made it to room six, Myra sat me down and began trying to find the right words to say.

"Robert," Myra said with a pause, "I want to be upfront with you."

"Ok," I said, awaiting the worst.

"I'm telling you this because I know you're new here and this isn't your culture. If I were in your shoes I'd want to know as well..."

Oh God.

"So," she continued, "Here you go: Whenever you see one of the teachers, you have to say hi to them. They won't say hi to you, but you need to say hi to them. It's a cultural thing - I don't blame you because you didn't know, but it's seen as rude if you don't greet them first."

I didn't know what was more shocking: The fact that we weren't discussing the potential oncoming annihilation of Ukraine, or that I had been offending the majority of my colleagues without saying a word.

"Oh, um, ok. I'm sorry, I had no idea."

"It's fine," she replied, "And I think they understand too. Don't worry too much about it. Also, another thing: On Sundays, when you communicate with your other co-teachers about lesson plans, you need to text them in the evening instead of in the morning. In the morning we go to Church, and don't start planning until the afternoon."

After the second comment, Myra took a sigh of relief and began to gauge my reaction.

Both were very helpful pieces of advice, which I took to heart and made sure not to forget for the rest of my time in Mukachevo, but I still couldn't get the Kerch Strait conflict out of my mind.

"Thank you, Myra, that's all very helpful."

"I hope you won't get too sad about this!" She said while standing up with a smile, "Everything is fine, and you're doing a great job teaching."

"Thank you," I said while racking my brain. "Please feel free to let me know about these things as time goes on. But," I said with a pause.

"Yes?"

I decided to go for it and breach the Kerch Strait subject. I didn't want to make anyone upset, but as my Peace Corps assigned counterpart, Myroslava and I had a relationship that made us closer than just colleagues.

"Did you see what happened in the Azov Sea?" I blurted out. She looked confused, which wasn't a reaction that I prepared for. "You know, the Russian navy attacked a Ukrainian ship, and took the sailors as hostages. Did you hear?"

"Oh, that," Myra replied nonchalantly, "Yes, I did." She paused, "It's very unfortunate, but these things happen. It's Ukraine. I wouldn't think about it too much, If I were you."

It felt like quite an odd response, seeing as she was a lot more relaxed about the existential state of her homeland than I was. However, I took the hint that the conversation was unnecessary and wouldn't do anything to subside my worries, and I decided not to press forward.

The bell rang (almost on cue), so I thanked her for her suggestions and for letting me talk to her about the incident.

"No problem, Robert. Feel free to come to me about anything. I'm happy we can communicate about things like this."

Seconds after the bell went off, students and teachers dispersed into the hallway. What I saw once again surprised me: It wasn't a wave of depression and solemn stares like I had envisioned walking into school that day. In fact, everyone was acting the exact same, even without a single light on in the school. The lower schoolers were running around and playing in the hallway, their teachers were trying their best to make sure they didn't run into each other, men were shaking each others' hands and the teenagers were being...teenagery. Even with the darkened hallways, everyone was acting like everything was going according to plan.

The only real change was that I started saying hi to the other teachers, who finally smiled at me and shot a friendly greeting back. At that point, I laughed. If there was an oncoming war, it definitely didn't show in School 16. Nevertheless, my theories for the lack of community-wide panicking soon began.

I initially thought that people here were disconnected from the problems in the east, seeing as we were in the most Western part of the country. But anecdotally I had already had a few discussions with some patriots who were both proud of their heritage and despised the Russian regime. Sasha, one of the custodians at school, and I would talk regularly about the "unfortunate situation" in the east, and he always wanted to hear my opinions about the U.S. and Russian relations. Indifference couldn't be the reason for everyone.

I then thought that perhaps because the situation was so new and had only happened the night before, that most people didn't know about it and were living in a happy ignorance until they checked the news later that day. But that didn't make much sense either. It's not like Ukraine is in the dark ages: Almost everyone I knew had a smartphone, and my host family watched the news every morning. Additionally Myra knew about it, and sure enough during lunch time Sasha wanted my take on the situation. He, unlike the rest of the school, was feeling down.

"What do you think will happen?" I asked as he plopped buckwheat on my plate.

"No one knows. We don't know what tomorrow will bring. I don't even know if we'll be at work tomorrow. It's a scary situation."

I was a little relieved to hear someone who was on the same page as me, but he was just about the only example.

A more fitting conclusion came from Myra's "this stuff happens all the time" attitude, because compared to Ukraine's brutal contemporary history, this may have felt like a minor incident. I'll share some of that history for some brief context.

Let's start in the early 1900s. After a four year war between the Russian Bolsheviks and newly independent Ukraine, in 1921 Ukraine was conquered and enveloped into the Soviet Union. Ten years later, with Stalin at the helm, collectivization policies forced Ukrainian farmers to give up one third of their grain to the Soviet government. The plundering of Ukrainian farmland led to a famine, which is considered by many countries as a Soviet instigated genocide that led to the death of three to five million Ukrainians. Cannibalism was all too common in Ukraine during this time, and many Soviet propaganda pamphlets were created asking citizens to not eat their parents and siblings.

A few years later came World War II. During this time Ukraine was taken over by the Nazi regime during their invasion of the USSR, and afterwards was once again taken over by the USSR. Seven million Ukrainians were killed during WWII, which is greater than the total military loss of the USA, Canada, British Commonwealth, France, Germany and Italy all put together. This included four and a half million civilians, many of whom died after being used as slave labor in German work camps (Gregorovich, 1995).

WWII concluded with Ukraine once again being under totalitarian rule, this time for forty years. Much of the USSR during this period was defined by extreme censorship, a Russian language mandate that made it illegal to speak the Ukrainian language, instigated a purging of intellectuals, and created massive distrust amongst neighbors.

Forty years later came the Chernobyl disaster, which happened right in the heart of Soviet Ukraine. Over 200,000 people had to evacuate their homes, and fear about radiation contamination spread rapidly through Ukraine. It is unknown how many people were exposed to contaminated food or air, but because of these fears, many Ukrainians made the heartbreaking decision to stop having children out of fear of what would happen during a pregnancy after a nuclear explosion. Here's an excerpt from The World Nuclear Association (2021):

A particularly sad effect of the misconceptions surrounding the accident was that some physicians in Europe advised pregnant women to undergo abortions on account of radiation exposure, even though the levels concerned were vastly below those likely to have teratogenic effects. Robert Gale, a hematologist who treated radiation victims after the accident, estimated that more than 1 million abortions were undertaken in the Soviet Union and Europe as a result of incorrect advice from their doctors about radiation exposure and birth defects following the accident.

The collapse of the Soviet Union happened five years later, which coincided with a prolonged recession to an already suffering economy. Corruption has plagued Ukraine since independence, as many politicians are controlled by various incredibly wealthy oligarchs throughout the country. Lack of adequate corruption reform has been holding Ukraine back from any sort of chance of getting into the E.U., unlike many of their post-soviet neighbors.

While the economy has stabilized in the past twenty years, the Peace Corps is there for a reason: Many of my co-teachers were making less than two hundred dollars a month working a full time job, which is only slightly more than many of the doctors on the front lines fighting COVID-19. For context, some of my friends in Kyiv rent an apartment for five hundred dollars a month, and my rent for a studio apartment in Mukachevo cost one hundred and thirty dollars a month.

In 2004 came rigged elections, which prompted a peaceful revolution called the Orange Revolution. This led to a fair election, but afterwards the new president was poisoned by Russian operatives. The next election in 2009 resulted in the winner of the 2004 rigged election, Yanukovych, winning fair and square. Four years later came the Maidan Revolution after Yanukovych refused to sign the European Association Agreement, which as we know provoked the annexation of Crimea along with an active and ongoing war in the east.

Compared to the past one hundred years, it made sense to me why this most recent Russian provocation at the Kerch Strait, while tragic, was met with a sense of fatigued normalcy.

But anyway, back to school.

Although I was still in a bit of shock, I decided to go with the mindset of "When in Ukraine, do as the Ukrainians do." Although Myra's words didn't exactly keep my mind from racing, I did my best to take on the laid-back disposition of my Ukrainian colleagues.

If everyone else was going to act normally, I might as well do the same.

I began the third period teaching seventh grade with my co-teacher Natalia, and soon found my stresses subsided once I finally began working. Teaching is such an active job, and teachers don't really have a lot of time to let their mind wander into endless possibilities about the future. For me there were so many different things going on at once, ranging from using the right vocabulary/speed of speech to make sure the kids understand my accent, to keeping an eye on them to make sure they're actively engaged and not checking their phones. My respect for teachers has amplified since joining the Peace Corps, because it's very draining to be juggling so many things for seven hours a day.

After working with some genuinely interested and engaged students (which wasn't always the case), for the first time in the day I felt calm. That is until after my lesson ended, when I checked my phone. During lessons I preferred to put it in airplane mode, which was the greatest mistake I could have made the day after Russian aggression.

I saw that I had eleven missed calls in the past forty-five minutes. Eleven. I checked Facebook to also find a litany of messages from one of the volunteer leaders, Cindy.

"PICK UP THE PHONE. URGENT!!!!"

After having a tranquil forty-five minute break, I quickly went back into panic mode. I immediately called her back.

"Cindy, what's wrong?"

"Oh, hey Bob! Thanks for calling. We were just doing a communication drill. Remember to keep your phone on at all times, haha. You heard about what happened, right?"

"Yeah, is everything ok?"

"We'll see. Just keep working for now and try not to think about it too much. Have a good day!"

After that I made sure to keep my sound on as I continued the rest of my day, and after some slight panicking, I tried to simply just get back to work. Compared to everything else going on, trying to calm down twenty fourth graders screaming in Ukrainian felt like the most normal thing possible.

Later that week, we learned that twenty four sailors and three ships were captured by Russian forces. Martial law was imposed throughout half of Ukraine, and men with a Russian passport ages sixteen to sixty were banned from entering the country. We were updated throughout the month by our Safety and Security Manager and were reminded to lay low, always have our phone on us, and not do anything too crazy.

I'm happy to say that tensions peaked during the first few days of the Kerch Strait incident. After some strong rhetoric and many days of PC Ukraine walking on eggshells, there was no invasion or escalation of war. Although there was an increased military presence in every region of Ukraine, life and school went on as normal. Martial law ended a month after it was announced, just like the President said it would, and the Alert stage ended on the same day. Aside from my conversation with Myra, no one in my community except Sasha brought up the incident or seemed too concerned by it. Life and school went on as normal, as students finished their last few weeks of assignments while the teachers celebrated the end of a long semester. My first semester at school soon ended, as did my anxieties about being evacuated and having my entire world ripped out from under me.

I felt proud to survive my first Alert stage and major geo-political tension. I would soon have to get ready for the next one in March, where a man playing the president on a popular TV show would run for real president against the incumbent, a billionaire chocolate tycoon who had led Ukraine out of the revolutionary rubble. But before all of that, I could finally take a breath and relax: The world wasn't ending, no matter how badly I had tried to convince myself otherwise.

References

Drum, K. (2018, November 28) *So What Happened in the Kerch Strait?* Mother Jones. https://www.motherjones.com/kevin-drum/2018/11/so-what-happened-in-the-kerch-strait/

Gregorovich, A. (1995) *World War II in Ukraine: Total Losses by Country.* Infoukes. http://www.infoukes.com/history/ww2/page-18.html

World Nuclear Association. (2021, May) *Chernobyl Accident 1986.* world-nuclear.org. https://world-nuclear.org/information-library/safety-and-security/safety-of-chern-accident.aspx#:~:text=A%20particularly%20sad%20effect%20of,likely%20to%20have%20teratogenic%20effects

Chapter Seven

Second Hand Stores

While I was truly blessed to be placed in such a developed town like Mukachevo, I soon realized a problem that wouldn't be going away anytime soon: My salary. Peace Corps volunteer salaries are meant to match what their counterparts make, and as I noted earlier, in Ukraine teachers get paid terribly. That means while there were tons of restaurants, cafes and entertaining places to go to, my three hundred and fifty dollar a month survival stipend forced me to make some tough decisions. If I ever wanted to take advantage of such a beautiful site and do something besides walking around and wishing I could go into places, by the end of the month I usually had to dip into my American savings account. Boo hoo woe is me whatever aside, I was really hoping to use that money for any sort of vacation during summer break. While I tried to avoid hedonistic overspending, the enticing release of a latte and a slice of pizza overwhelmed my weak twenty-two year old willpower on a regular basis. The problem was that going out to eat even once or twice a week would cause me to go over my budget, and if I didn't find a way to curb my spending I would basically be giving up a trip or two to Europe.

At the same time, I desperately wanted to do something other than go to school, window shop, and go home. In Hryshkivtsi the monotony and boredom caused more mental and emotional struggle than I ever could have conceived, and I desperately didn't want that to repeat for two years in Mukachevo.

Thank goodness for second hand stores.

There are tons of second hand stores almost everywhere you go in Ukraine, which is weird because there isn't a developed sense of thriftiness embedded into their culture. There's no Ukrainian Macklemore with a fur coat telling everyone that it's cool and hip to buy used clothes, and in fact, second hand shopping is seen by many as only something you do when you don't have enough money to buy new clothes.

"Where are you going?" My host mother Inna asked me on an early Saturday morning in December.

"Second hand," I said with the face of someone who was about to get a lecture.

Her answer was always the same: "Robert," she would say while shaking her head, "Why second hand?"

With my limited Ukrainian at the time, it was difficult to express how second hand shopping was one of the only fun and affordable things I could do in my free time. Going from store to store and sifting through old tracksuits to high end dress clothes was a perfect activity for someone like me who had to count every penny. After a few months in Mukachevo, I ended up finding a walking route that took me to five different second hand stores, all of which were on the same street. It would easily take me an hour just to sift through every one of them, and in Peace Corps that's about as good as it gets when it comes to leisure time.

Early on thrifting became one of my weekend traditions, and although my host mother would look slightly frightened after going through the mangy sweaters, colorful jackets, and bright orange construction worker outfits, she and the rest of the people in my life eventually got used to the fact that ninety percent of my wardrobe was going to be second hand.

After a few weeks of thrifting, I noticed a few key distinct differences between American and Ukrainian thrift stores. First of all, I discovered that the majority of clothes donated to Ukrainian thrift stores are from the E.U., specifically from Switzerland. This meant that while each store had the typical fun and unique thrift store finds, there was also a plethora of really nice clothing. As a result, the majority of the fancy clothes I wore in Ukraine came from the kind nature of the Swiss people, which I highly appreciated after not bringing over any nice or well-fitted clothing from America. I didn't often get compliments on my wardrobe, but when I did it was on a Swiss button down or pair of pants that I had bought for a couple bucks the weekend before. The irony was that if anyone knew where my new high-end clothes came from, their perception of them would negatively and irreversibly change.

The cool Swiss garb in those second hand stores isn't the only big difference between thrifting in the U.S. and Ukraine. Another one is the pricing: Of course the prices in Ukraine are cheaper, but when I say pricing, I specifically mean how the prices are created. In the United States, you find something in a store, it has a price, and that's that. Well, you pay the sales tax, but after that that is pretty much that. It's quite different in Ukrainian thrift stores, because nothing has a price tag. Instead, prices are based on weight. Yes, weight. After you find everything you want, you bring it to the counter, they weigh it, then charge you accordingly.

This system is just begging to be abused, and while working for an organization that rationed off water during training, I was ready to go full speed ahead and take advantage of this unique but fatally flawed pricing model. I usually only bought very light but yet extremely nice clothes at a fraction of what their normal price should be. Shorts, ties, hats, bathing suits - anything lightweight was a huge bargain. I still bought my heavy stuff there, because even with the heavy weight tax it was still cheaper than buying a heavy coat in the city center, but these businesses definitely could've been making a lot more if they had a more typical way of pricing.

Another pricing quirk is that the price per kilogram (2.2 pounds) is different on different days. The most expensive day of the week is when the truck of new clothes arrives, because on these days there is the highest variety options available. I personally tried to stay away from shopping on those occasions, mostly because of the price but also because the stores were crowded. So while the masses went to the least expensive place on the most expensive day, I could be the hippest hipster, lurking in the shadows and waiting for the cheapest available time.

I typically needed to wait five or six days. The price goes down each consecutive day after the truck arrives until it finally reaches the cheapest day of the week, a.k.a. the day before the truck arrives again. While the most expensive day could charge up to eight dollars for a kilo, the cheapest day was almost disgracefully cheap. Most places I found charged less than a dollar for a kilo on the final day, and most of the time I'd leave with a bag full of clothes that cost less than a couple packs of frozen vegetables. Sure, sometimes all the good clothes were gone and I was left going through a bunch of gym shorts and striped button downs about three sizes too large, but if I found just one piece clothing that I could wear on a work day, my trip would be more than worth it.

I remember one Saturday I went shopping with a fellow volunteer Jack, and we were lucky enough to find one of the better thrift stores during the least expensive day. Jack picked out a few ties, some nicer than others, and I found a couple pairs of dress pants and suit jacket.

When the cashier weighed Jack's stuff first, we couldn't believe it.

"Six hryven," the cashier said.

"What?" Jack said. Sometimes Ukrainian numbers are hard, and after hearing that four ties cost twenty five cents, we were sure that we hadn't heard her correctly.

"Six hryven," the cashier said again, "Would you like a bag?"

"How much is the bag?"

"Two hryven."

And there you have it. One plastic bag cost more than one of the polo ties Jack laid down on the counter. Even for Ukraine that was ridiculous, not that we were close to complaining. My haul of multiple pairs of pants and suit jacket cost three bucks, and for the price of a latte and two sandwiches from a bodega, we were just about ready to go to a wedding. It was times like these when I felt like I found a cheat code after playing life on hard mode for so long.

Going to thrift stores was a regular part of my life, seeing as it was the cheapest way to get any sort of cultural experience. I would go on a walk, breeze through the center, say hi to a couple people I knew, then browse through the multitude of stores. During my time in Ukraine I bought close to seven or eight T-shirts, three long sleeved button downs, a pair of corduroys, two pairs of blue dress pants, a pair of khakis, jeans, jorts, a bathing suit, multiple sweaters, a winter coat, two Soviet track jackets, and a pair of tight construction shorts that were more likely worn at a rave than at a construction site. It was a nice way to de-stress, and after only bringing a couple collared shirts to the most fashion-conscious culture I had ever been around, second hand shopping turned out to have extreme practical and therapeutic value, as long as I made sure not to tell anyone where I got all my new clothes from.

Chapter Eight

Showers

I took a tour of what would become my first adult apartment in January 2019, a few months after I moved to Mukachevo. Per Peace Corps policy, we had to live with a host family for a minimum of three months, and I wasn't trying to go a single day over. As much as I appreciated my host family, being reminded that my second hand sweaters weren't pristine enough to wear to work, needing to make my bed everyday, and getting side eyes whenever I didn't wear slippers in the house got pretty old pretty quickly.

I plunged into the Peace Corps with the expectation of living without modern amenities and possibly dealing with no running water or cleaning supplies. This wildly inaccurate view was much aligned with my college experiences, where I lived in dilapidated off campus housing where my roommate and I decided to live with the fleas until they eventually died off in the winter. Having always struggled with tidiness and always sooner or later driving various roommates crazy, I was actually excited to have no cleanliness expectations. If only I had known the first thing about Ukrainians and their obsession with immaculate and spotless living spaces. My host family wasn't really asking me to do anything extraordinary, but being a twenty-two year old with a, let's say, "different philosophical mindset" about tidiness, I couldn't wait to finally find my own place and fulfill my Peace Corps dream of drudging it out in some hardcore grime.

I was lucky enough to find an apartment that was only a ten minute walk from my school. The Head of the English Department, Maryana, heard that I was looking for a place, and offered to show me around an apartment that her family owned. I gladly accepted, seeing as I had about ten days to either find somewhere to live or sign up for another month with the host family.

I made my way over to Maryana's through ice covered sidewalks, walking like a penguin unlike most of the locals, who had somehow mastered the art of not slipping and falling on their asses. You really can't appreciate American infrastructure and salting in the winter until you've walked like a penguin for twenty minutes, only to let up for a second and bruise your butt while falling and smashing a bag full of eggs on the sidewalk. That actually happened to me, but a teenager was kind enough to hand me my groceries after having a quick laugh at the American.

Without slipping, I made it to 16 Luchkaya Street, a place I was praying would become my future home. The daunting metal gate in front of the complex was the first good sign. The apartment was only about a one minute walk from the train station, also known as the only twenty-four hour facility in town, meaning that a huge population of sketchy people would regularly chilling in my neighborhood. I knew a one way ticket to not getting housing approved would be any sort of safety risk, so the big metal gate screaming "do not enter" was a good start.

My sitemate, a volunteer leader named Emma, met me there to make sure that the apartment was up to Peace Corps standards. Her leadership title gave her administrative duties as a volunteer, and she was one of the few who took that role as serious as it demanded. Emma's by the book nature drove up my stress levels a bit and casted doubts about the nature of any place we toured together, but I guess it was better than the alternative of PC leaders who didn't really care about the protocols and may have sometimes overlooked a hazard or two.

Maryana welcomed us to their complex, and took us to what would become my apartment for the next thirteen months. We walked up some stairs onto a balcony that faced a decently sized yard, which was covered in snow, and soon we progressed into the apartment. I would have lived in a decently sized trash can at that point, but even with my rose colored glasses on, the apartment ended up being exactly what I needed. It was a one room, one bathroom place, with the hallway in between serving as a kitchen. The room was fairly large, having a wooden dining table at one end and a bed facing the opposite, with enough space in between to meander around and do some exercises. It had a decently sized dresser, multiple windows, a carpet on the floor (instead of the wall), and a stove top that had to be lit with a match. It had a heating system for the winter, a balcony for the summer, and a garden across the balcony where my neighbors grew various fruits and vegetables. Additionally, the ceilings were high enough for me to walk around without the fear of hitting my head, which couldn't be said for the places of some other volunteers. Even better, the apartment was located above a garage, so I wouldn't have to worry about disturbing any neighbors living below me.

Also, the location was perfect: It was a twelve minute walk to school, which would without a doubt would let me off the hook whenever I woke up a little too late. And finally the proximity to the train station made it easy to sneak away from site whenever I had the inclination. It was a wonderful place to set up shop as my first apartment since graduating college.

However, before any of that could come to fruition, we had to get it approved.

"Do all of the windows open?" Emma asked Maryana, checking her clipboard for various boxes to check.

"Yes, no problem with windows."

"What about the bathroom? Does the water run?"

Maryana went to the bathroom to turn on the sink. Worked like a charm.

Emma spent the next ten minutes peppering Maryana with various questions from her checklist, and because Maryana was an English teacher, the whole process went very smoothly. Neither Emma nor I had enough language skills to get through this comfortably, so after being thankful for my potential landlord's English abilities, the routine tour almost ended before it started. However, oddly enough, there seemed to be a translation barrier when Emma asked about the heating system.

"What about heat?" Emma asked Maryana. Maryana paused. Oh no. I started to hold my breath, praying this wouldn't be the thing that would pry me away from the fantasies I already started to have about this place.

"Well," Maryana said, "We have heat, but if Robert ever wants to use it, he has to call us to turn it on. He must call my mom, the landlord, Maria."

Emma shot a quick look at me.

"Are you ready to ask her mother for hot water every time you need it?"

"Yes," I said immediately.

"Bob, are you sure that you'll-"

"Yes Emma yes I don't care yes I want to live here it doesn't matter it's fine Emma."

Emma shrugged and checked another box. If that was the only impediment in the way of me finally getting to live on my own, then I would have no problem finding Maria whenever I felt the need to be clean. I only showered every three days or so anyway and only used cold water to wash dishes, so I didn't think it would be too big of a deal. Also Maria's house, along with Maryana's apartment, turned out to be right next to my potential place, so if I had to knock on her door two or three times a week to take a shower, then that would be a small price to pay for freedom.

The apartment ended up passing every safety standard, my housing was approved one week later, and the first day I was allowed to I moved into my new apartment at 16 Luchkaya Vulitzia (street). A couple of Emma's friends, Volodiya and Yuri, drove me there and gave me a celebratory beer and a jar of condensed milk.

"For your new home!" Volodiya said, putting the two side by side in my empty fridge.

It was an incredibly sweet gesture, but I was later disappointed to learn that there wasn't some sort of cute "beer and milk move in" Ukrainian tradition. No, they just gave me a beer and some milk, but it didn't matter: I had finally arrived and now could at last live by myself in filth like I had always dreamed of.

That was a dream I had no trouble actualizing. I'll spare most of the details of a twenty two year old's journey of learning how to take care of an apartment, but I probably made my bed double the amount of times living with my host family than my entire time living alone. Vacuuming was a rarity, dishes tended to get comfortable in the sink, and my friend Ellie was later thoughtful enough to explain that the black stuff in between the tiles in the bathroom is mold, and that mold is bad and you should get rid of it. Black mold aside, I was ecstatic to finally be living alone and paying for my own apartment, and with that came a sense of freedom I had never experienced before.

The benefits showed themselves immediately. Throughout my time in that apartment I hosted dozens of volunteers passing through, who heard that I had a place only seconds away from the train station in one of the bigger Peace Corps sites in the country. Some would stay for the night as a pit stop before their train to Slovakia or Budapest, while others stayed a week at a time, wanting to do some in-country sightseeing. Either way I was happy to provide some sort of help and was giddy to finally have guests who I could chat with after three months of social isolation.

The apartment was also fruitful when there was no one around at all. After a long day of work I could decompress without any possibility of my host brothers knocking on my door to play some cards and practice their English. It additionally helped professionally by giving me the ability to invite volunteers to do a few lessons at my school. This scored me some points with my teachers, who were more than happy to have Peace Corps Volunteers give lessons that provided them a break from their hectic teaching schedule.

Even in a country where I didn't understand most of the people most of the time, this experience of living in the first apartment, one of the first steps into adulthood and independence, was one I knew I was sharing universally. I was doing my best to soak in every second of it, wearing whatever sweaters I wanted to without needing to listen to someone with good intentions tell me that they must be ironed. Sometimes I would sit in the arm chair in the corner, just looking at the space, eternally satisfied with where I was and how I had gotten there.

Of course, as time went on, I started to notice the downsides. I knew this would happen, as it doesn't take a seasoned veteran of life to know that things grow a little stale after an initial period of bliss. Honeymoons and the subsequent souring period also feel universal, but the Ukrainian aspects of this universal experience made things more inconvenient than usual.

I soon learned the balcony wasn't for my personal use, but rather was actually meant for hanging everyone's washed clothes. Not only was view of the garden was always blocked by someone else's T-shirts and underwear, but this also meant that my fifty-five year old landlord Maria would come to my balcony every day with a front row view of me and the condition of my apartment. This would be fine if there were curtains, but there weren't, and I often found her peering in at the mess I was living in.

Furthermore, due to the lack of curtains and the close proximity of all my neighbors, it was easy to see me meandering around unless I was sitting in the armchair in the corner or laying in my bed. I soon got into the habit of suspiciously looking around whenever I wanted to take my pants off, something that in a Pavlovian way still haunts me to this day.

Additionally, I didn't have complete freedom. For example, whenever I needed to wash my clothes, I had to figure out a time that worked for Maria because the only washing machine was in her bathroom. While I was thankful that I could use her washing machine and that she took the time to hang my clothes on my balcony, there were multiple occasions when I had to wear a smelly collared shirt to work because I couldn't find Maria when I needed to. The clothes always needed a couple days to dry, and since Sunday's are essentially a day of rest in Ukraine, if I was ever away for a weekend or forgot to wash clothes on a Saturday (like I often did), I would be rolling into first period that Monday hoping the students and teachers didn't notice the stains I was attempting to hide.

My key also broke multiple times trying to get in and out of the front gate, so sometimes I would have to alert Maryana or another neighbor whenever I wanted to leave or come back. I appreciated that I had a community to let me in, but then again if I wasn't in Ukraine my key wouldn't be breaking nearly as often. I remember one time having to wake up Maryana close to 11:00 pm after breaking yet another key in the gate, which would have been only slightly uncomfortable if she hadn't delivered a baby a few weeks earlier. To her credit she was pretty chill about it.

And of course, my apartment and running water weren't warm unless the heat was turned on in my apartment, which is something that only my landlord controlled.

The first winter I hardly had any issues with this. Even though heating in Ukraine is extremely expensive, in my place it was always turned on, so I rarely had to find Maria. She was a stout woman, rocking a short black haircut much like many of the older women in Ukraine, and always seemed to be doing something or another in order to maintain the various apartments she was renting out.

Whenever we crossed paths our conversation typically stayed the same.

"Robert!" She would exclaim, "Hello. How's life?"

Good! How's life?"

"Incomprehensible speech"

"That's great!"

"Robert, how's the heat? Are you cold?"

"Nope, all good"

"Great!"

This would be the extent of the conversations we had once a twice a day, and they always concluded with her asking if I was feeling warm enough.

It didn't take me too long to find out that Ukrainians don't just dislike the cold: They despise it. I always joked with some of my buddies that for people who live in a country where snow is on the ground for months at a time, they just cannot stand the cold. Don't get me wrong, winter is rough in Ukraine, but I thought that after hundreds of years they would sort of embrace it, or at least get used to it.

Nope, they hate it, and it's not just the cold weather: They hate everything cold. Ice in drinks is not a thing, ice cream in the winter is thought of as completely irrational, and some Ukrainians keep windows shut due to a fear of getting sick from a cold draft. One time I was even drinking cold water while going on a walk in November, when one of my colleagues caught me in the act.

"Robert!" Marina exclaimed, "You can't drink cold water outside. It will make you sick. It's bad for your throat, you know!"

"Oh," I said, "I didn't know, sorry about that."

"And where's your hat? Robert, it's like you're trying to catch a cold!"

On another occasion after I overslept on a Tuesday morning, I walked into the break room and was greeted by a collective scowl from my fellow English teachers.

"Sorry everyone, I slept in."

"Robert," Myra said, "We are not mad at you because you overslept."

"We are mad at you," Marina butted in, "Because you went home without your jacket last night! It was snowing, you know!"

After almost half a year of people doing their best to make sure I wasn't experiencing the cold, it was no surprise that my very caring landlord regularly made sure that everything was warm enough.

The summer was a different story. When the cold months finally pass in Ukraine, it becomes a time to celebrate both the warmth and the huge reduction in utility bills. Around April, Maria turned off the heat in my apartment, and I quickly understood that along with the general heating system the water also wasn't heating up. When I realized what was going on, I simply did what I had been training for over the past few months: I went outside, found Maria, and asked her to turn the heat on. With a thumbs up, she went inside the garage, and after a minute or so told me to go for it. I went to my bathroom, and after a couple minutes of cold water, it finally became hot. After patting my back for doing something that functioning adults do, I got in the shower and I assumed that would be the end of it.

Well, after about a month of me interrupting Maria when she was cooking, cleaning, peeling potatoes, and doing various other landlord tasks, she eventually got tired of it and brought me down to the garage under my apartment to show me how to operate the heating system. *Easy enough,* I thought, except for the fact that I rarely understood a single word Maria said.

Maria speaks a dialect called "Rusyn," or commonly referred to as "Zakarpatt-ian." The land Zakarpattia, which translates to "Behind the Carpathians," has a long history of being occupied by other states: For hundreds of years it was a part of the Austro-Hungarian empire, then Slovakia after WWI, then the Soviet Union after WWII, and then Ukraine after independence in 1991. All in all, this diverse region has been a part of four different territories with four different languages over the past one hundred and twenty years. Hence, the local dialect, "Zakarpattian," is a beautiful and confusing mix of five or six different languages, sometimes sounding closer to Hungarian than Ukrainian, while also having Czech, Slovakian, and even Russian influences. After spending three months learning survival Ukrainian, I was taken aback at times when I had trouble understanding basic situations in Mukachevo. I initially assumed that I was just bad at Ukrainian, but my ego was relieved when I learned that a good chunk of people were speaking a Slavic/Hungarian mega-language that would be impossible for me to learn.

While this bit of information helped my ego, it definitely didn't help me practically. Maria and I could communicate well when we were using gestures and a phrase or two here and there, but me listening to instructions was a completely different story. While Maria eloquently explained the heating system over the course of thirty seconds, pointing at the various buttons and switches, I nodded my head, threw in the occasional "da," and read her body language and tone of voice to show that I was understanding her perfectly. When she gave her patented thumbs up to see if I understood, I shot her a thumbs up back, thanked her, and walked to my room, not having a single clue how to turn on the hot water. I gritted my teeth, took a two minute freezing cold shower, and decided that later on I would ask Maryana how to turn on the hot water so that I would never have to do that again.

That next day, when I saw Maryana, I froze when she brought up the water situation.

"How is the water, Robert?

"Working well, thanks," I said, lying.

"Hot enough?"

"Oh yes, very warm, thank you."

I ended up taking cold showers for the next six months. I'm not a very confrontational person and often choose suffering in silence over potential conflict, and in that specific moment I just didn't have the guts to tell Maryana that the heat wasn't working and I took a freezing cold shower the day before. Because of this mentality, I was forced to continue the miserable and freezing two minute hell ride indefinitely.

It wasn't simply a coldish shower. Instead, it was as if someone was actively trying to make it as cold as possible. Before this if you asked me about the differences between cold showers, I would have told you that they are all probably the same. Nope. There is a huge difference between a shower which uses some heat, and a shower that is as cold as it can possibly be, the latter of which is nothing short of painful. I am grateful that no one was living under me, because they would have heard the occasional gasp and scream two to three times a week. That was my experience for six months, all because I was too embarrassed to ask again how to turn on the hot water.

At first, I took it on as sort of a challenge because I knew that many other Peace Corps volunteers were having a lot harder of a time than I was. I'm sure the majority of sites around the world didn't have cafes, a park with a ferris wheel, a movie theater, and a castle, so I decided that this could be one of my hardcore Peace Corps experiences. Getting through that shower was a short lived pain that I could feel prideful about afterwards, and that was enough to keep me going for the first few months. True, I was always slightly terrified before stepping into the tub, so much so that on multiple occasions I went seven days without showering, but after a couple of months I found the best way to go about it.

107

I started off with my feet and legs, two somewhat nonsensitive parts of my body. This was in order to welcome myself to the miniature nightmare to come. I always thought that if I did my legs first, then the rest of my body would get used to it, and the whole experience would be a little less abrasive as I moved up. That never turned out to be the case, but I always drudged on. I would then go to my arms, then to the top of the head. My hair would blunt the initial frigidity, and afterwards enough water would drip to my face to where I wouldn't have to hold my breath and wash it separately. Most of the time as the water hit my body I simply gasped lightly. The chest, which was the most unbearable portion of the experience, was the only time when I would yell involuntarily. However, right after the ice water grazed my torso, enough of my body would be covered so that I could finally turn the water off, soap myself quickly, then turn it back on and wash myself in a frenzy in order to finish and dry off as fast as possible.

There was nothing good about this process, but at least I didn't have to ask Maryana one question. By then, even if I wanted to talk to Maryana about it I couldn't: Each day that passed was just another day I gave a forced thumbs up, letting them know that the hot water was working fine, further entrenching me in the lie. If I ever wanted to experience hot water I would either have to fess up and tell them I had been taking cold showers for the entire time, or say I somehow forgot how to turn on the heat, neither of which would translate very well cross culturally.

I decided to try to make the best of it, and after a few months of misery I began to notice a benefit or two. On the positive side, cold showers feel amazing when they are over and done with. It's like the feeling of finally laying in bed after a long work out, except this time you don't have to lift a finger. Someone also told me that they are good for your skin, and I decided not to verify that claim and just accept another benefit. Yes, I soon had a honeymoon period with ice-cold showers, which looking back on it revealed the scary revelation of how easily humans can adapt to something that makes them feel miserable.

However, this wouldn't be the first time for me or any other volunteer: In the Peace Corps you have to rationalize a lot of tough conditions in order to go on for twenty-seven months, and this was just another part of that process. The only difference was that I brought this on myself and could have ended it anytime I wanted to, but I try not to think of that too much.

The only time it really inconvenienced me was when I would have volunteers over for multiple days at a time. One of the unfortunate souls was Ellie. When Ellie stayed over for ten days over the summer to help out with a camp, she had the nerve to desire a somewhat regular shower and hot water. How posh, right? We ended up figuring out a system where I boiled water in pot, poured it in a different pot, then I'd place it in the bathroom sink next to Ellie. She then mixed the almost boiling water with the water from the shower, creating an ideal water temperature to start a sponge bath. We repeated this two or three times for every shower, and we ended up boiling about twenty pots of water during our stay together.

That was fine with Ellie, because as a Peace Corps volunteer she was used to being flexible and dealing with not so ideal conditions. This was a little different when I first started dating my girlfriend, Alina, about a year into my service. About two months into our relationship, I invited her over to spend the night at my place for the first time. I had been to her place a couple times, which was as spotless and as orderly as I expected it to be. Now, it was my turn, and when the opportunity to host presented itself, I offered without hesitation.

I'm not exactly sure why I was so keen on having her over. To review, Ukrainians are an extremely clean and pristine people, while for me one of the most exciting reasons for having my own place was that I didn't have to clean after myself. Ukrainians also hate the cold, but the heat in my apartment didn't work and I had been taking freezing showers for the past six months. Not to mention that there were the usual inconveniences, like having almost no privacy due to the lack of curtains, and that I didn't know how to use the oven.

They were perfect conditions to show that I am a great guy to be dating.

Thankfully she didn't need to take a shower that first night, and she was actually thoroughly impressed by how clean my apartment was. I waited a few months to tell her that I had spent most of the day cleaning, only for Maria to come in later and ask me why my place was such a wreck. Maria, the kind soul that she is, ended up sweeping and fixing up my apartment with me right until I had to leave to pick up Alina at the bus station. So, that night I dodged a bullet: My apartment was clean, we cooked on the stove top, and no one needed to take a shower. The date was completely normal, which is the only thing I could have asked for.

The only complaint, one I should have seen coming, was that my apartment was unbearably cold. It was autumn of 2019, and by then I still hadn't done anything about the heat, and while it's not the coldest part of the year by any stretch, it is a time when gas and heating starts to become a factor in the life of every Ukrainian. However, I had enough blankets to deal with it on my own, and I wanted to delay using the heating system for as long as possible. I of course still didn't want to tell Maria I still didn't know how to use it, but also if I could grit through the winter, like my sitemate Emma somehow did, I could forgo paying for heat and essentially receive a thirty percent raise on top of my Peace Corps salary.

However, being true to her Ukrainian roots, Alina, whose teeth were chattering even under my pile of blankets, broke a couple hours into the night.

"Robert," she blurted out, "I'm cold, I'm freezing cold! Why is it so cold??"

I didn't really have an answer, not one that would put me in a positive light anyway, so I shrugged and said it felt fine to me.

"Talk to Maria," she demanded, "I'm sorry, I just don't want to be cold anymore."

If it were another volunteer I probably would have found an excuse, but for my new girlfriend I didn't really want to go into my penny-pinching and non-confrontational behaviors.

After six months of gritting my teeth through the lack of gas, in October I walked to Maria's house and finally asked her to turn on the heat. She seemed confused by the question, and not wanting to even begin to explain why I was asking her, I just shot a confused face back and shrugged my shoulders. She soon put on her slippers and once again showed me how to turn on the gas, which in the end was pretty simple. All it involved was flipping a switch and twisting a handle. Alina and I then continued our night with heat, albeit not much, but enough to get us through the evening without any more issues.

Even with the heating back on, it was still way weaker than I remembered. My water only stayed hot for a little more than two minutes, then went cold, then gave one final burst of hot water before staying ice cold indefinitely. It was a pattern I discovered after previously thinking that the hot water only came on sporadically. After needing a month or two to master the heat pattern of the shower, I began to treat them like a sauna, making sure I had cleaned myself thoroughly before enjoying the final switch from hot to cold.

This, again, was fine for me, because by that point two minutes of hot water seemed like an excessive luxury. But Alina, who eventually had to shower at my place, did NOT feel like handling it. After our third or fourth round of boiling water on the stove, we mutually agreed to only spend the weekends at her place, and if she ever had to come over it wouldn't be for multiple days at a time. All in all, this experience was a good sign for our relationship. Even through all of that she still wanted to be with me, so if you want to figure out if someone really loves you, make them take ice cold showers.

As for myself, I continued this little shower/sauna tradition for the rest of my time in Ukraine, and chose to take mostly cold showers even when I had the option of hot water, like at her place or in hotel bathrooms. I just sort of got used to it, which funny enough can encapsulate my (and I'd bet every other Peace Corps Volunteers') entire volunteer experience.

Chapter Nine

Some Help

On a grey winter weekend where the clouds matched the same color as the sidewalk, I left the comfort of my new apartment to begin my weekly trek of grocery shopping, which was usually a bit of an ordeal due to the lack of available supermarkets around in my neighborhood. The only shops by the train station were small bodegas that were only intended for people who needed to grab a bite to eat right before traveling. The only food products there besides the typical ready-to-eat snacks such as chips, candy bars, and pre-made sandwiches, were frozen dumplings and low quality sausage links. If I was ever desperate I could force myself to have a sausage and dumpling dinner, but most of the time I just settled with a sandwich.

On top of the low quality options, due to the proximity to the train station, these crummy bodegas were way more expensive than any other shop in Mukachevo. Therefore, if I ever wanted to buy actual groceries or anything within a normal price range, I usually had to walk to the town center, which took close to an hour round-trip.

Due to the energy-sucking and encompassing winter weather, I was a little too lazy (and hungry) to haul myself to the grocery store, so I conceded and made my way to the train station. I walked in the first bodega I saw, and after passing a wall of liquor and bottled beer, I began going through what kind of sandwiches were available. I could feel the clerk's presence, who stared at me the entire time, and when I was ready to check out, like always she didn't bother saying anything except for the total.

"103 gryvnas," she said.

"Card?" I asked, showing her my debit card.

She looked at me, groaned, and pulled out the terminal. This store, like a ton of other places in Ukraine, preferred cash, but at the time I only had a 200 hryven bill on me. Not having exact change makes cashiers way more angry than making them whip out the terminal, so I decided to keep quiet about the purple bill in my pocket. After waiting for the terminal to turn on, I paid the exuberant price and left in silence.

I hated that place, but whenever I was too hungry to walk to the center on a cruddy day, this option was the quickest and easiest thing possible.

While walking back with a salami sandwich in one hand and a link of cheap sausage in the other, a middle aged woman began walking towards me with a smile. A smile? It was immediately off-putting, because Ukraine isn't exactly the place where strangers smile at you while passing by.

I must know this woman, I thought while taking my first bite of the stale sandwich. But how? At that point in my service I had met hundreds of students and parents, so while I didn't know who this woman was, I could only assume it was someone associated with School 16.

I tensed up, not because I was afraid of speaking to her, but because of what was in my hands. Ukrainians place a lot of importance in the quality of the food they eat, and seeing me with a pre-made sandwich and cheap sausage would make any Ukrainian slightly shocked and more than slightly disappointed. I soon found out that this woman was no different.

"Hi Robert, how are you?" she said with a smile, which she quickly lost after looking at the monstrosities in my hands.

"Oh good, just getting some lunch," I replied while trying to get out in front of the subject.

After staring at my lunch, shook her head. "Oh Robert, where did you get that sausage?"

"Over there," I said, pointing at the crummy bodega.

"Oh, you shouldn't buy from there. It's too expensive. Are you free?"

I was caught off guard by that question, so even though I just wanted to get back home, I didn't have any wit to make up a quick excuse.

"Well, I, not really-

Before I could think of something, she gently grabbed my arm and led me past my apartment on the route I usually took while walking to school. Except this time, instead of turning right to the school, we kept going forward.

While avoiding puddles walking through a neighborhood I had never ventured out to before, I couldn't make out much of what she was saying. However, somewhere in her monologue I heard the words, "Better, fresher, food, bread." I kind of got the gist, but I made sure to tell her I wasn't understanding ninety percent of what she was saying.

"It's ok," the woman said slowly, "It's good you can understand me at all. By the way, we're already here."

She brought me to a small bodega called "ABC." It was nearly identical to the one I had gone to countless times by the train station, and when we got inside, everything pretty much looked the same. I saw a few older men drinking and and chatting in the corner of the bodega, which was a small difference, but on the outside it didn't look too different from anything I'd seen before.

"Here, look Robert," the woman said, pointing at a wall of sausage links, "See that sausage? Cheap and fresh. Buy sausage here. But not chicken, don't buy the chicken. Look, the chicken looks bad, doesn't it?"

I took a glance at the slimy and aging chicken breasts behind the counter, and I could almost see the smell coming off of them.

"Yes, it does look bad," I mustered up in broken Ukrainian, trying to not let the clerk hear me.

"You're right. Only buy sausage. Much cheaper than at the station."

We left the first bodega without buying anything and continued the tour.

"Only buy chicken in the center. But here," she explained while pointing at another identical shop just a few seconds away, "Fresh bread. You should buy your bread here, especially in the morning. Where do you buy your bread?"

"In the center," I remarked while passing the second bodega.

"Where in the center?"

"The supermarket," I revealed while trying not to make eye contact. One of the first things I heard about Ukraine is that it's the breadbasket of Europe, so I knew buying cheap supermarket bread wouldn't please my tour guide.

"Robert," she said with a motherly tone, "Don't buy bread in the supermarket. It's not fresh."

We continued our tour by taking a right towards another residential neighborhood. Before walking too far we took a sharp left down an alley, where we found a couple of people selling fruit out of the trunk of their car.

"You can buy fruit here. It's very cheap and it's from their garden. Fresh from the garden," She said this while buying a few apples, which we ate on the spot. "Fresh, isn't it?"

I had to agree. The apple tasted like the ones from Larysa's apple tree in Hryshkivtsi, and the prices were from the village as well: Two apples for ten cents was an amazing deal, even in Ukraine. In fact, all of the prices from the tour were incredible compared to that crappy place by the train station.

The only problem was that although we had only been walking for a few minutes, I wasn't sure how the heck we even got there. At that point I probably couldn't have made it home if I tried, even though we were mere minutes away. We were down some side street in a neighborhood I had never explored before eating fruit out of someone's trunk, and I worried that I'd never be able to return without a detailed bodega map or this woman by my side. All I could do was hope for my muscle memory to lead me back here, because my sense of direction always left much to be desired.

With seemingly each side street we passed another bodega, where she stressed buying only a select number of specific products, from the cheapest candy to the best homemade frozen dumplings. Additionally, she advised me which bodegas to avoid, and although I didn't quite understand why, I got the message after various thumb down hand gestures. She did all this while using the simplest Ukrainian

115

possible, which was quite considerate of her, because almost no one besides my host family had ever watered down their Ukrainian for me. I typically went through life not understanding the majority of most people's conversations, but she was kind enough to make sure I was absorbing the vital information she was providing.

After our eighth or ninth bodega/car trunk stop, we took one last right, which led straight onto the main road towards the train station. By the time we returned to my apartment, we had gone through enough places to fully stock my fridge and pantry at a fraction of what I had been paying, as long as I could remember how to find everything. Later on it took me a few more tries on my own to get the lay of the land, but after enough attempts and experimentation I finally found the best, cheapest, and closest bodegas in my neighborhood. For the rest of my time in Mukachevo, going to the center solely for chicken was much more comfortable than hauling back three or four grocery bags of dumplings, bread, and other essentials.

"That should be everything," the woman said in front of my gate, still smiling. "And now you don't need to shop by the train station again!"

"Thank you so much," I told her, still mystified that this woman would take thirty minutes out of her day to help me out.

"It's no problem. My son is in third grade, and he says hi to you everyday. He really likes you, and when he comes home he always talks about you!"

Third grade. I didn't even teach third grade. He must have been one of the seemingly hundreds of kids I fist bumped in the hallways, but I had no idea I could have that type of influence on a student I didn't even teach. Quite the revelation on a dreary afternoon.

"Thank you," I told her. I wish I could've said more, but that was all I could muster up at the time after only a few months of Ukrainian practice.

"No, Robert, thank you. Have a good day!"

And with that she left to continue her Sunday. I didn't even catch her name.

Chapter Ten

Meet the Locals

A handful of times a year, PC Ukraine hosted professional conferences, where volunteers could meet up, network, develop projects, and cut loose with like minded Americans. For most of us, this usually meant some professional development during the day and going bar hopping during the night and early morning. In that sort of atmosphere, amongst well over one hundred Americans who had all been socially and emotionally starved for months at a time, an electric and nervous energy thickens the air. This led to us predictably getting carried away, drinking too much, staying out too late, and regretting some decisions the next morning. However, I was with some of my closest friends in the entire country, so while most of us were a shell of ourselves by the final morning of each conference, I always left with happy memories, even if many of them were clouded by hangovers.

Those hangovers, however, are no match for the emotional hangover that shows up the first week back at site after one of those conferences. It's like when you feel a little extra down the week after a long vacation, except times twenty. There's only a fraction of a percent of people in the world who understand the experience of being a Peace Corps volunteer and being an American living in Ukraine, and for five to seven glorious days we were all in the same hotel. Inevitably this escape from reality ends and we all go back to the site, where most people don't understand anything we say, let alone relate to us. Without exception this catalyzed a week or two of depression, which always made me question if these sort of conferences did more harm than good.

In mid-February, about a week after the PDM (project development and management) conference, I realized something while in the midst of a heavy slump. I almost stopped in my tracks while cleaning my new and messy apartment.

I haven't made any friends in Mukachevo.

My post-conference depression had pushed me to that thought, but it didn't make the thought any less true. I hadn't met any locals outside of my workplace, let alone any young and personable ones I could grab a beer with. Sure I had hung out with my sitemate Emma every now and then and got some drinks with some of her Ukrainian friends, but I hadn't met anyone by myself. At that point I had only been in Mukachevo for four months, but by then I began to wonder...is there something I'm missing out on? While some of my PC friends were posting Insta stories of their various hangouts with cool young Ukrainians, the most I was doing on a weekend was going on walks and occasionally having a short conversation with a student or parent I saw along the way. I didn't have the funds to be going out and about, not that I'd even know where to go, but I still felt like I was missing out on some sort of essential Peace Corps experience: Getting to know the locals.

A couple Sundays after PDM, as I was preparing for a full slate of Monday classes, I got word that my school was going to be under quarantine.

Quarantine? National lockdown? CORONAVIRUS?

Nope, this was 2019. Quarantine was a common phrase in Ukraine long before 2020 came around, and every winter it was extremely common for schools to be under a Karantine for a set number of weeks. The purpose on paper is simple: When too many kids are sick, schools go under quarantine in order to restrict transmission of illnesses. It made sense at the time, but I soon found out from other volunteers the real reason schools went under quarantine.

Heating costs a ton in Ukraine, and in order to alleviate some of the bills, schools undergo "quarantine" until they no longer need to turn on the heat or at least until winter is almost out of sight. It's a sad situation because schools effectively shut down because the heating bills are too formidable, but with that said, both students and teachers alike happily embraced quarantine and treated it like a week long vacation.

There was a moment in the break room a week or so earlier, where I saw a couple of my colleagues with their heads slumped over in their chairs, reeling from the work week and practically begging the powers that be to give us a quarantine. I couldn't quite believe what I was hearing, but after later learning about the real reason, I too began to wish for the stiff but necessary safety precaution of taking off multiple weeks of school in the middle of winter.

On a Sunday night near the end of February, I got the message from Maryana I had been hoping for all weekend.

"Quarantine in school," is all Maryana wrote, but she could probably hear me celebrating a few seconds later. After basking in my newfound vacation, I chatted with one of my old training buddies Noah to see if he wanted to hang out that week.

"Absolutely," he said, "Why don't you come by? You can do English club or something, so that way you won't have to use any vacation days. My school would be down."

"Perfect," I wrote back. I soon bought the tickets to Noah's site in the neighboring region of Ivano-Frankivsk. In any other part of Ukraine, a mere one hundred and forty miles away would only be a three or four hour bus ride. However, because of the Carpathian mountains, I would have to go up and around the mountains in order to get to his site. This meant that it was going to be a seven hour travel affair, which started with a four hour train up north to Lviv.

That night I bought the cheapest and earliest train to Lviv: The Elektrichka. The Elektrichka, as my father described five months later when he visited me over the summer, is a tin can of misery. Each cart is filled with metal benches, which have three seats each and face each other in rows of twos. This means that on the Elektrichka, you will be face to face with three other people during the entire ride. There is minimal leg room, so someone always has to stretch their legs out into the hallway, while the rest of the group has to scrunch their legs in between one another, making sure to sit absolutely still in order to not bump into anyone else's leg. There is no air conditioning or heating system, and the windows are often shut due to the unfortunate myth in Ukraine that drafts are a major cause of illness.

In short, it sucks.

But, three dollars is three dollars, and if I could shave two hundred percent off ticket expenses, it was a no brainer on my minuscule Peace Corps budget.

The morning of my excursion, I got up at 6:30 for my 6:56 train. I packed, mixed some instant coffee in some cold water, chugged it, grabbed my sandwich out of the fridge, brushed my teeth, and then headed out. I left my apartment at around 6:45 and got to the train station about one minute later. When it was all said and done, the proximity to the train station was by far the biggest perk of living in that apartment, as I was a full ten minutes early for my train after waking up just fifteen minutes beforehand.

Once my train finally arrived, I got on the Elektrichka and did my best to find a comfortable spot. On the Elektrichka, naturally, the seating is a free for all. It's a low stakes decision, because you can always switch seats later on, but I always did my best to avoid any unsavory characters if I was able to.

As I walked through the hot tin can, I saw a young couple sitting alone, looking normal and not scary. I decided to park in front of them and shoot them a modest smile that they couldn't ignore. Due to the nature of the Elektrechka, it's pretty much impossible to not occasionally make eye contact, and the only way not to is to blatantly ignore your train buddy by intently staring out the window. When that close to someone, it's additionally almost impossible and also extremely awkward to not strike up a conversation of some sort, unless they're looking tired, hungover, shady, or all three.

Trying not to be rude, my new travel partners did the bare minimum of smiling and then went back to their phones.

I took that as an opening. It was about seven in the morning, but after my recent panic sadness of not making any friends in Ukraine, I was in the mood for a conversation. I decided right then and there to make friends, like a normal person does, and to stop acting like someone who was afraid of the locals. By then I had been studying Ukrainian for five months, and had enough successful interactions to have the confidence to start talking to a couple of strangers. After a few minutes of carefully reciting the Ukrainian in my head, I decided to shoot my shot.

I darted my eyes towards the guy, who's beanie and heavy metal T-shirt hinted that he was a strapping cool youth like myself. When he made eye contact, I made a move.

"Hi" I said in Ukrainian, "How are you all?"

"Good," the man said.

"Good," the woman said, "And you?"

"Good," I replied.

"Blah blah blah blah blah," the woman said while smiling.

Not having any idea what to say, but not wanting to show my lack of Ukrainian, I went with my patented, "Haha, yes yes."

I clenched my jaw and felt blood rushing to my face. Thankfully I was saved.

"Do you speak English?" the man said to me, effectively ending my attempt to speak Ukrainian.

"Uh, yeah, hi, I'm Robert."

"Hi, I'm Pavel, this is Alona. Where are you from?"

"I'm from the United States," I said.

Pavel laughed and asked, "Why are you here?"

I got that response a lot in Ukraine. While blunt, it's not everyday you see an American in Ukraine anywhere outside of the major cities, or anywhere at all.

"I'm a part of the Peace Corps," I replied.

"Is that with the Red Cross?" He asked, pointing at the Red Cross jacket I had won after donating a couple pints of blood a few years back.

"No, but my organization is sort of like the red cross. I'm an English teacher"

"Sho vin skazav?" Alona chimed in.

When Pavel replied, Alona looked at him wide eyed and spun her head in my direction

"Sorry," Pavel continued, "Alona doesn't speak much English."

"No problem." I said while turning to her. "I'm an English teacher," I said in Ukrainian.

Her eyes widened even more, no doubt because I was able to mutter anything at all in her native tongue. This was another response I often received because most American expats in Eastern Europe at best only know Russian, and at worst only know English. Compared to Russian, which can be used pretty much anywhere in Eastern Europe, Ukrainian isn't even used all throughout Ukraine, so it's almost impossible to find a foreigner who can mutter a few phrases. I'm sure these thoughts were racing through Alona's mind on that dreary morning riding through the Carpathians.

"Where are you two from?" I asked, relieved I had found an English speaker. This was going to make the whole "making friends thing" a lot easier.

"Well I'm from Kharkiv in the east, where she's from Mukachevo. She studies in Kharkiv, but we're both visiting for the holidays. We're only going to be here for about a week, and right now we're actually on our way to go skiing."

"Oh, that sounds fun!"

Alona said something to Pavel, asking for a translation, and Pavel relayed back to her our short conversation.

"Where are you going skiing?" I asked.

"Oh, in a small village in Carpatia. It's a couple hours from here."

"Oh nice," I said, "I didn't know there was skiing so close-by."

"Do you want to come with us?"

I could hardly muster a response to that question, even in English. Was it really this easy to make friends in Ukraine? Strike up a conversation with someone, and then five minutes later you get the invite to go skiing? What the hell had I been doing for the past six months?

As much as I wanted to go on a skiing adventure with some of the locals, I couldn't just ditch Noah and his English Club. I made the right decision, but that didn't make it sting any less.

"Oh, sorry," I muttered, "I'm actually going to be busy for the next couple of days."

"Oh that's fine," Pavel replied, "Just call me later and maybe we'll still be up there. Here, I'll give you my number, will you hand me your phone?"

And with that, I made my first Ukrainian acquaintance, and over the next hour the three of us used multiple languages to talk about our lives during one of the cooler conversations I've ever been a part of. I would say something to Pavel, he would translate to Alona, she would say something in Ukrainian to me, I would try to understand and say something back, and if I couldn't then Pavel would translate. I was having that Peace Corps experience that you read about in romanticized blog posts, all with the frosty Carpathian mountains in the backdrop.

After about an hour our conversation naturally ended, which was then followed by another hour of occasional eye contact and polite smiles because we were still facing mere feet away from each other. At the beginning of the third hour of the ride, Pavel and Alona got up and grabbed their bags from the headrail above us.

"This is our stop," Pavel said, turning to the snow covered mountains that stood just outside the window. "We'll be skiing for the next few days. Just let us know when you're free and we can meet up."

"Perfect!" I said, trying to conceal my excitement. I never thought that my forced and planned out initiative to make friends would come to such a success, but as luck would have it, I'd be skiing with some of the locals in no time.

A couple days later, after doing a successful English club and catching up with Noah, I called Pavel with the real phone number that he actually gave me, excited to see what my new friends were up to.

"Hey Robert, we are actually leaving skiing a little earlier than we thought," Pavel told me over the phone.

"Oh," I said as the energy left my voice. Somehow I knew that skiing with a cool young Ukrainian couple was good to be true. "Sure, I understand."

"We are coming back to Mukachevo, though. I will ring you when we get back, we can go to a bar or something."

"For sure!" I said with a newfound excitement, "When are you coming back?"

"Tomorrow night," he replied, "I'll message you then."

While I was disappointed that I missed out on the slopes, I was still elated to have an opportunity to spend some time with Pavel and Alona.

A couple days later, while I was back home watching stand-up comics on You-tube, I got the message from Pavel about my plans for that evening. It was still quarantine at school, so I could finally say yes to one of these invitations without any Peace Corps duties getting in the way.

"What bar do you want to go to?" I messaged him.

"Actually, Alona asked if you want to have dinner with us and her family."

It felt like a big step after only a couple hours of chatting on the train, but after the skiing invite, these types of invitations to a stranger didn't seem too out of the ordinary.

"For sure," I texted back, "Where does she live?"

"We'll pick you up," Pavel said, "They live a little bit outside of Mukachevo. Is that ok?"

It wasn't ok, because I technically wasn't allowed to leave my site without properly notifying the Peace Corps with an "absence from site" form. Admin stressed through a constant stream of emails that any breach of the rules (especially with the travel policy) could result in termination of service. I felt a little uneasy, but I wasn't about to throw my first hang out with Ukrainians down the drain because of the overly restrictive policy. Some of my friends had gone to Lviv tons of times without notifying the Peace Corps, and they never seemed to get into any trouble. What harm could be done if I went five minutes out of town to have dinner with these people?

"Sounds good," I texted back, "See you then."

A few hours later, a white van rolled up in front of my apartment complex. A shorter woman, who looked like she had been out in the sun too long, was driving. She smiled and waved at me while I hopped into the van.

"Hey Robert," Pavel said from the back seat, "This is Alona's mom, Maria."

"My mom," Alona said pointing at her chest, "No English."

"Pryvit Robert!" Maria said, welcoming me into the van. As we drove past the metropolitan area, Maria talked to me the entire time, speaking a Zakarpattian dialect that thankfully had more Ukrainian than Hungarian. I managed to more or less understand her and have a coherent conversation, which was a victory in itself, other than a couple of times I looked over to Pavel to help me out with a phrase or two.

After only a few minutes of driving we were officially outside of the city center, and the surroundings soon began to look a lot more like Hryshkivtsi. We were on another road sandwiched in between one story houses, all of which were protected by gates. The only difference was that most of the gates were different colors, instead of the green style that dominated my training village.

We arrived at her house just a few minutes later. Alona hopped out of the car to open up the gate, and waiting or us was a man who, unlike most of the people I'd encountered in Ukraine, towered over me. As I got out of the car, I went to shake his hand, which ended up completely encompassing mine during the exchange.

"This is Alona's father," Pavel said, introducing us, "If you ever have a problem in Mukachevo, this is the man to contact!"

The father spoke some Russian to Pavel, and after nodding his head, Pavel turned to me.

"Follow us."

We crossed the street and walked through another gate, which led to a windowless cinderblock shack. Alona's father opened the wooden door with a long brass key that looked straight out of a movie, which led to a narrow wooden staircase that looked like it had been built a century beforehand. Going down some stairs in a window-less shack with a stranger felt a little too close to potential rob and murder territory, but after putting faith in a man I'd met only a few days earlier, I followed the two down the tight and rickety staircase.

We all needed to crouch forward to save our heads from hitting the concrete ceiling. The bottom of the shack was incredibly dark, and with no railing all I could do was put my palm on the wall and hope that I didn't trip and fall over my hosts. Luckily we all made it to the end of the stairs unscathed, and after Alona's father turned on the light, I was greeted by a cellar-like room filled with shelves of glass jars, which were holding enough marinated vegetables to last for weeks. It was almost identical to the shack at my host family's place, except for one major exception: At the end of the room stood two giant wooden barrels which almost took up as much room as the four of us did. Pavel took a few plastic cups from one of the shelves, crouched over to the barrels, pulled the nob, and outflowed a dark red liquid into his cup.

"Zakarpattian wine," he told me, "The best in Ukraine, and it's homemade."

The father handed me a plastic cup and gently nudged me to the barrel.

"Bitter or sweet?" Pavel asked.

That felt like a trick question. "Bitter, please," I said in front of these two tall strapping Ukrainian men.

"Good choice," Pavel replied, winking at me. Manly test passed. He poured a cup for me and a cup for the father.

"Robert, there's one more thing," Pavel mentioned while he finished pouring, "When you drink this wine, you have to squat like a Ukrainian. You know, Slavic squatting, I'm sure you've seen it here before."

"Yeah, I think so," I said back to him. Since arriving I had also seen various memes of bald men in Adidas tracksuits squatting, and come to think of it, I had seen Ukrainians squatting in various places pretty much every other day while drinking coffee or smoking a cigarette. Now, standing in front of two bald Ukrainian men (minus the track suits), it was my time to shine.

Pavel and the father squatted down, and I joined them, trying not to listen to the crying cartilage in my knee.

"That's perfect, Robert," Pavel said, "Now cheers! In Ukrainian we say 'Budzdorivia.'"

"Boodroviya?"

"Pretty much. Budzdorovia, Robert!"

"BOODROVIYA!" I shouted back in excitement.

I gotta give kudos to Pavel. He definitely knew what he was doing, because drinking homemade Ukrainian wine from a wooden barrel and Slavic squatting with a couple of the locals was an incredibly authentic Ukrainian experience for a young American like myself. He knew what he was doing, but even with that said, it was still hard to believe how far I'd come in less than a week.

While reveling in the moment, I almost forgot to sip the wine. I smelled it, just like I had seen in the movies, and then took a taste. It was extremely bitter. I wasn't much of a wine drinker at the time, with the majority of my experience coming out of a bag or a box during my college days, so needless to say I hadn't acquired any sort of pallet. It was a bit of a shame that the wine, which was probably of extremely high quality, only tasted like chalk, but while squatting in that cinderblock shack with my new Ukrainian friends, the taste was the last thing I cared about.

That night we enjoyed a robust Zakarpattian dinner, which once again included more spices and flavors than any of my dinners in central Ukraine. The borscht was a little bit spicier, the dumplings were a little more savory, and the wine still tasted like chalk. The family was pretty curious about my experience so I gave my usual spiel, but I was also happy enough to try to listen and understand the conversation they were all having. It was a mix of Russian, Zakarpattian and Ukrainian, along with a little bit of English whenever Pavel filled me in on what they were talking about. Feeling the buzz from the wine and the stronger buzz of finally branching out, I tried to savor every moment possible, knowing that it wouldn't be lasting for as long as I wanted it too.

This was because, unfortunately, Pavel and Alona were only staying for a few more days. As I made it home that night, Pavel mentioned that they'd be leaving by the weekend.

"We should hang out one last time," he said while dropping me off back home, "We can play billiards or something. Do you play billiards?"

"Yeah, I do. I played a lot in the States." That was a stretch. Although Pavel and Alona had been nothing but nice and non-judgmental during our hang outs, I still wanted to portray a facade of coolness during our last day together.

"Great, we will be a bit busy tomorrow, but how about we meet up, uh, pislazavtra. How do you say that in English?"

"The day after tomorrow," I replied.

"See?" he said while patting my shoulder, "You're getting better already."

A couple days after our dinner, I met Pavel and Alona at some billiards bar I had never been to. While a few years beforehand I could hold my own in pool back in the states, I unfortunately wasn't aware that there is a different type of pool played in Eastern Europe: Russian Billiards. As expected, it's way harder and more frustrating. First of all, all of the balls are the same color: White. They are also way bigger, and the holes are smaller. So not only does the table lack the rainbow design of American pool, but it's also insanely difficult. Nearly impossible, I would say.

I learned this moments after we entered the dimly-lit bar. There was enough room in the place to have four pool tables and a dance floor, but at the time we were the only ones there. We all ordered a beer and put our kopeks into the coin slot, and soon after a sea of giant white pool balls rushed onto the table.

"Would you like to go first?" Pavel asked.

"If you don't mind," I said nonchalantly, ready to show off my cool guy pool skills on our last night hanging out together.

128

In two rounds, I hit zero. Zero. I started off by whiffing on the break, which should have been easier because the ball is so much bigger, and it went downhill from there. Pavel was decent, getting the ball in the hole every fourth or fifth try, but for the longest time Alona and I didn't have any luck. That is until the second round, when Alona hit two in a row, much to her excitement and my dismay.

In typical fashion, while trying to look like I knew what I was doing, I fell on my face. This was pretty much a nutshell of my first six months in Ukraine. Sometimes I could get by while following the "fake it till you make it" advice I had gotten from the veteran volunteers, but there are some things you just can't fake, such as speaking a second language, teaching for the first time without any prior experience, and playing Russian billiards.

Pavel was nice about it, though, "I know American billiards is very different," he said trying to cheer me up, "This is a lot harder. It probably takes a while to adapt. Don't worry Robert, it's just for fun."

After a few pathetic games of billiards, we walked back towards the city center. I couldn't tell you what we talked about, because all I could remember was the conflicting pain and euphoria in my gut on the walk home. I was grateful that I had serendipitously met two young and hospitable locals, but at the same time it pained me to say goodbye to the only friends I had made to that point.

"It was nice meeting you, Robert," Pavel said to me at the train station before we departed. "We'll be back sometime in the summer after the semester ends for Alona. We'll reach out whenever we come back to Mukachevo, and we can do something like this again. Maybe American billiards next time."

"Thanks so much, Pavel. I've had such a great week. I'm really glad I sat next to you two on the train."

"Crazy, right?" Pavel said, patting my shoulder.

"Goodbye Robert," Alona said slowly in Ukrainian, "It was really nice to meet you." She then turned to Pavel and said something.

129

"Alona says that you should feel free to call her mom any time you like. You'll always have them in Mukachevo if you ever need any help, and her mom wants to invite you back to dinner."

"Thank you Alona," I told her in Ukrainian, "Have a good trip and thanks again."

"Thanks Robert. Stay safe, and hopefully see you soon. Call us when you make it home."

I promised to text them about returning home safe, even though my apartment was less than a minute away, and with that we went our separate ways. The potential of returning to Alona's mom's house softened the emotional blow, but for the next few days I was more sad than after the Peace Corps conference.

I had just made a breakthrough, I thought that night, as I once again sat alone in my apartment. *And now it's over. It's over.*

Although I was down at the time, with hindsight it's clear that my week of quarantine was a huge step in my journey in Ukraine. The experience of making small talk with a stranger on the train, which led all the way to squatting in a concrete shack and drinking wine from the barrel, gave me enough confidence to put myself out there more during the rest of my service.

It was a first step to greater adventures, and even though I didn't know it, that week with Pavel and Alona marked a turning point in my service. In the subsequent months I had a lot more conversations with strangers on the train during the rest of my time in Ukraine, and while most of those conversations ended at our respective stops, I was no longer scared of initiating conversations. Even with Pavel and Alona gone, all it took was a simple greeting on the train to completely change the rest of my service.

Chapter Eleven

Election

I first heard the name "Volodymir Zelensky" long before every news anchor in America gave their shot at pronouncing it in the summer of 2019. Many of them got it wrong: Volodimyr (Vuh-low-di-meer) is the Ukrainian equivalent of Vladimir, but I don't blame anyone who called him Vladimir, because why would they know the difference? Only a microcosm of a sliver of the American population is caught up on Ukrainian politics, but here came this Ukrainian president storming into the middle of the American political sphere by playing a part in one of the biggest American political stories of the decade. You're probably one of the millions of people who heard this man's name a few times in the summer of 2019, and then never really thought about him again, but just how he became president in and of itself is worth understanding.

The 2019 Ukrainian presidential election was only the second election after the Maidan Revolution. The first one in 2014 was two months after the pro-Russia government was overthrown by the people, as Ukraine began a strong push towards Europe and away from Russia. This next election five years later would be a true litmus test for the Ukrainian state. Would Ukraine be plagued by yet another fraudulent and corrupt election, or would it continue its path towards a free and fair democracy?

There had already been a rigged election in 2004. The pro Russian candidate, Viktor Yanukovych, initially claimed victory, but election observers widely determined the election as fraudulent. This led to the Orange Revolution, a largely peaceful protest movement that swept Ukraine, where millions of people took to the streets and made their voices heard. This included a protest of over 500,000 people in Kyiv's city square, which was unlike anything this post-soviet country had ever seen before.

As a result, after a close review the Ukrainian Supreme Court declared the election as fraudulent. The initial results were thrown out, and Ukraine then conducted a second election. This time, the pro-western candidate, Vikor Yushchenko, who had been poisoned by Russian operatives during the middle of the election cycle, won 52% to 44% (Kuzio, 2005). Yushchenko served for the next five years until 2009, when Yanukovych challenged him again. Facing a weakened incumbent marred by corruption scandals, this time Yanukovych won fair and square.

Technically, the election resulting in Yanukovych's victory in 2009 was a fair vote, but seeing as the winner began to effectively sabotage Ukraine's European intentions from the inside, I wouldn't say that the election should be seen as a raging success solely because it wasn't manipulated with directly. As you read earlier, Yanukovych was the Russian puppet who fled the country after the 2014 Maidan Revolution. Yes, not one, but TWO revolutions were a result of this guy running for president.

So after two separate revolutions, which included one nonviolent one in 2004 and one violent one in 2014, the eyes of the world were glued to Ukraine in 2019 to see if they could get through a presidential election cycle without any bumps in the road.

The incumbent at the time was Petro Poroshenko, who was elected in 2014 to steer the country towards stronger ties with the European Union, United States and the West. Poroshenko had been involved in politics for a couple of decades up to that point, but he first rose to national prominence through his chocolate company, Roshen. Roshen began in the early 90s, and by 2012 it was named as the 18th largest candy manufacturing body in the world ("2013 Top 100 Candy Companies," 2013). It brought Poroshenko's net worth up to more than a billion, which soon slightly tumbled after Russia discontinued shipments as their relationship soured with Ukraine.

Poroshenko campaigned on "Army, Language, and Faith," vowing to build up Ukrainian's army against the existential Russian threat. His campaign and presidency promoted national identity and heritage by creating a Ukrainian language mandate in schools, which angered many people in the primarily Russian-speaking provinces. Additionally, under his presidency Ukraine formed a new Ukrainian Orthodox sect of Christianity, chipping away at Russian influence by officially separating from the dominant Russian Orthodox Church, which had towered in Ukraine for decades. Lastly, while Poroshenko was in office, Ukrainians finally obtained "visa-free travel" in the EU. In the past, Ukrainians would have to apply for a visa to travel in the EU, which would cost up to fifty euros. Now, they could travel unimpeded, which has opened up the rest of the world a little bit more to Ukrainians.

It makes sense that after a pro-Russia candidate sparked a violent revolution, Ukrainians wanted a guy like Poroshenko to steer Ukraine into a more western and autonomous direction. Many Ukrainians looked at post-revolution life with fervent optimism, but even with everything I've mentioned above, over the next five years that optimism deteriorated. My anecdotal view is that Ukrainians became sick of Poroshenko and his government due to corruption and economic stagnation, much like with every other president since Ukraine's independence in 1991. Corruption is rampant in Ukraine, so story after story of cabinet members taking bribes did nothing to help Poroshenko's re-election hopes. Russia had a huge effect on the economic stagnation, because they annexed a the popular tourist port region of Crimea, and started a war that dissuaded western investors from putting their money into Ukrainian projects. Thus, the economy (like it always is) was blamed on the president, and that combined with endemic corruption made Poroshenko's bed.

It didn't take too long for the general public's view to sour on Poroshenko, and by late 2018, most people were ready for a change.

In comes Volodymir Zelensky. By trade, Zelensky started out as a comedian/actor, who became nationally known after starring in a popular Ukrainian political comedy, Servant of the People. Here we had a man deciding to run for president with no political experience after raising his national profile through a hit TV show. Sound familiar?

Servant of the People, however, is vastly different from the reality show that helped a certain American president get elected. It's a show about a history teacher (Zelensky), who in the first episode goes on a rant against the endemic corruption in Ukraine. A student takes a video of the rant and uploads it to Youtube, where it goes viral and eventually gets him elected the president of Ukraine.

Yes, the man who eventually became the real president of Ukraine gained national prominence after starring in a TV show as the president of Ukraine.

I'll repeat that. He played the President of Ukraine on television. Then he became the real president.

Servant of the People began airing in the fall of 2015, and through comedic and clever writing, the show poignantly pointed out and criticized corruption in the Ukrainian political system, at times blatantly calling out the oligarchs who run the country. Servant of the People is on Netflix, and if you've made it this far then I suggest you give it a shot. It's a pretty good watch, and it's only three seasons, ending in 2018.

That timing is no coincidence. Servant of the People aired on the popular TV channel, "1 + 1," which happens to be owned by a Ukrainian Oligarch, Ihor Kolomoyskyy. Kolomoysky is one of the richest people in Ukraine, and plays a huge role in many different Ukrainian industries, ranging from politics, media, and banking. If you've picked up the general vibe of Ukrainian politics by now, it shouldn't be a surprise that Kolomoyskyy and the incumbent president Poroshenko absolutely despised each other, and Servant of the People, which ran on the television station that Kolomoyskyy owned, was used as a way to get Poroshenko out of power.

Kolomoyskyy is worth 1.8 billion right now (Forbes, 2022), but in 2012 his new worth was closer to three billion, with his most lucrative venture being in finance. Kolomoysky established Privatbank, which is one of if not the most commercially successful banks in Ukraine. Anywhere you go in Ukraine you'll find a Privatbank ATM, although I've come to loathe those devilish green machines in the wall. The ATM gives you your card after you've already gotten your money. Multiple times I've taken out cash, only to get super excited and leave my card in the machine. It's completely backwards, but that's neither here nor there.

Problematic ATM practices aside, Kolomoysky earned a killing with Privatbank, making him one of the richest men in Ukraine. However, controversy arose in 2016 when rumors started swirling that the bank defrauded the Ukrainian people, and stole upwards of five billion dollars from its customers. An investigation found Privatbank guilty of fraud, and in response, the Poroshenko led government nationalized the bank, effectively taking over all power and control from Kolomoysky. (Funny enough, Prvivtbank in Ukrainian means "private bank," and in 2016, the private bank became nationalized.) Along with absorbing Pryvatbank, the government froze over two billion dollars of Kolomoyskyy's assets, cutting his net worth by more than half.

Now, you may be asking yourself: Did Privatbank actually defraud the Ukrainian people, or was it a political move by Poroshenko to limit the power of one of his rivals? Probably both. The FBI is currently investigating Kolomoyskyy for financial crimes, and in 2021 the United States laid sanctions on Kolomoyskyy for financial crimes which he perpetrated in the U.S., as well as being a threat towards Ukrainian democracy (Dickinson, 2021). He's a corrupt oligarch who despised Poroshenko, although Poroshenko can't say much either - as of February of 2022 Poroshenko has been charged with treason. It's a mess.

But that's getting ahead of ourselves - back to Zelensky. By 2016, when Privatbank was nationalized, Servant of the People had been airing for about a year, displaying the courageous actions of Zelensky's character against a corrupt and oligarchical controlled political system (remember that Kolomoyskyy is the owner of the channel that is current broadcasting Servant of the People). The series continued for a couple more years, as Zelensky's character started to face more and more punishment for not going along with the corruption. At the beginning of season three he is thrown into exile, only to storm back into Ukraine and to take back the government for the people. This heroic case study against corruption captured the imagination of Ukrainians, and in 2018 they were ready to make their imagination a reality.

In March of 2018, before the last season of the show, the Servant of the People became an officially registered Ukrainian political party. In December 2018, a few months after the finale, Zelensky declared on New Year's Eve that he would be running for president, represented by the Servant of the People party and primarily running on an anti-corruption campaign.

That's a lot to digest, so here's a quick recap: The Oligarch Kolomoyskyy defrauded the Ukrainian people through his bank, stealing billions of dollars. Poroshenko's corruption plagued government then nationalized the bank and froze two billion dollars of Kolomoyskyy's assets. During this time Kolomoyskyy's TV channel aired a show about a history teacher turned president, which criticized corrupt Ukrainian political practices. Two years later, the actor who played the president on Kolomoyskyy's channel decides to run for president against the person who led the charge against Kolomoyskyy.

And then you know what? The TV president won by a landslide, and two months later he was solicited by Donald Trump to dig up dirt on Biden, or else America would withhold three hundred million dollars of military aid from Ukraine, which it needed for an ongoing war with Russia.

But more on that later. We first had to get through the initial election.

The first round of voting was in March of 2019. Many volunteers, including myself, didn't know anything about the Ukrainian political dynamics at the time. All we knew was that merely months after being under high alert due to martial law, Ukraine was preparing for its most important election since its independence in 1991.

That didn't sit well with most of us, especially our country director, William. After receiving some ominous election-security emails the summer before orientation, rumors began to fly about our inevitable evacuation due to the election.

From orientation until election day, no more than a couple of weeks would go by without getting an email reminding us of the significance of the election and how big of a security risk it could potentially cause. This was printed into our minds even before the Kerch Strait incident, and after martial law ended in January we remained on high alert, waiting to see how Ukraine would respond to its first democratic election after the Maidan Revolution.

And, with Peace Corps' number one responsibility being the health and safety of their volunteers, the anxious volunteers like myself were bracing for the trigger happy country director to press the abort button and send us all home. At least by now I would have served for about eight months and gone on a few adventures, so if I got evacuated I would've been severely less salty than if it had happened in November. I still would've felt robbed, though.

In February, we received an email from our safety and security manager going over the game plan for the election and the subsequent run-off. We learned that volunteers couldn't travel to any region center for about a month, and afterwards we would have to stay tuned for the runoff election. There had already been a bit of political violence in a few places and we were more or less told to sit tight until all of this election stuff blew over. None of this was surprising, but the part that actually caught my eye came at the end of the email:

We appreciate you continuing to avoid large crowds, rallies, and demonstrations and strongly advise you to stay away from the schools on Election Day where voting will take place. Please let us know if ballot counting continues at your (school) sites on April 1-2 and if you feel this is a risky place for you to be.

The first thing I did was text Maryana to see if our school was a polling place. It was, so the first thing I took from that email is that I wouldn't have to work during the election.

"Sorry Maryana, it's due to safety precautions. You know, Peace Corps, out of my hands."

"No problem, Robert." What a great boss.

If it meant getting out of a day or two of work I was intent on following rules, but by March that happened to be one of the only occasions when I abided by Peace Corps Policy.

During the Kerch Strait incident in November I had just moved to Mukachevo, and I wouldn't have been caught dead traveling when I wasn't supposed to. After less than three months in Ukraine, I didn't want to do anything to risk losing my job as a volunteer. That changed dramatically in March.

As a grizzled volunteer of seven months, I finally understood something that most of my cohort realized a few months earlier: The Peace Corps has no idea what you do and where you go on a day to day basis. There are hundreds of volunteers dispersed throughout thousands of miles of Ukraine, and the only people who can catch you and get you in trouble live in Kyiv. If you just refrain from being an idiot and don't post stuff on social media, you could travel whenever you wanted, as long as your organization/school was cool with it. And as long as volunteers showed up to work and did our job (which I did by the way!), we pretty much had free rein to do whatever we wanted to in our free time.

By March even my naive-self had figured this out, albeit later than the rest of my cohort. By then I had trekked over to Lviv on the Elektrichka a few times, and while I spent most of the experience hyperventilating over the stupid risk I was taking, by my fourth and fifth trip that anxiety began to be replaced by the sense of renewed adolescent coolness that comes from breaking the rules.

However, the election was definitely not the time to be testing out the Peace Corps' travel policy, and I had no intention on leaving site. By the time the initial election rolled around in late March I was more than happy to hunker down in Mukachevo. I mean, it's still Mukachevo, and I was grateful that I had a relatively comfortable and interesting city to stay in. Maybe I'd go exploring or hang out with some of the locals or buy some ice cream and ride on the ferris wheel by myself. You know, typically Peace Corps stuff.

My plan was swiftly decimated after matching with one person on Tinder. We matched in mid-March, about a week before the "do not travel under any circumstances" stage started, so timing couldn't have been better. After texting for a few days, Khrystyna, a law student in her third year, invited me to Lviv.

"Hey," I replied, sad, "I would love to come to Lviv, but my organization isn't letting us do any travel because of the election."

"What? Why not?"

"Well, there could be violence or protests or something."

"Oh Robert, that's not going to happen. It's going to be perfectly safe here."

Bob, don't do it.

She replied before I had a chance to, "You could just break the rules ;)"

Devil, no.

"I don't know," I replied, "I could lose my job if they catch me."

"How could they catch you? They're all in Kyiv, right? I think it'll be ok."

"What about in early April?" I begged, "We are allowed to travel from the fifth through twelfth."

"I'm sorry, I won't be in town :("

Crap. A week after that I won't be able to travel either. Will I really have to wait a month and a half before I could go on this first date?

"Ok," I texted back, "I'll see you on Sunday."

"Great :) I'll see you then."

Sunday. The day of the election. Nice one.

....

Under normal circumstances maybe I wouldn't have travelled eight hours round trip during a volatile election to meet up with someone from Tinder on a Sunday afternoon, but after more than half a year of isolation, the choice was simple: Go on this date, or never meet anyone ever for the next two years. Naturally, the less responsible part of me won out, and not wanting to pass up the only date opportunity I had come across during my service, I bought the train ticket and got ready to go.

139

I'll spare the details of the trip because (thankfully) nothing extremely interesting or intriguing happened. Just imagine a guy getting on a train, consistently looking over his shoulder and trying to look as small as possible in the least crowded train car. After touching down in Lviv he immediately walks to his hostel while doing his best to conceal his identity with a hat, sunglasses and scarf. Then, after staying in his hostel the whole night out of fear of losing his job, he wakes up the next day only to wait in the hostel a few more hours before his date in the park. That was me.

The date rolled around about 2:00 pm on Sunday, after spending most of my time in Lviv almost giving myself an aneurism from over thinking. I took an Uber to one of the bigger parks in Lviv, where Khrystyna was waiting for me on one of the benches.

We walked around for a couple hours, using both English and Ukrainian to try to get to know each other better. Khrystyna's English was pretty good, and I tried to fill in the gaps with my Ukrainian skills if she ever couldn't find exactly what she wanted to say. Often I didn't know the Ukrainian equivalent, so whenever we hit a lull we typically tried to quickly just change the subject. Even after six months in the country, my Ukrainian skills were far from where I wanted them to be, although like most Ukrainians she was impressed that I knew more than "hello."

It was nice to go on a date after nine months of living like an asexual hermit, but I can't deny how close I was to an emotional breakdown. This wasn't because it was my first date since college, which of course led to some heightened nerves, but it was mostly due to the fact that during our time together I couldn't do anything to conceal my identity. A ball-cap, sunglasses and scarf would have been too strange, even with her acknowledging the risk that I was taking. I knew that all of my superiors were in Kyiv, but Lviv is a pretty big city, and there was always a chance that an administrator could be visiting on official Peace Corps business, especially during the election.

However, after an hour passed, I noticed something strange. None of my superiors jumped out of the bushes with cameras. None of then walked behind me, tapped me on the back, and said, "We gotcha, Robert. Caught red handed. You walked right into our clever rouse to test your morals within Peace Corps, and you failed miserably. Now off you go back to America." My worst fears, as usual, were't realized.

Near the end of our date, when I was feeling a bit more bullish, I even began playing some music from my phone which was recommended by my students. It was Russian pop-rap, which I initially only liked ironically, which of course soon turned into an unironic passion.

"I'd turn that off if I were you," Khrystyna told me nonchalantly, "On a day like today people may come up and start to fight you."

Oh, Right. Russian music is extremely popular and widespread in Ukraine, but in a city like Lviv, which is much farther down the nationalist side of the political spectrum, blasting the language of Ukraine's biggest enemy wasn't quite the move on the day of a presidential election.

"Oh," I muttered, "Thanks for the heads up."

She later took me to a museum in a part of Lviv I had never been to before. Although my slightly nervous energy didn't mesh well with the quiet museum, as I read about some classical Ukrainian writers I was able to temporarily forget about the huge risk I was taking.

That is until 3:45, or about an hour until my train. Just twenty-eight hours after I arrived, it was already time to head back. We headed out of the museum and she took me to the bus stop, making sure I knew exactly which bus to get on in order to make it to my train on time.

"Thanks, Khrystyna. I'll let you know next time I can come back."

"Hopefully we won't be at war," Khrystyna joked again. "I hope to see you again."

"Yeah, hopefully. Until next time."

That day was my only opportunity to meet Khrystyna, and although I had grown a few grey hairs, I had the chance at a second date. That's all I could ask for, as well as not losing my job.

Mission completed, I thought while on the bus back to the train station.

I made it home unscathed at 8:45 pm, right before the initial results came in. Zelensky (comedian) took first place with Poroshenko (chocolate tycoon) in a distant second, and they were set for the run-off election in April. To that point there had been no bombings or other violence, which made sense after experiencing the calm and laid back atmosphere in Lviv. While tensions were high during the post-revolution election in 2014, this one felt like just another day in Ukraine.

The tranquility was a stark contrast to what I and most of my fellow volunteers expected, as our tense expectations were undoubtedly influenced by the Kerch Strait episode months before. Better safe than sorry, I guess, but that didn't make me any less anxious the following week, as I waited with terror to receive an email that I had been caught in Lviv and must immediately travel to Kyiv to await punishment.

That email thankfully never came, and even better the run-off went off without a hitch. In April Zelesnky beat Poroshenko by a margin of 73% to 27%, in one of the bigger blowouts you'll ever see in a free and fair election (BBC, 2019). He had captured the nation's imagination, which like all politicians in Ukraine he soon lost in the years afterwards.

The election itself, however, was an unquestioned success. No polling stations were bombed, there wasn't any significant violence or intimidation at polling booths, and election observers from across the world agreed in unison that the election was free and fair. Poroshenko, to his credit, peacefully gave up power, and didn't end up using martial law or any other nefarious methods in order to stay in control.

That isn't to say that things didn't get petty. Right before Poroshenko left, Poroshenko's people had the audacity to remove all of the computer servers from the Ukrainian "situation room" (NBC, 2019). Poroshenko said that, well, he paid for them, so if he were leaving, he was going to take them with him. How petty is that? In one of his last actions as president, Poroshenko ripped out government servers as a final F-U to Zelensky. Zelensky's incoming administration complained that it was a major national security risk, but I'm sure those servers were replaced rather easily by the new billionaires who were about to run the country. However, with Ukraine's recent political history in mind, a former president removing government servers is one of the more tame scandals to happen in modern Ukrainian politics.

Pettiness aside, Zelensky was inaugurated one month after the runoff, and in the process the EU, election observers, many Ukrainians, and all of the Peace Corps took a collective sigh of relief. By the end of the second run-off I knew that I was in the clear regarding my Lviv shenanigans, and for the Peace Corps the result of this whole process was the best-caste scenario: There was no violence, no election fraud, no revolution, no evacuation, and no volunteers were caught breaking travel restrictions.

After a long two month affair, the election came and went, the weather got warmer, and at least ¾ of the country was satisfied in the new hopefully less corrupt direction the country pointed towards. Peace Corps could also finally put their second potential evacuation time-bomb in the rearview and was able to bring back to life as normal.

And then, less than two months later, in Zelensky's first call with the President of the United States, Trump threatened to withhold hundreds of millions of dollars unless Zelensky began to dig up dirt on Biden. Just imagine what went through Zelensky's head! A year ago his TV show hadn't even finished, and now he was being blackmailed by the most powerful person in the world. What was supposed to be a honeymoon period for Zelensky turned into flocks of reporters coming to Ukraine to ask him about something he had absolutely no interest shedding light on.

And get this: Not one Ukrainian brought it up to me. Not one person! It was headline news for months, and led to just the third impeachment in our nation's history. Yet with all that said, not one Ukrainian asked me about it. Not my colleagues, not any students, not even anyone on the train. And it's not like Ukrainians were afraid to ask personal/political questions, because I got questions about Trump and Obama all the time.

Eventually I brought it up to some students at my adult English club, who all proceeded to laugh and said, "Oh yeah, haha, I guess that's a thing." My anecdotal interpretation is that to them, corruption and blackmail are just par for the course in Ukraine. Myra's words from November rang in my head, "This kind of stuff happens all the time here."

Once again I had failed to properly gauge the response of the locals after a major political event, but I couldn't get too greedy: My date went well, I wasn't kicked out of the Peace Corps, and our entire cohort wasn't evacuated after a revolution resulting from a rigged election. I counted myself lucky, and afterwards began to focus more on life in Mukachevo, like I had planned all along.

References

Associated Press. (2019, May 29). *Ukraine's ex-president accused of removing computer servers from situation room*. NBC News. https://www.nbcnews.com/news/world/ukraine-s-ex-president-accused-removing-computer-servers-situation-room-n1011286

Dickinson, P. (2021, March 9) *US Sanctions Ukrainian Oligarch Ihor Kilomoyskyy*. Atlantic Council. https://www.atlanticcouncil.org/blogs/ukrainealert/us-sanctions-ukrainian-oligarch-ihor-kolomoisky/

Kuzio, T. (2005). *The Orange Revolution*. Elections Today. https://ciaotest.cc.columbia.edu/olj/et/et_v12n4/et_v12n4_003.pdf

 # 1750 Ihor Kolomoyskyy. (2022). Forbes. https://www.forbes.com/profile/ihor-kolomoyskyy/?sh=2b96692651dc

2013 Top 100 Candy Companies. (2013). Candy Industry. https://www.candyindustry.com/top-25-candy-companies-2013

Ukraine Election: Comedian Zelensky Wins Presidency by a Landslide. (2019, April 22). BBC. https://www.bbc.com/news/world-europe-48007487

Chapter Twelve

Talent Show

In the spring of 2019, School 16 hosted its annual "English Week." I learned early on that at an institution like School 16, English Week is a big flex. As a specialized English school, School 16 conducts five English classes a week rather than the typical amount of three, and the English department is by far the largest department they have. It's safe to say that English is definitely School 16's thing, and English Week is a chance to show everyone (especially the parents) that we do English and take it seriously. It was especially important to my colleagues in the English department, who were surely going to be evaluated on the spectacle, and being the shiny new American I of course was expected to participate and help them shine.

I wasn't too sure of what my role would be, and that didn't change for much of the semester. I didn't get much info in the months leading up to the biggest week of the year, and after a brief meeting in January 2019, all I knew was that it would be happening sometime in May and that my colleagues wanted volunteers from other parts of Zakarpattia to participate.

"Ok no problem," I said, "When should they come?"

"Oh," Yana replied, "We aren't sure yet, but we will let you know!"

"Ok, well, what do you want us to do?"

"We're not sure about that either. We will let you know!"

I had already gathered from my time thus far that most plans needed a bit of time to get the ball rolling in Ukraine. I found that whenever I forced any discussion, whether it be about lesson plans, activities, or scheduling, I was always met with a non-answer and side eyes. I learned early on to just hang back and wait for the right time to come, so I figured they'd get back to me sometime or another.

The only problem was that I had no idea what to say to the other volunteers whenever they asked me for details. I told the volunteers that I had invited, Sophia and Josh, that I'd need them sometime in mid-May, and that they should have their travel forms ready whenever I got the official word. While they were a bit anxious about the Peace Corps tight travel policy and getting their forms in on time, they also had experience with how scheduling typically works in Ukraine and made sure not to hold their breath.

Soon enough the beginning of May rolled around, and I was still in the dark. Just as I finally started to get a bit anxious, I got a text from Maryana to meet in the teacher room during the big break. Generally, the vibes were rather lighthearted in the teacher's room, where we would typically drink coffee and chat while escaping the screaming children in the hallways. However, with just a week before the big show and little to no planning, things took on a more serious tone.

My colleagues soon started speaking in Ukrainian. Fast. I hardly understood a thing that any of them said, aside from the occasional "Robert," and all I could make out was that there would be competitions and dances of some sort. Twenty minutes into the discussion the bell rang, and everyone left looking like they generally understood the plan, except me of course. After the meeting I asked Myra to give me a run down.

"Oh, right," she said, probably after forgetting that I didn't understand much Ukrainian. "So, the good news is that besides next Thursday, you won't have to do anything. We are going to plan all of the competitions and activities, and all you have to do is host a workshop with other volunteers."

"What kind of workshops?"

"You know, like, the workshops you all do in Peace Corps. We are going to invite English teachers from all around Mukachevo to come, so get the volunteers to come on Thursday, if you can. That's all you'll need to do."

Perfect. The pro-sustainability volunteer in me was happy to hear that the department was taking most of the initiative in setting up and executing the events.

On top of that, I was looking forward to finally doing some of the pedagogical workshops that Peace Corps strongly encouraged us to implement at our sites.

"So what do we want to do these workshops on?" I asked, "Games, critical thinking, stuff like that?"

"Yeah totally, whatever you think. Games for sure, maybe something with technology. Whatever you all are comfortable with."

"Alright, perfect," I said. This was going smoothly.

"Also," Myra said smiling before walking to her classroom, "Ask Yana about the talent show."

"Talent show?"

Yes, a talent show. Ukrainians love to put on a performance, so it made all the sense in the world that a grandiose celebration of talent and wit would culminate one of the more important weeks of the school year. It was hardly a surprise, especially since it wouldn't be my first performance at School 16.

In the fall semester, we put on a Harry Potter Christmas musical, which was the first project that Myroslava and I worked on after my arrival. Every week for about two months Myroslava, some older students and I spent time together memorizing lines, doing blocking, instilling choreography and perfecting english pronunciation. While I thought we would be writing our own script, we ended up copying lines from the actual film and implanting them in the musical. Plagiarism aside, it was a great way to cap off my first semester at the school, and it really helped me bond with a group of students who at that point I had only seen in the classroom.

The entire performance was in English, except for my role where I had to attempt to speak Zakarpattian, much to the amusement of the parents, teachers, and administrators sitting in the crowd. Although that part in particular was more of a struggle than teaching dance numbers to a bunch of edgy and hip Ukrainian teens, all and all the crowd was pretty nice and encouraging while I butchered their native tongue. I felt that they appreciated my effort, and since the beginning of most Peace Corps services is looking like a fool in front of your colleagues, I was glad at least this time it could help me with immersion. I look back upon the whole experience as one of the finer moments of my service.

By March of 2019 I was no novice to performances at School 16, and since the show was spearheaded by another one of my colleagues, Yana, I fully expected to play a role.

"Robert," Yana whispered to me while our sixth graders were taking an exam, "We would like you to host the talent show. Does that sound ok?" My 'just say yes' mentality was in full swing, and hosting a talent show would be no problem at all.

"Sure! Why not. What do you need me to do?"

"Oh, It shouldn't be too much. You just need to introduce yourself, kick things off, and maybe sing a song of your choosing."

"Sing a song?"

"Yeah, choose an American song. You know how to sing right?"

She said this with a straight face, which made it seem like Yana assumed that I knew how to sing simply because I was an American. Not wanting to break the stereotype, I was intrigued by the idea of showing off my high school musical theater prowess in front of my students and colleagues. My only solo ever came in eleventh grade, when I had a ten second bar in our school's musical, 9 to 5, only to be starved of the spotlight for the seven or so years since.

"Yeah, well, I've sung before, sure-"

"That's perfect. Pick a song today or tomorrow and send me the music. Thank you!"

"Yana," I mentioned, "I don't know about this. Don't you think that it'd be a better idea for one of the kids to host?"

"What?" She exclaimed, "Why do you think that?"

"I just want to make sure that you all are running the show, and I'm not taking over."

"Robert," she said, sighing, "That won't be the case. The kids will be doing most of the work, and you're just going to start things off."

149

"And besides," she continued, "You're our American volunteer during English Week. You gotta do something!"

I was already at my limit for minor confrontations during the calendar month (one), so I conceded.

"Ok, I'll do it. I'll let you know about the music."

"Amazing! Let me know by tonight."

That night I began brainstorming an American-ish song that I could show off and share with my school. My first choice was Hotel California. That was quickly shot down, after Yana listened to it once. My next choice was Wagon Wheel, which was a lot more in spirit, dare I say wheelhouse, of the show. Growing up in Tennessee and spending a lot of time in North Carolina, an upbeat catchy song like Wagon Wheel seemed a lot more appropriate coming from me than a six minute song about a haunted hotel that most of the audience wouldn't understand. I got the approval from a much more enthusiastic Yana the next day, and soon began rehearsing.

However, before my Ukrainian music debut, we had to get through the actual English Week. Again, my role was simple: The English staff would handle most events during most of the days, while I had to invite a few volunteers to Mukachevo with the intention of putting on pedagogical workshops for English teachers in the area.

Getting volunteers to come to Mukachevo was easy. Sophia and Josh were the only two volunteers who I asked, because they both said "yes" almost immediately after I texted them. It wasn't too hard of a sell.

In the Peace Corps, any sort of change is welcomed. Being isolated in a village without any sort of amenities or any native English speakers takes a heavy toll on volunteers. No one is designed to be that isolated from their family and peers for a two year span, and even the strongest wills and coping mechanisms deteriorate after the eighth or ninth month of having no friends or sense of community. The isolation and loneliness is by far the most difficult part for the majority of us, and it's no surprise why such a toxic drinking culture is rampant amongst cohorts worldwide. If you are deprived of community, connection and human contact, which by design is the universal experience of every Peace Corps volunteer, you're going to find something else to fill the void.

With all of this in mind, it was easy to get Sophia and Josh to come to Mukachevo, seeing as it would be be nothing but good for all of us to reconnect and spend a few days connecting with another human being.

After confirming the plans, my job was pretty much done until Thursday, so for the first few days of English Week I had it pretty easy. The classes were completely planned by the teachers and were filled with contests, scavenger hunts, group projects, trivia, and games on games on games. The students were active and engaged all week and seemed to be really loving the change of pace from the normal class style of lectures and grammar drills.

If only they did this every week, I thought, *They might not need a volunteer.*

On Wednesday night, after having a few days off from teaching, Sophia and Josh showed up after taking the trip from their relatively rural sites. Sophia's site, Mizhyria, was a village of about 10,000 in the thick of the Carpathian mountains. Tristan's was a little closer to the ground, but his site was just as rural.

Just like I imagined, their jaws almost dropped to the cobblestone road when they first saw Mukachevo, and after a ride on the town's ferris wheel and a tour of some of the cafes and mini malls, we headed home to figure out our game plan for Thursday.

"Alright, Sophia," I said while sitting on my carpet, "You'll go first with your presentation on technology in the classroom."

"Does your school have internet?" she asked, sitting in the arm chair, which was the only chair in my apartment.

"Yes, I've already talked with my teachers. Internet should be ready to go. Will you need anything?"

"As long as you have a projector, I'll be fine."

"Perfect. So after Sophia, Josh, you'll do your talk on learning styles. Then I'll finish it off with critical thinking."

151

"How long do we have?" Josh asked.

"We have two and a half hours total, but we'll need a few minutes to change presentations, so I'd say to be safe try to cut it at forty minutes."

"I don't know if I can do forty minutes," he replied. "Do you want some peanut butter?"

Peanut butter is a rare delicacy in Ukraine, and I had no idea where he found it in that village of his.

"I'm OK for now, but definitely remind me later. That's fine, you can go a little over on time. Since I'm going last, I'll be able to see how much time we have and cut it short if I have to."

"Ok," he said while indulging solely with a spoon, "I'll need to print out some stuff."

"No problem. We have a printer at school, so we should get there a couple hours early to set everything up."

"Great, that should be it for me then."

"Awesome," I said, getting off the floor, "Thanks for coming, guys."

"Seriously Bob," Sophia said, "It's our pleasure."

I remember sitting in silence with them for the next hour, fervently preparing to present sustainable pedagogical seminars to our biggest audience to date, and other than our keyboards it was mostly silent as we frantically edited and re-edited our presentations.

Due to our job mainly focusing on creating sustainable change, workshops like these were as much of a part of our work as the actual English teaching. If we could get the teachers to really absorb some of the information from our workshops, that would go a lot further than the important yet temporary work of hosting an English club once a week. We were also going to be presenting in front of at least twenty teaching professionals who knew what they were doing, so we wanted to make sure to at least look like we knew what we were talking about.

Unfortunately, no matter how hard we tried to prepare, nothing could have gotten us ready for our first ever big time pedagogical seminar. Things started collapsing shortly after arriving at the school.

Thirty minutes before our presentations, after all of the printing, reviewing, and setting up, Yana told us the internet was out.

"WHAT?" Sophia blurted out.

"Yes, it's not working. Will your seminar still be ok?"

Sophia, who was presenting on technology in the classroom, didn't reply, but we all knew the answer. Of course it isn't ok. Sophia is doomed. Most of her slides instantly became irrelevant, and because she was first, she had only fifteen minutes to prepare what to do.

Fifteen minutes wasn't enough. Throughout her entire presentation in front of rows full of English teachers from throughout the region, she ended up repeating the phrase, "Well, this is a great website to use, but it doesn't really work right now. If we had the internet, then you'd see..." and, "This website is actually really cool, you all should really check it out when you can. If you give me your emails I can send it to you.." Brutal. She sat down after her shortened presentation deflated, and neither Josh nor I had anything to say. There was nothing to say.

It didn't get better from there, either. Josh's workshop went on for almost an hour and wasn't any easier on the eyes. He wanted to have an interactive workshop where all of the teachers would participate, but the only problem was that no one wanted to speak up. Whenever Josh tried to get the teachers involved, he was met with blank stares and long and awkward silences. Additionally when it came to teaching new games, most of the instructions were either lost in translation or simply were apathetic about playing games at four in the afternoon on a Thursday. I have to hand it to Josh, because he tried his best to get as much as he could out of the tough crowd, but just like Sophia, after he concluded he slumped over in his chair and stared into the distance.

Then, I was up. I had to speed through my Critical Thinking workshop in thirty minutes due to time constraints, but I was confident that we could at least end on a high note.

I started off with a riddle, as most good presentations do. My first slide revealed, "What gets wet as it dries?" Seeing some intrigued faces, I was excited to get the ball rolling and pump up some interest.

Before I could say, "If you already know this one, don't say it," one of the teachers immediately yelled, "A TOWEL, IT'S A TOWEL, I'VE DONE THIS BEFORE!" After sadly giving her a piece of candy for her contribution, I saw Yana pointing at the clock and telling me to speed things up. I proceeded to lecture as fast as I could through the twenty-five slide workshop while hardly taking any questions or having any discussion. The irony isn't lost on me that a non-stop thirty minute lecture is far from the best way to build critical thinking skills, so just like Josh and Sophia I sat down afterwards with a thousand yard stare, wondering what the hell just happened.

"Thank you all!" The teachers said after my presentation while racing out of the room.

"You're welcome," We faintly replied.

After everyone left, we all sat down together to debrief. Emma, my volunteer leader and sitemate, was nice enough to show up right before our presentations started and got to experience the whole disaster as an audience member.

"What did you learn?" Emma asked, as if she were a mother who had let her kids fall off a bike for the first time.

"Make sure there's internet if my presentation is about the internet," Sophia said.

"Do more group work instead of calling on them," Josh replied.

"Choose less popular riddles," I muttered. It was a typical experience of floundering early to get better later on, but it didn't feel that optimistic at the time. It just sucked, although the teachers at School 16 cheered me up later on by saying they found a lot of the information useful and were going to start using it in the classroom. That didn't fool me, but I appreciated the pick me up from my colleagues.

After the long buildup and the complete failure that followed, we decided to get some drinks. The talent show was the next day, but after such a stressful ordeal at school, the only thing Sophia, Josh, Emma and I wanted to do was blow off some steam. We went to an Irish Pub, the likes of which Josh and Sophia hadn't seen since swearing in as volunteers in Kyiv five months earlier. Then, for a few magical hours, we had the rare chance to talk at a normal speed and pretend our lives were normal, if not for just one night. Aside from ordering a couple "Beer Towers," there was nothing too exciting or noteworthy about our time together, other than the fact that we drank more than we planned and got home later than we wanted.

The next day I woke up without an alarm. My head was throbbing, my mouth tasted awful, and I was dreading to check the time.

I turned over to pick up my phone. It was 8:00. I had thirty minutes until the talent show.

Thirty minutes! Crap!

I had just enough time to eat the first thing I saw in the fridge, brush my teeth, put on a football jersey (which I convinced myself was somehow English Week related) and get out of there. Thank god my walk to school was only twelve minutes long, or I would've been completely out of luck. I tried warming up my vocals on the walk, but my belting baritone was nowhere to be found, which only added on to the hangover-induced anxiety. It's not like I was trying to sound like the next coming of Prince, but I sure as hell didn't want to embarrass myself in front of a crowd, either. However, I didn't have much of a choice: While rushing through puddles on a crummy Friday, it dawned on me that I was going to experience my second train wreck in consecutive days. The only difference was that this one was completely avoidable.

I hustled into school, mind scattered, thankful I lived less than fifteen minutes away. I entered the front doors with two minutes to spare and darted to Classroom 27, where the talent show was set to kick off. By then the headache still hadn't subsided, and my dehydration hadn't let up even after my second water bottle of the day.

The environment at the school only magnified all of my discomfort. It was dark, literally, and as I climbed my way to room 27, the students, who were all rushing just like me to get to class before the second bell, were tightly smushed together throughout the halls and on the stairwell. I jockeyed for position and made my way up the stairs while trying not to make eye contact with anyone in my weak and hungover state. All I focused on was trying my best to get in the right mindset to execute Wagon Wheel, while also attempting to not look as flustered as I actually felt.

As I made it to the third floor I practically ran into Yana, who stopped me in my tracks. Somehow her disposition looked worse than mine.

"Robert, awful news," Yana said hastily, "The electricity in the school is out, and we can't put on the show. I don't know what's wrong but we're going to have to delay the talent show until Monday."

Yana said some stuff after that, but I couldn't hear her over the feeling of complete elation that was strong enough to temporarily put a pause on my hangover.

"Oh, that's terrible," I said while forcing myself to subdue the oncoming smile.

"I know. It's ruined, just ruined."

"Well, I'm sure we'll reschedule it. Try not to worry too much Yana. But, what should we do now?"

"I don't know. Find Myra."

I found Myra in room 27, where she was bouncing off the walls trying to figure out what on earth to do. We had to continue with some sort of activity, because English Week couldn't end with a promise of a talent show and nothing to show for it. In a span of a few minutes, with about thirty tenth and eleventh graders waiting on us in room 27, Myra concocted a trivia game. She started things out by writing seven different categories on the board.

156

"I will say a letter," Myra announced just as the period started, "And you must come up with a word for each category starting with that letter. Whoever gets them all down first wins!"

Myra looked at me, shrugged, and went ahead with it. It was a pretty decent game, especially being last minute and given the lack of electricity. The older students, who usually were too cool for games, quickly formed into groups and started strategizing without any direction from Myra or myself. The loud and excited cheers after every round only amplified the throbbing in my head, but after a crazy morning, we were all relieved that while English week didn't end with a talent show as planned, it didn't end with a dud either.

After somewhat successfully getting through the culmination of English week without electricity, we rescheduled the talent show for Monday, hoping the electricity gods wouldn't punish us for a second time. Sophia and Josh went home on Friday on what I can only assume was a miserable bus ride, while I had the whole weekend to get over the hangover and get back to hitting all the right notes. I made sure to have a tame weekend, and I was able to wake up early enough on Monday to eat breakfast, shower, and warm up my voice.

Feeling somewhat confident, on Monday I walked into room 27 about an hour early, surprised to see that everything was already set up and put in place. There were tons of streamers, a makeshift stage, and posters saying "School 16 talent show" all around the room. I guess that the monumental stress of the previous Friday was too much to handle, even in a leisurely work culture like in Ukraine, so it made sense why the set up was ready before people started even showing up to school. I went to Yana's room to check in on things and to see if I could help, but the sustainable volunteer in me was happy to hear that there was nothing I needed to do. All I had to do was prepare.

The show started at 8:30 on the dot.

"Hello everyone," I announced with a working microphone, "And welcome to the School 16 Talent Show!"

After a thunderous applause by some of our students and school administrators, that twangy tune started playing from the speakers, and it was finally my time to shine.

I didn't sound as good as I did whenever I showered, but I only needed to catch my breath once, and I had more than enough air and energy to finish the song with a bang. Later on in the day I watched the video and realized I was pretty off pitch, but I don't think anyone really cared too much. We were all just happy to get the Talent Show underway, electricity and all.

The show went off without a hitch, kids of all ages showed their talents, awards were handed out, and everyone left in bright spirits. After the workshop and electricity debacles from the week before, on that Monday morning everything somehow went according to plan. Thank god.

Chapter Thirteen

REENA

I had great luck getting placed in Mukachevo for a ton of reasons, and one more was that a refugee rights NGO (non-governmental organization) was smack dab in the middle of my town. The NGO "REENA" is funded by the United Nations High Council on Refugees (UNHCR), which is one of the leading human rights agencies in the world. While I enjoyed teaching, I saw the Peace Corps as a great opportunity to get my foot in the door of some sort of international or human rights related field, and once I learned about REENA being in Mukachevo I became overwhelmed with excitement.

Put in a little bit of work here, I thought, and *this could open up some pretty intriguing doors.*

After learning about REENA from one of the admin at Peace Corps, I first contacted them after finding their email on some website that took me the better part of fifteen minutes to find. I emailed the org one day in late 2018 while walking home from work, and on that very same walk I got a reply within minutes.

Hello Robert,

Perfect. Let's meet tomorrow. 13 Rashinka Street. See you Soon.

Nadia

The next day after school, I walked to 13 Rashinka Street, which was only about a twenty minute walk from School 16. I found myself in the parking lot of a church, and I quickly assumed I had made a wrong turn or something. However, as I walked around I found the entrance, where an older woman was standing at the front steps waiting for me.

"Robert," she said, outstretching her hand, "I'm Nadia. Let's get something to eat."

With such a fascinating job of running a refugee NGO in Eastern Europe, I was eager to pepper Nadia with questions about her life and experiences. She looked to be in her seventies (and sported a short haircut), so I also wanted to hear about her life in the Soviet Union, the collapse, and how far Ukraine had come since then. Before all of that, however, I was prepared for the typical Ukrainian introduction of getting stuffed with food. I followed Nadia up a couple flights of stairs to a kitchen, where she sat me down and turned to the coffee maker.

"Is an espresso ok?"

"Yes," I replied, "Yes, thank you."

"It's no problem. Please, Robert, tell me, how did you find us?"

"Oh," I said, not knowing what to say, "Well, one of the Peace Corps administrators told me about REENA. Once I learned that I would be placed in Mukachevo, she reached out to me telling me to get in contact with you."

"Oh, that's good," she replied, "I'm glad you heard about us from Peace Corps. We don't want to be found very easily."

It made sense. Working with vulnerable black and brown populations in a country where some groups of people, such as active far right white nationalist organizations, wouldn't take too kindly to REENA's mission, is a recipe for a potential disaster. To her point, the only sign I noticed was inside of the office, and it said something about REENA being an environmental organization. They were sort of if not all the way undercover, which only made things that much more intriguing during my first visit there (REENA isn't actually this organization's name, so don't worry about me blowing up their privacy).

"I've worked with the Peace Corps for a long time," Nadia continued, "In fact, many years ago I lobbied for the Peace Corps to send volunteers to Zakarpattia, and I was the first one to host a volunteer in the region. I know how little they pay you, it's a tough job."

"Well, it's not too bad-"

"Robert, it's ok. I understand the things you have to deal with. The salary, the school, those kids. How is it working with all of those teachers and teaching all of those kids?"

"Oh, it's really great! I'm really starting to enjoy it, and it's been a good experience overall."

Nadia smiled, and looked like she was suppressing a laugh.

"Mhmm, yes, it sounds lovely. I for one can't stand the education system in Ukraine. At one point I was the head of English Department of Mukachevo State University, you know, when we were under the Soviet Union. I eventually became fed up with the corruption. There are bribes everywhere in the education sphere. You'll never see it, but it's true. It's everywhere. The corruption here is awful, just awful. I've never let anyone bribe me, but it was rampant during Soviet times, and unfortunately not much has changed since then."

"Interesting," I said.

"Interesting and sad," she replied, sipping her coffee. "After I quit, I began working with refugees and stateless populations with the mission of helping them obtain proper legal documentation. The documentation process is a mess in Ukraine, but without it, these vulnerable populations can't do anything. They can't work, own a home, and some can't even send their kids to school."

"Of course," I said, wanting to feign some sort of knowledge about refugees.

"Would you like anything else? We have some holoptsi in the fridge. Are you hungry?"

"No, I'm ok."

Once again she didn't believe me. She walked to the fridge, pulled out a huge plate of holoptsi, a delicious Ukrainian dish of meat wrapped in cabbage, and put it in the microwave.

"Robert," Nadia said after pressing the timer, "I'm so glad you emailed me. We would love to have an English club with you. As a native speaker your work would be incredibly valuable in a place like REENA. Would you be open to doing a club with us?"

161

"Of course!" I said, feeling a jolt of excitement for the first of hopefully many days of working in human rights, "I would be happy to help in any way I can."

"That's great, that's wonderful. I'm sure our students will be thrilled to speak with a native speaker. Are you ready to meet them?"

"The students?" I finally said, taking the plate of warm holoptsi, "Are they here?"

"Yes, they're upstairs. Take your time eating, and afterwards we can do a club. We have a white board and markers up stairs. Will that be enough?"

I hadn't prepared anything because I assumed the club would start, well, not my first day meeting Nadia. But I didn't want to bail on my first opportunity with REENA, especially after getting an espresso and a second lunch.

"Sure, that'll be great," I said, "When can I meet them?"

"Take your time. Eat."

After scarfing down my third meal of the day, I followed Nadia up another flight of stairs. We walked down a thin hallway to a conference room, where I was quite surprised to find Ukrainian teenagers instead of refugees. At that point I understood that as a twenty-two year old American with no background in refugee rights, I would be more useful conducting English clubs than trying to interpret international migration law, but I thought at least at REENA I would be teaching refugees.

On the other hand, ten minutes beforehand I didn't know I would be teaching a club at all, so the Ukrainian students nervously looking at me didn't throw me off too much. They looked just as intimidated as the students at my school.

"Hello," I said to the wide-eyed Ukrainian teenagers.

"Hi," they all said in monotone unison. I had never facilitated an English club before and I doubt they had ever been to one either, so neither me nor the kids knew what to do next.

"Well, I'll just let you all get to it then!" Nadia said while shutting the door.

We started things off with some simple introductions: Name, age, and what you want to be when you grow up.

162

"My name is Anastasia, and I want to be a stewardess."

"My name is Yuri, and I want to go to business school."

"My name is Nastia, and I like international law."

"Very nice," I said after each introduction, trying to assess their English ability.

"What do you want to be, Robert?"

I wasn't expecting to hear that question. For the past few years I had been totally focused on the Peace Corps, so much so that I hadn't planned for anything afterwards. But here a sixteen year old was asking me the same question I was asking him.

"You know, I'm really not sure. Probably something in government, but I don't really know."

They continued to stare at me blankly, probably being confused why the adult in the room didn't know what he wanted to do with his life. The government answer also didn't seem to inspire the teenagers.

"Well," I said, trying to rebound, "I like international law too. Maybe I'll become an international lawyer like Anastasia."

"Cool," Anastasia said, "That's cool."

After a clunky first club of "getting to know you" games, I wasn't confident that there would be a second one. Luckily, I was happy to find the same kids back the next week. I don't know if their parents were making them or if this was some sort of Church program, but I was grateful to have another chance after having a week to actually prepare something.

Early on, we started every club with some general discussion. In those days I used a projector to go through some online flashcards, but after a few glitches I ditched that effort and decided to use the large strips of paper REENA provided to talk about new vocabulary. While they listened attentively to the various idioms, phrasal verbs and listening exercises that I brought to class, a couple months into the club I figured out that they mostly wanted to learn about American culture. More specifically, they wanted to know if the things they saw in the movies were real.

163

"Mr. Robert," Anastasia asked after a few weeks of clubs together, "Are the parties in the movies the same to the parties you went to in America? Like the university parties, are they real?"

I didn't want to flat out tell this teenager that many of the things about college partying in the movies are true, but at that point we all started to form a nice connection, so I didn't want to flat-out lie to her either.

"Well," I began, "Most of the stuff you see in movies isn't one hundred percent real. American movies are largely exaggerated, I mean, they are more interesting than real life. But it is true that there are a lot of parties in college. We call it college in America."

"What about popular kids?" Yuri chimed in, "Are there popular kids in America, like in some of the TV shows?"

Throughout the hour we essentially had a Q/A, and I realized that the clubs didn't necessarily have to be as formal as me standing next to a whiteboard teaching them how to ace standardized tests. They all ended up asking me all of the questions they had on their mind for the past two months, while I asked about parts of Ukrainian culture that I had been wondering about.

"So," I remarked, "I've noticed that everyone here is very fashionable." Before I could get to my question, the students started laughing and nodding their heads.

"Uh, is that funny?," I continued, "Are people not fashionable? Because people seem-"

"It is funny, Mr. Robert. It's funny because here everyone cares too much about the clothes they wear," Nastia, the most fashionable one, said, "It's so stupid."

"Why is it stupid?"

"Because it's not real," another one of the students chimed in, "Lots of people have the newest iPhone, but they can't put bread on the table. It's an old Soviet Union thing. The economy was bad, and no one could have anything nice. Now people want to show off to prove that they're not poor. That's why fashion is important, but none of the Gucci bags are real. It's all fake Gucci you can buy at the mall for ten dollars."

Now we were getting somewhere.

"Do you all care about fashion?"

"Yeah, we have to," Yuri said, "If you don't look good you'll get made fun of for being poor."

This breakthrough set off a series English clubs that soon became the best and most fulfilling part of my week. I had full reign of the club without any Ukrainian government mandated lesson plan or Peace Corps policy breathing down my neck, as well as a group of motivated and introspective students who went out of their way to learn English every Tuesday afternoon. Although this was the last thing I expected to come out of REENA, this externality made me consistently happier than anything else throughout my service.

However, even with all that said, I was still hoping that I could eventually get more into the nitty gritty human rights stuff. During our various meals together, Nadia would occasionally bring up that they were working on notarizing a permit that would let me enter the refugee camp in Mukachevo.

"Once we get the permit, you can start working with us. It's coming soon, I can tell you."

I was elated to hear this the first time, but after the fifth or sixth, I stopped taking it too seriously. After getting my hopes up time and time again, I coped by doing my best to remember that I had no experience working with refugees or stateless people, I didn't know their language, I didn't know what they needed, and if I did start working with them I had no idea what sort of services I could offer. Much of the work Nadia and her team focused on was with the employment office, where they worked on documentation so that the refugees could start getting paid formally instead of under the table. I had no clue how to go about doing that, and after six months of clubs at REENA I resigned to the fact that my greatest skill in Mukachevo was being fluent in English, and if all Nadia ever needed me to do was an English club, I was more than happy to contribute.

165

However, I had given up too soon. Right as I thought I'd never get the chance to do anything with REENA besides the English Clubs, in the Spring of 2019 I was presented with my first big opportunity with UNHCR (United Nations High Commissioner for Refugees). One day after school, I got a surprise facebook message from Victoria, the PC administrator who told me about REENA in the first place.

"Head of UNHCR wants to see you. Samuel will be in Mukachevo soon. Have time to call?"

This was finally the mega opportunity I had been looking for. After some intense fist pumps and screaming into a pillow for a few minutes, I collected myself enough to call Victoria later that day, who confirmed my initial excitement.

"This is an opportunity for you, Robert. Make no mistake about it. Samuel collects impressive people, so you should do your best to impress him. Lindsey, a volunteer from a couple years ago, got a grant to do a project with stateless populations. She did a good job, impressed the right people, and then got a UNHCR internship in Benin. Now she makes twelve-thousand dollars a month working in Geneva. That could be in store for you if you make a good impression."

I tried writing down everything Victoria said on one of the flashcards I had bought for Ukrainian practice. Geneva, impress him, collect people, got it.

"When is he coming?" I asked.

"On Wednesday night, so that should give you two days to prepare. He knows about you already, so talk to Nadia. She'll figure something out for you two."

So, this was it. This was my opportunity to shmooze with the human rights guy in Ukraine. All the work I put in with REENA had finally brought a legit opportunity to make my way into the field of Human Rights.

Future fantasies of working in human rights started to rush into my mind. *This is it,* I thought, *This is what you've been working for.* Of course I wasn't solely working in order to scheme my way into a human rights internship, as my more machiavellian tendencies subsided after being burned one too many times by various toxic relationships my sophomore year, but getting into the human rights field was a dream of mine, and this was the best chance of making progress towards that dream.

I talked to Nadia the next day, who had confirmed she already talked to Victoria.

"We'll make sure that you and Samuel can get acquainted," Nadia said at the kitchen table, as I once again stuffed my face with whatever they had in the fridge that day.

"Tomorrow," she continued, "We'll pick him up from the train station around 5:30 or so, and we'll then welcome him to REENA. You of course are welcome to join us at the meeting. Will you be available?"

"Of course I will!" In fact, the meet up was set to be about an hour after my English club, and in the very same conference room no less. It was absolutely perfect timing.

"Wonderful," Nadia said, "You can stay in the kitchen while the rest of the team sets up for Samuel. I'm sure you won't mind lounging there until then. You can help yourself to whatever's in the fridge."

....

The next day I walked to the church and had the usual club. Only a couple of students showed up that day, and an hour came and went pretty quickly. Afterwards, just as I was instructed, I went to the kitchen. I spent about thirty minutes journaling about my day, and after I became exhausted from writing every tedious detail of a typical Wednesday, I trolled the fridge. Nadia had already fed me earlier in the day, but I was wondering if there was any extra rice. No luck, just some cakes that I assumed were waiting for Samuel.

My intuition was correct, because a bit later some of the social workers rushed in to bring the cakes to the conference room. By then it was 5:15, but after already waiting for forty five minutes, I started to pass the time by playing chess on my phone. I played a few rounds against the computer, and after a couple humbling losses on easy mode I checked the time. 5:35, and still no word. They were running late. I decided to play a few more rounds.

During the next couple of rounds, I finally started to understand the computer's strategy. I took my time to carefully construct my moves, and in a relatively short round I ended up beating the computer for the first time. I won the next round, and after I made it three in a row I upgraded the level. I was getting better, and quickly.

That's when I got a bit lost in the flow of chess. Instead of carefully listening for footsteps and people speaking English, like I had been doing since the moment I stepped into the kitchen, I instead gave all my focus to outsmarting the level two computer. I became so focused on the game that at one moment I barely even noticed the bus driver, who had popped his head in the kitchen.

"He's here!" The bus driver said.

"What?" I said, not taking my eyes away from the virtual chessboard.

"He's here," he repeated while shutting the door.

He's here? What did he - Oh my gosh, Samuel is here!

I soon heard various people speaking English and walking up the stairs to the conference room. I planned on getting to the conference room early after everyone had set up, but I had gotten so lost in my match against the damn chess bot that I had thrown my carefully curated plan out the window. I hastily tossed my computer in my backpack and left the kitchen, only to see the backs of Nadia, the bus driver, and a man wearing a very nice suit.

Samuel.

Dang, it was Samuel! And I was behind Samuel, and after devising such a detailed plan to chat with Samuel before the meeting started, I had no way to slither past them and beat them to the conference room.

I hurried behind them to catch up, but I quickly caught myself inches away from running right into them and knocking them over. Toppling Samuel as he walked up the stairs probably wouldn't land me a six-figure job in Geneva, so I fell back and began to creep up the stairs as slowly as I could. I'm not sure why I went from sprinting to slow-motion tip toeing, but at the moment I thought it'd be better if they didn't notice this frazzled and slightly sweating twenty-three year old following them up the stairs.

Just walk behind them unnoticed, and things should be fine, I thought, carefully plotting my every step.

The problem was that Nadia and Samuel were walking so slowly. Even with me tiptoeing, I had to slow down my pace even more than I expected. In the span of going up just one story of stairs I had to stop twice to keep from getting too close, worrying for some incomprehensible reason that they would notice me coming from behind.

By the time we made it to the conference room, instinct and adrenaline had taken over. Somehow they hadn't felt my looming presence, and as we entered, the four of us were greeted with a chorus of cheers.

"Welcome Samuel!" Everyone exclaimed. REENA had really gone all out: The table was covered in cakes, water bottles and candies, and the majority of the folks were wearing party hats.

This disoriented me even more, as I began catching much of the secondhand jubilance and cheering directed towards Samuel. Luckily, my animal-like instincts took over the steering wheel, and as Samuel and Nadia turned right I bolted to the left and began pretending to talk to one of the social workers.

Perfect, I thought, *It's like I was here all along, being normal.* At that point I was noticeably damp, but I was positive that Nadia and Samuel hadn't noticed me stalking behind them.

Over the next couple of minutes Nadia introduced Samuel to the staff, most of whom looked more star-struck than I did. After watching the scene for a few seconds, all of a sudden it added up: Samuel wasn't just an extremely successful and influential person in the field of human rights, but he was also the head of the organization that funds this small NGO in Western Ukraine.

He probably approves their funding.

At that point it all clicked: Due to Samuel's enormous influence over the future of REENA, the staff had much more of a reason to impress him than I did. Hence the set up, party hats, and general anxiety in the air.

After a few minutes of introductions, Nadia finally turned to me and said, "Oh, of course! This is our Peace Corps volunteer, Robert." I wasn't REENA's volunteer, but neither Nadia nor I had any interest telling Samuel otherwise. After taking a deep breath which I tried to conceal, I walked up to Samuel, looked him in the eye, and extended my hand.

Right as I was about to say my rehearsed, "Nice to meet you, I look forward to speaking with you later," Nadia spoke up again.

"And guess what Samuel?" Nadia exclaimed, looking at me, "Robert speaks Spanish!"

Spanish? I speak Spanish???

Oh yeah, Spanish.

Earlier in the year, I off-handedly told Nadia that I knew some Spanish. More accurately, I off-handedly lied to Nadia that I knew some Spanish. You know how you study Spanish in high school and don't remember much of it, but when people ask you if you know any other languages, you say "I know some Spanish?" That's what I said earlier on to Nadia, in order to sound smarter and more impressive than I actually was. Who would've known that this little white lie would bite me in the biggest of all moments.

Samuel, who may have been one of a few dozen native Spanish speakers in Ukraine, looked delighted to finally find someone in this Slavic country who could speak in his native tongue. At this point the whole room was watching, jobs on the line, waiting for me to do my part to make Samuel like us.

Still frazzled from being in an intense chess battle, almost bumping into Samuel and Nadia, creeping stealthily behind them, sweating bullets and finally being showered by a wave of greetings and joy, guess what happened?

I froze. I absolutely froze. I wouldn't classify myself as someone who is cool and collected under pressure in the first place, so it was unsurprising that no memories from my ninth grade Spanish class came flooding in.

Not even an hola.

After a couple seconds of staring at one of the most powerful people I had ever met, I came to my senses and blurted out in Ukrainian, "Haha maybe later." Before anyone had any chance to respond, I laughed again, said "Bye everyone!" and left the meeting.

That walk home was...dark. It was grey and slightly raining, and although I had an umbrella, I hardly even used it. I let the rain fall on to my ashamed brow, and with each passing step I realized more and more the mistake I had made.

I left..I left... Why did I leave? Why did I LEAVE????

I stayed at REENA for an hour and a half after the English club, waiting for my opportunity to score a meeting with Samuel, only to shake his hand, not speak Spanish to him, and leave due to embarrassment. With each step I began to slowly process the biggest goof of my life, and by the time I made it home, it hit me.

You messed up your one chance to work for UNHCR.

With that thought I threw my umbrella into the middle of the street. It landed directly on some horse poo. I should have been looking out for that, as the many Roma in town use a horse and buggy to get around, but in my raging state I wasn't exactly what you would describe as attentive.

Landing in horse shit: A great metaphor for what just happened.

I would have laughed if I wasn't in the midst of an emotional breakdown. I decided to call my dad and tell him the story, hoping it would help me process what just happened.

"Hahahaha oh my god," my dad said, who afterwards was kind enough to say, "It's alright Bob, I don't think you messed up too badly. Victoria said he wants to meet with you, so you'll probably get to talk to him again. When does he leave?"

"In a few days," I said in the rain with a stained umbrella.

"See, you'll be fine. You didn't mess up, you'll get your chance. Just try not to think about it, ok?"

"Ok, I'll try thanks dad."

I continued to think about it non-stop, and over the next few hours I called four more of my friends and family. Each time the story took about twenty minutes to tell, and after they all laughed at my luck, they pretty much had the same response: You didn't screw up, that's hilarious, you'll get another chance, you'll probably be fine. Just make an effort to see him again, you did nothing wrong!

None of their words made me feel better. I felt the same sense of dread and was even more agitated than earlier. I was also being a little dramatic about it by sitting in the dark in my apartment while making each call. It wasn't a good night.

Finally, in that pitch black room of sorrow and darkness I finally called my friend and Peace Corps colleague Aiden, who was serving in central Ukraine. Aiden and I met on the bus, where he tried teaching me how to pronounce "Hryshkivtsi," and we had this relationship where every few months I would call him out of the blue and tell him a thirty minute story. He would listen, make a few comments, and then go on about his day. This time, after laughing at my stupidity, he was the only person to give it to me straight.

"Yup Bob, you messed up. Shouldn't have left that meeting, shouldn't have told Nadia that you know Spanish. You screwed up, but it's ok. Just sleep on it and try to meet with him tomorrow."

"Thanks Aiden," I said, "You're the only one who told me that."

"I'll always give it to you straight Bob. But don't worry too much about it. You'll get another chance."

And with that, I felt a little bit better and turned the lights on.

A couple days later, Nadia texted me to meet her in the city center. On occasions like this we would typically get coffee and discuss my life, the state of REENA, and potential projects. However, she had been hinting in the days since my debacle that I'd get another chance to meet Samuel and finally impress him with my Spanish, and I was desperately hoping that this meet up in the center would be that opportunity. They had been busy over the past couple days touring refugee camps throughout the area, and by Friday night I knew that Samuel was set to leave for Kyiv early the next morning.

Now or never, I thought, while preparing myself for a last chance interaction with Samuel. While I didn't get my hopes up, I still made sure to wear some business casual attire without any wrinkles, which took a bit of time because my iron had been on the fritz. A year earlier I would have gone to that meeting without even thinking about the wrinkles, but after nine months in Ukraine there was no way I wasn't going to look as presentable as possible.

However, I was having some problems. My iron recently had been staining a lot of my shirts because a portion of the iron had turned black. I read online that the black portion was due to burnt dust and dirt sticking to the iron, and that while a variety of methods were recommended to solve this issue, covering the iron in toothpaste for ten minutes seemed to be the most effective way.

That obviously didn't work, so thirty minutes before meeting Nadia in the center I was wiping toothpaste off of my iron. I ended up knocking on Maryana's door to borrow her iron.

"What is wrong with yours? Marayana asked.

"It's a little burnt," I mentioned, being stealthy enough to leave out the whole toothpaste part.

After quickly flattening out the wrinkles in Maryana's apartment, I darted towards the center, not wanting to be late in case Samuel was there waiting for me. It was once again sprinkling, so I did my best to avoid puddles as I sped walked to the center.

I made it to the statue by the Ratusha (city council building) right on time, and as I approached, I saw Nadia and, yes, Samuel walking towards me.

HELL YEAH.

My heart almost leapt out of my chest when I saw Samuel accompanying Nadia and nobody else. I did my best to contain my excitement, which desperately tempted me to scream out in victory, and thankfully this time my cooler side won out.

"Samuel, this is Robert," Nadia said to me as I outstretched my hand.

"Yes, I think we met on Wednesday. How are you Robert?"

"Estamos mucho emocionados que tu esta aqui." Flawless, just as I practiced during the entire twenty minute walk.

Samuel laughed and said something that I didn't understand, but at that point in my service I was already pretty good at pretending to understand something in a different language. I nodded, laughed back, and said, "Si."

"So," Nadia said, "You two enjoy dinner. I told Samuel that you two should go to Bograch and get some Zakarpattian cuisine. Does that sound ok, Robert?"

Nadia looked at me with a sly smile that silently said, I came through, didn't I?

"That sounds great," I replied.

"You know how to get there, right Robert?"

"Yeah, it's a pretty close walk."

"Ok then, I'll let you two be. Enjoy your dinner."

And that's how, on the last possible night, I finally ended up meeting with Samuel. He was tired from spending three days going to various refugee/Roma camps and facilities in Zakarpattia, but he still made the time to talk to me about UNHCR, his work over the years in various different places all around the world, and his personal experience working so far away from home. It was a perfect end to a stress-filled week that took a few months off of my life, and I'm grateful that although I almost completely butchered the opportunity in a fit of adrenaline induced stupidity, I got to meet with the head of a really cool agency that I wanted to work with in the future. And as a volunteer nearing the end of my first year in the country, that's all I could have really asked for.

Chapter Fourteen

One Year In

My second semester at School 16 ended on May 31st, a few weeks after the REENA fiasco. I once again sang Wagon Wheel, this time at graduation, and after the ceremony I walked home, proud of getting through my first full semester in one piece and more than ready to finally embrace summer vacation.

I spent the initial few weeks of summer participating in a whole host of Peace Corps camps throughout the country, and afterwards when I was truly free of all work obligations, I decided to go back to where it all began: Hryshkivtsi. It was right around my one year mark in Ukraine, and what better way to celebrate than to go back to my roots. When I first made it to Hryshkivtsi, I could hardly mutter a phrase, buy soap or use public transportation. I was completely helpless, and rightfully so. But now I would be traveling alone by train to return to the lovely grandparents who provided me a home, hoping to shock them with my much improved Ukrainian after spending my first two months using shoulder shrugs and miming as our primary form of communication.

Unsurprisingly, the trip from Zakarpattia to central Ukraine was going to be burdensome: According to my schedule, I'd have to leave at 11 pm, ride the train to Lviv, hop off at 3 am, wait in the train station for three hours, and then take a nine hour train ride to the region capitol of Zhytomyr. After making it to the capitol, I needed to take an hour and a half bus ride to Berdychiv, which is the only city that has a bus route to Hryshkivtsi. It was quite the trek to get back to my first home in Ukraine, but that was nothing compared to everything Larysa and Valik had done for me during the three months of training.

The hardest part was going to be hanging out in the Lviv train station from 3:00 am to 6:00 am. Train stations aren't known for attracting the most cultured bunch, and I would need to force myself to stay awake in order to make sure that no one would steal my stuff. Additionally, I would be sitting for the nine hours on my train from Lviv to Zhytomyr, so I wasn't banking on getting any extra shut eye on the ride there. The trip wasn't going to be easy.

Additionally, in an unsurprising lapse in judgement, I thought it would be a great idea to only bring a limited amount of cash and leave my debit card at home. Somewhat thematically, while many of my mistakes in Peace Corps were not my fault and seemingly inevitable, there was a fair chunk of them that were completely my own doing, and me leaving my debit card at home obviously fell into the latter category. This was in an attempt to curb some of my overblown spending habits, which had become more and more inflated by the month. I had my ticket there and a ticket back, so even if things got a little tight I'd still be able to return home without a problem.

I was all set to take a week-long trip without a debit or credit card. What could go wrong?

After falling asleep on the comfortable bed in the deluxe wagon heading towards Lviv, I woke up around 2:30 am, about half an hour until I had to get off. My resolve to tough out three hours in a bus station was a lot weaker after only a few hours of sleep, so I was begging that the conductor would forget about me. It was a pipe dream, but in my dreary state, I was holding out hope that there would be some sort of lucky miscommunication.

Just when I started to believe my pipe dream would come true, I heard a knock on my door. I cracked it open to see the conductor, a plump woman with (you guessed it) short black hair, telling me it was time to go. I begrudgingly woke up the passenger in the bunk below me so I could get my stuff from the compartment under his bed, and trudged along to the hallway of the train.

This was a terrible plan. I felt awful, and soon I would have to force myself to stay awake to fend off the drunkards in the train station. I made the mental note to under no circumstances tell Larysa and Valik about my journey, as without a doubt my actions and decisions would only frighten and confuse them.

I stood solemnly in the train hallway, listlessly looking out the window and hopelessly wishing there would be a malfunction that would force the train to somehow skip the stop in Lviv. Soon becoming bored with the flat fields that define most parts of the country outside of Zakarpattia, I let my eyes wander to the train schedule posted on the wall. I couldn't believe what I saw.

This train, the one I was about to depart, was a direct train to Berdychiv. I was at a loss for words, never for a minute having considered the thought of looking up a ticket from Mukachevo to Berdychiv.

As I explained earlier, the only way to get around the Carpathian Mountains is to go to Lviv first, so there are tons of trains going from Zakarpattia to Lviv. However, by chance my current train to Lviv, which I was only using to make a transfer that could eventually take me to a city two hours away from Berdychiv, was going straight to where I needed to go.

It seemed incredibly unlikely that a train from a small city in Zakarpattia would have a direct route to another random small city hundreds of miles away in central Ukraine. But this one was, and in a few minutes I would have to get off. I cursed under my breath, realizing my hubris had gotten the best of me: I underestimated Ukraine's railway infrastructure, and now I had to pay.

However, I knew that trains typically stop in Lviv for about twenty minutes. After a quick mental calculation, I guessed that twenty minutes would be just enough time to rush down to the ticket booth, buy a ticket for the same train, and hop back on before it left. I hadn't financially planned for this type of splurge, especially with the lack of debit-card, but I would be kicking myself in that dark and cold train station if I had gotten off the ride that was heading directly to my destination. I estimated the ticket would cost me maybe half of the cash I had for the trip, but my desire for sleep won out, as it typically does.

While not trying to think about the fact that I would be buying a third train ticket for a trip in which I would be on the same train the entire time, I prepared myself to make a sprint for the ticket booth. I was a bit nervous about the whole situation, so I walked up to the conductor to ask if she knew if there were any more tickets to Berdychiv. I can't exactly say why I did this, but I think in my dream-like state I was hoping that I could simply buy a ticket on the train, which was silly because it was something I had never seen before during my year in the country. I felt like it couldn't hurt, and any sort of guidance at that point would have calmed my nerves.

"Hello," I said close to three in the morning. She looked up at me and waited, although I wasn't sure how to continue.

"Well say something," she said.

I didn't know how to explain my situation in Ukrainian, which was still far from an advanced level.

"I get off now. But I want to stay on. I go to Berdychiv. This train goes to Berdychiv. Is there another ticket?"

It didn't get through. She stared at me blankly.

"I want another ticket," I mentioned again as it became harder to keep my eyes open.

"A ticket? But you are getting off."

"Yes, but I don't want to. I want to stay on. Is there another ticket?"

This time she stared at me again, but with a different look on her face. It wasn't a blank stare. Instead, it was like she was calculating something.

"You need a bed?" she said.

"Yes, I need a bed. I get off now, but I want to stay on. Is there a bed?"

"Yes," she said, "We have a bed."

She then gave the "follow me" hand gesture, as we walked up to the front of the wagon to a room without a number on it. I heard her shuffle around some stuff, and after about five minutes she waved me in. There wasn't much space to fit my bags, but I eventually got everything in there and laid down in the bed she had just freed up. At that point, she told me not to leave the room, and put a finger against her lips.

Although I was in a dream-like state, it all dawned on me after she gave the "shush" motion. Yes, the "extra ticket" that I had wished for was simply me hiding out in the conductor's room. Only when I laid down on her bed it became clear to me that this was not an official ticket, but rather something off the books.

Almost by accident I had walked into a situation that every volunteer at one point in their service dreams about: Giving a bribe.

I hadn't bribed anyone yet in Ukraine, and once I figured out what was happening I was actually quite delighted. I felt like a rugged off the grid cowboy volunteer, making bribes and swingin' deals whenever I was in a pinch, although I tried not to focus on the fact that my incompetence got me into this situation in the first place. I calculated that about five-hundred hryven (twenty dollars) would be a fair price, and sure enough after my savior returned she told me my "ticket" cost five-hundred hryven. I handed it over with a smile.

"Thank you," she said, "Try not to leave the room."

"No, thank you," I said, fantasizing about the extra sleep that was waiting for me.

It hurt to give up a huge chunk of my trip budget, but my tired mind gladly ignored the perils of sunk cost and fell asleep in the conductor's bed. I'm not sure where she slept - or if she slept at all - but I'm confident that we were both pretty happy about how everything went down.

I closed my eyes and opened them about five hours later to the conductor once again waking me up.

"Berdychiv, right?"

"Right."

"We're almost here."

Man did that feel good. Not only did I get an extra five hours of shut eye, but I also had the pleasure of arriving in Berdychiv four hours earlier than expected. I got off the train after thanking the conductor again, and had more than enough time to walk around, drink some coffee, buy Larysa some flowers, and reminisce. Berdychiv was my training group's occasional escape from the village and all of the stressors that came with it. It was easy for Berdychiv to have a special place in our hearts, and I was grateful I had an extra few hours there due to the bribe I had made earlier. It bought me time and brought back a lot of memories that I forgot existed, which made the reduced travel budget worth it.

After more than enough time of aimlessly walking around, I made my way to the bus stop to complete my journey to Hryshkivtsi. It was an extraordinary cold day in the heart of the summer, which caught me by surprise after experiencing the ninety five-degree days during the previous August. I didn't bring a jacket, with the assumption that staying warm enough in Hryshkivtsi was going to be the least of my problems. Unfortunately on the day I returned it was about fifty degrees, and I shivered the whole time in the marshutka (bus). With flowers, chocolates, and a lack of jacket, I began to wonder which one Larysa would notice first.

I arrived at the house, where the green gate was already unlocked. After petting the dog that at one time in my service only greeted me with intense barking, I made my way to the front door. Larysa was already waiting for me.

"Welcome Robert," Larysa said with a smile.

"Thank you, it's so nice to see you."

That simple Ukrainian phrase was more than enough to surprise her, seeing as it was more coherent than anything I said to her the year before. She soon noticed my bare arms on a windy and cold summer afternoon and began shaking her head.

"Where is your jacket? Aren't you cold?"

Ah, my host grandmother worrying about me. It felt just like old times, and I happily entered my old village home and accepted the jacket she grabbed off of the couch.

After walking inside and seeing the yellow walls of the house, memories started to flood. Since the last time I had seen the inside of that house I had met hundreds of people, started my first job out of college, sort of learned a new language and figured out how to survive in Ukraine on my own. The most surreal part, however, was being able to understand someone for the first time after knowing her for almost a year.

"Thank you for not forgetting us," Larysa said as we sat on the couch watching daytime television.

"How could I?" I replied, "I wouldn't be here if it weren't for you."

I owed her more than she could know, and the sting of buying three train tickets for a one way trip quickly faded once I settled in and started catching up with her.

"Are you hungry?" she asked, "I made dumplings."

"Yes, I'm starving."

"Perfect, let's get you something to eat."

Just like old times.

Over the course of that first day, my routine was the same as it had been a year before. Larysa made the same dishes, which throughout the day consisted of dumplings, the mixture with diced eggplant and olive oil, and that delicious meat that I still didn't bother asking about. After our meals we watched old Soviet movies I didn't understand and the Ukrainian version of Maury. Occasionally I would walk outside to greet the dog, who was still as loud and chained up as ever, and then I would venture over to the backyard, where apples were already rotting on the ground after falling from the various trees sprawled around the property.

When night time rolled around, Larysa said something to me that I didn't hear throughout all of my time in Hryshkivtsi.

"Robert," she said, "Will you help me with something?"

"What is it?" I asked, delighted.

"Raisa is coming for dinner tonight. Will you help me set up?"

"With pleasure," I said, trying to hide the pride in my voice. During training, when I was overwhelmed with simple communication and everyday tasks, there's no way Larysa would have asked for a hand. Even when I asked to help with the dishes she declined, so I took her asking me to help set up dinner as a sign of my progress and maturity over the past year. Maybe I was overthinking it, because she had already cooked everything and all I had to do was set the table, but all I could think about was how I was finally starting to pay Larysa back for all she did for me, albeit in a microscopic manner.

Raisa, Chloe's old host mother, walked over from her home in the early evening.

"Raisa!" I said, embracing her, "It's so nice to see you."

"Likewise," she replied, smiling. She then turned and started speaking to Larysa. Even though throughout the day I had been understanding Larysa about ninety percent of the time, when those two spoke I could barely make out any part of the conversation.

While Larysa made sure to only speak Ukrainian with me, over dinner I was reminded once again why it's often so difficult to communicate in Ukraine. In Hryshkivtsi and hundreds of other villages, the common language isn't quite Ukrainian, and it isn't quite Russian. It's a mix called "Surgic," and it's not simply something that an outsider can learn. This is because there are different types of Surgic in almost each individual village or region. There is no one "Surgic," and while most people from all around Ukraine will be able to understand each other, it causes all sorts of problems for someone like me who only speaks Ukrainian. To be fair, it's an extremely rare occurrence to find someone who only speaks Ukrainian and not Russian, but on that cold summer evening, that rare occurrence was me, sitting dumbfounded in Larysa's living room.

However, the Peace Corps prepared me for this. Throughout the dinner I casually nodded my head whenever I didn't understand something, and laughed whenever they laughed. I also later on admitted that I often couldn't understand them, which was fine, because that was nothing out of the ordinary. Our host families knew us when we didn't even know Ukrainian, after all. In the end we were all just happy to see each other, and as Raisa left right as the sun began to set, she turned to me and said something I could finally understand.

"Robert, say hi to Chloe for me. Tell her to visit, because I miss her. We miss you all very much."

"Of course, Raisa. Thank you."

It's touching how much these women cared about us. When they first brought us in, none of our host mothers had ever met an American before. Yet, with no prior experience, they agreed to house us and take care of us during one of the most vulnerable periods of our life. Sure they were overbearing sometimes, but it was only because they viewed us as family. Maybe they viewed us as adult sized children, which, as I looked back at myself from a year ago, may not have been too far off. It was all coming from a place of love for people they had never even met before, which was hard to appreciate at the time. But back in Hryshkivtsi, I felt it all at once.

I went to bed that night feeling warm. Extremely warm.

Over the next few days, Larysa and I got back into our old routine. Although we loved catching up after such a long time, we knew each other well enough by then to make some time for personal space. I went on a ton of walks, walks at one point I dreaded, but now embraced while going through some of my earliest memories in the Peace Corps. I trekked back to where Natalia stayed, to where I saw the goat during my first week, and later to a patch of grass next to the train tracks where I'd sometimes read and write bad poetry.

The nostalgia ladened pleasure lasted for a while, but not long enough to stave away the inevitable boredom. Other than the walks, there wasn't a ton to do, and even though Larysa's precious volunteer was back, she still had to go to work. Although I should've been expecting this sort of lull in the quaint village of three-thousand, by the third day I spent more time staring at the ceiling and Instagram than doing anything remotely stimulating.

Luckily, in the evening after another slow hour browsing through social media, a volunteer that I didn't really know, Dean, sent me a message.

"Yo Bob," he wrote, "Whats up man. Are you in Berdychiv?"

"Well, sort of. I'm in Hryshkivtsi."

"Where's that?"

"It's a village near Berdychiv. Why what's up?"

"That's awesome, man. I actually switched sites and I'm in Berdychiv now. You should come hang out, we can get pizza or something!"

The last time I saw Dean was at one of the Peace Corps conferences the previous October, and I probably wouldn't see him again until finishing service. We had only chatted briefly at that conference, but we were in a fantasy football league, so that was a good enough reason as any to get lunch together.

We met up at a pizza place, which I jogged to because I was training for a 10k and I wanted to kill two birds with one stone. It was fairly cold outside, so not wanting to come back in a damp t-shirt and shorts, I ran with a plastic bag filled with a jacket and sweatpants I could change into at the restaurant. I ended up getting there about twenty minutes early, no doubt due to my speed and endurance, so I relaxed on a bench, thankful for the sweatshirt and sweatpants concealing my wet clothes on a cold and windy summer day.

I soon saw Dean across the street.

"Bob!" He said, smiling and waving.

"Dean!" I said, trying to ignore the stares of surprised Ukrainians.

Even though we barely knew each other, we gave each other a big hug, and the feeling of Dean's smile and embrace instantly provided more warmth than any plastic bag of sweatpants had to offer. Remember, the isolation and sadness doesn't go away, and seeing Dean's grinning face was a breath of fresh air.

"How ya doin' buddy?" he said loudly as we walked into the restaurant.

"Amazing Dean, amazing. It's good to see you."

"It's good to see you too! You're wet!"

"Yeah, I ran here!"

"That's awesome."

Finally, not only another American, but another American my age I could hang out with! There was nothing too exciting or spectacular about our lunch together, but any occasion where I could connect with someone in my own language would be the highlight of my month. At one point during our lunch, Dean was telling a story, and half way through I thought of a joke.

184

Oh, this is going to be great, I thought while trying to pay attention to Dean's story about his previous Peace Corps stint in Nicaragua.

When he finished his story, I went for it and put my best foot forward while trying to push aside my anxiety in order to soak in the joy of telling a joke. Sure enough, Dean started laughing.

"Is that why you were smiling while I was talking?" Dean asked while grabbing another slice of pizza.

"Yeah," I replied, "It's just that I can't remember the last time I told a joke."

Dean laughed and began nodding. "That's so true. You know, on my way here I actually started smiling just from the idea of potentially sharing a laugh with someone. I haven't done that in months."

"Yeah," I said, "Yeah..." A long silence followed, as we were brought back to the sad realization that something as simple as sharing a meal and a laugh is one of the most important things that volunteers can do for each other. If I've learned anything from the Peace Corps, it's about how desperately we need to interact and make connections with people. It's a lesson that many learned the following March, but more on that later.

After a two hour lunch with Dean, we said our goodbyes (see you next year, man), and I made my way to the bus stop. I took the bus back (I had ran enough for one day) and settled in for my last night at Larysa's. Her husband, Valik, earlier had arrived from Kyiv, and while he only spoke Russian, we all figured out a way to communicate. Just like with Pavel and Alona, I spoke Ukrainian to Larysa, who translated it to Russian for Valik, who then spoke Russian to Larysa who translated it to Ukrainian for me. I bet Larysa never thought in a million years that she'd ever be in a situation like that, translating a conversation between her husband and an American speaking Ukrainian.

That's what was so cool about the Peace Corps - it puts people in extraordinarily unique situations, and not just the volunteers. It's an experience that neither Larysa nor I will ever forget, and I'm incredibly thankful we were both able to reflect on such a significant experience during my return. It's disturbingly easy to forget about even the most impactful experiences throughout the course of our lives, but as my visit to Hryshkivtsi concluded, I made sure that this experience wouldn't fall forever into the subconscious.

The next morning I packed my bags once again and got ready to go to the train station.

"Thanks for having me, Larysa. I'm really glad we got to see each other again. And thanks for helping me last year, I'll never forget it."

"Oh, it's nothing. Thank you, Robert. Thank you for not forgetting us. Call me when you're at the train station, ok?"

"Ok Larysa. Thank you."

"Will you come back next year?" she asked.

"Of course, we'll figure something out! There's a direct train from Mukachevo, so it should be easy enough."

Larysa smiled, hugged me once again, and sent me off. I waved goodbye to her through the bus window, sad to leave but confident that I'd return once again. Thank you Larysa, for everything.

Like any good host mother, she made sure that I got to the train station with more than enough time and money to spare: After being fed for four straight days, my wallet was way fuller than I expected it to be, which ended up making a huge difference. After the bribe, the flowers, the chocolate, and the pizza with Dean, the purple blue and green bills nestled in between my wallet were just enough to buy a direct ticket from Berdychiv to Mukachevo. I only had enough hryven left over to buy a bottle of water, but with all the food that Larysa had packed for me, I was going to be far from hungry on the overnight train home.

After using the train station outhouse with the toilet paper I had packed myself, I waited listlessly near the tracks, surprised that my plan of being hundreds of miles away from home without a debit card didn't result in disaster. As my train slowly glided in on another cold morning, I rushed to my wagon, not wanting to miss my only opportunity to get back to Mukachevo. While walking up the stairs to the train-car, I looked up, and made eye contact with someone I immediately recognized.

It was the conductor who I bribed just a few days before. After making eye contact we smiled simultaneously, connected by our small secret.

"Good to see you again!" she said, "Ticket?"

"I have one this time," I said, proudly showing the beige piece of paper I bought ten minutes earlier.

She looked at it for a second and began laughing.

"Not quite! This is the wrong train, your train is next!"

"Oh, uh, thanks."

Well, maybe I wasn't quite the competent and savvy volunteer of my imagination just yet, but still glowing from such a fulfilling visit, I was more than happy to get off and continue to wait. I had more than enough to think about.

Chapter Fifteen

The Swing of Things

It's January 2020 and I am in a groove. Just a month earlier I traveled back to the States for the first time since orientation, and it couldn't have come at a better time. While up to that point I had loved my time in Ukraine and wouldn't have changed my life there for anything else, back in America I had absolutely no problem basking in the sweet luxuries of hot water, salted sidewalks, and Cheetos. I had never craved Cheetos at any point in my life, that is until I was deprived of them for fifteen months. You'll never know what you'll start yearning for after too many months of eating sausages and frozen potato dumplings.

The Cheetos, as well as spending time with my family for the first time in about a year and a half, was just the mid-service pick me up that I needed. Although I had hit my stride during the second half of my service, nothing could match a luxurious nine days of being pampered by first world infrastructure and a caring mom.

I didn't want to get too comfortable, though. The last thing I wanted was to soften myself up with a dishwasher and dryer, only to force myself back to the frozen and unforgiving Ukrainian tundra. So after a week and a half of tearful reunions and celebrations, I flew back to Kyiv on December 28th, which was just in time to celebrate the biggest holiday of the year, New Years, with my girlfriend and a couple of Peace Corps buds.

Yes, I was able to somehow convince someone to be my girlfriend. Let's rewind a few months: Alina and I met on August 20th, which happened to be the one year mark of my service. What better way to celebrate the one year mark than a little pobachenya (date) with a beautiful woman? There was only one problem: Alina, who was a grad student at the time finishing up a master's degree in law, only knew Ukrainian. And me, being a complacent volunteer rolling into his second year, only sort of knew some Ukrainian.

We initially hit things off on Badoo, the Eastern European version of Tinder. I hadn't been too successful on Tinder in Ukraine, and by that I mean I had absolutely no success whatsoever. Besides that one date in Lviv with Khrystyna, which never lead to anything, I hardly got any matches, no matter how much I tried and how much I cried. I decided to switch things up, knowing that it was the app and not my looks or personality that must have been the problem.

To warn any and all matches, the only thing I wrote in my shiny new Badoo profile was "Please help me study Ukrainian." Alina, being the open-minded gal that she is, decided to give me a chance, and after a couple weeks of texting, where I used google translate to decipher the majority of her messages, we agreed to meet up in Uzhhorod.

Uzhhorod, the capitol city of Zakarpattia, is just like Mukachevo in the fact that it's closer to a city you'd find in Central Europe than in Eastern Ukraine. The neoclassical churches, charming townhouses and of course cobblestone walkways create a perfect atmosphere for romance to bloom, especially compared to the concrete and industrial Soviet style that encompasses the majority of Ukraine. Thank god for the beauty of Uzhhorod, because I needed everything I could to impress this woman, especially with my lack of communication ability.

After studying more Ukrainian in the two weeks leading up to the date than I did for most of the summer, I still couldn't help but to second guess all of the pre-planned phrases and conversation topics that were roaming around in my head. At that point my Ukrainian was probably above average when compared to other volunteers, but being able to impress my friends with a clear and grammatically correct order at a restaurant paled in comparison to a date with a native Ukrainian speaker.

All I could do was hope for the best.

We met up by a chocolate shop in the city center on a warm and sunny Sunday afternoon. Unlike most of the Ukrainian women in my life at that point, Alina's brown hair fell down past her shoulders, although she greeted me with a classic shy smile that I was no stranger to after a year in the country. She looked just like how she did in her picture, which I was thankful for, and I was hoping that she was thinking the same thing. After a quick hug and a few pryvits (hello!), we began walking out of the center towards the river, which like in Mukachevo cuts through most of the city. In a matter of minutes we were strolling on a pathway surrounded by trees, and if I didn't know any better would have made me forget we were in the capital city of the region.

"Do you like Ukraine?" she asked early on on our walk.

"Yeah, I do. Do you like Ukraine?"

"Yes," she replied, "But it's a very traditional country. I'm from a small village, and sometimes I feel like I'm in a culture from one hundred years ago."

"Yeah," I muttered, "Ukraine is very traditional."

"Yeah, everyone wants to have kids when they are twenty-two. I don't want that type of lifestyle."

"Yeah, that's way too young. It's better to be progressive."

"Yeah, I agree."

Boom. A connection. We made a connection while having a coherent conversation about our values, just like normal people do. It felt like a real date!

She soon started speaking incomprehensibly, using various hand gestures to add emotion to her impassioned speech, and after a forty-five second monologue all I could do was nod and pretend I could understand her.

"Oh yes, very cool," I said, hoping to change the subject as quickly as possible.

Knowing Alina now, it's clear to see that she caught on to my language ability pretty quickly, and was thoughtful enough adjust her language for me to understand. As she began to filter her speech I soon started comprehending more and more, which made me believe that I was more or less just getting used to her accent.

After a two hour walk by the river, which cut through one of the bigger parks of Zakarpattia, we continued our date back in the center. Although throughout the date she sometimes had to repeat herself and I nodded through a bunch of things I couldn't understand, we were able to get a little bit deeper than simply some shallow icebreakers.

After our walk we went to a pizza restaurant, where the background music made it even more difficult for me to get what she was saying. More smiling, nodding, using context clues and sometimes admitting that I couldn't really hear what she was saying. Nothing I wasn't used to, but on a date it made things ten times more nerve-wracking.

Afterwards we walked to a park and spent some time talking on a bench, where she showed me some photos of her and her friends at a music festival. It was all rather typical, other than the massive language barrier. Before too long the sun began to set, and before it got too dark Alina was kind enough to call me a taxi to get me home. Thinking that I had crushed it, I departed this beautiful woman with a strategic hug, after being told by volunteers and my co-workers alike that it is NOT OK to kiss someone on the first date in Ukraine. As I hopped into the taxi with some pep in my step, I was feeling good about my second date chances.

I ended up getting a second date, and a third, and eventually enough to where she could be honest with me about how our first date really went. A few months into our relationship, Alina finally confessed that contrary to my initial beliefs, throughout our first date she didn't understand half of what I said because of my heavy American accent.

"Really?" I asked as the energy left my body. It looks like I wasn't the only one who was pretending to understand. "Then why'd you want to go on a second date with me? I mean, if you couldn't-"

"I understood enough," she conceded, "And more importantly I could understand that you were a good guy."

"How did you get that?"

"I don't know," she replied, "Just a feeling."

Thank goodness I gave off any sort of energy other than the nervous anxiety that I thought was melting off of me, but even with that said, it was still a tough pill to swallow.

She could barely understand you, I thought, How much can she understand right now?

During the early days of dating Alina, I began to feel incredibly insecure about my language abilities, and subsequently our relationship. Other couples can talk about anything, but with Alina it took quite the effort to string together a few sentences about my values and general thoughts about life. About a month after we made things official, I asked her if she felt weird that I couldn't understand everything she said every time she opened her mouth. She laughed.

"Robert, there are some people who speak the same language but never truly understand one another. We always get each other and if we don't, we take the time to figure it out."

That is true. Alina had never gotten impatient or frustrated when re-explaining something.

"I appreciate that. Thanks Alina."

"There's nothing to thank me for," she would always reply.

"But you still don't think my Ukrainian is a problem?"

"You know what" she quickly retorted, "It's not a problem at all. Actually, I think our languages make us even better at communicating. Think about it! Whenever we talk, we need to be one hundred percent sure we are communicating as openly as possible. You see, it's actually a good thing, Robert. I think this is why I communicate better with you than anyone else I've dated."

I couldn't believe how much I had lucked out - how could I find someone this awesome randomly from a dating app? Although I was elated that our relationship was actually working out, speaking to her on a daily basis forced me to truly confront my weaknesses with the language. It's easy to avoid make mistakes if you avoid your second language altogether, but whenever I was with Alina, I found myself often sheepishly muttering "ya ne rozumiu" (I don't understand). Without fail, she would explain her point a second time, sometimes with simpler words so that I could get what she's saying. Alina's patience is one of many factors that has kept our relationship together, although it always hurt my ego when she had to water down what she was saying. All that effort had to be a burden for her, but if she hadn't been willing and able to go through with it, our relationship wouldn't have been able to work out.

"You're speaking Ukrainian," she would say whenever I was feeling down. "You should be proud of yourself. I don't know English, I mean, you're the one speaking my language. I have no problem explaining myself a few times for you to understand me."

What a gem.

With Alina by my side, the fall semester of school was a breeze, even as I went through the Peace Corps patented "mid-service slump," which is a phenomenon where volunteers almost universally go through a wave of depression at some point during their second year. I don't know why it's so common - maybe it's because nothing is shiny and new anymore, yet we still have twelve more months of dealing with the hardship of living in a second-world country. The weeks start to mesh together, and while at one point I almost begged for this sort of normalcy, especially during my hectic and stressful first few months, going through that fall semester again was quite the comedown after a great summer of camps and seeing friends all throughout the country.

Even though I felt waves of depression I couldn't understand, heading over to Alina's every weekend softened the blow. She soon became my closest confidant in a place where I pretty much had no one else to talk to except other volunteers who were a little too far away. She was the soft landing spot that I desperately needed at the end of each week, and soon that feeling of connection that all humans so desperately desire turned from a rare treat to a weekly tradition.

By January Alina and I had been dating for five months, and by then things were really starting to really take off. My language had been improving rapidly after busting out of a half-year long plateau, and the motivation of communicating deeply with the woman I was falling in love with drove me to work harder and harder. We started talking more and more, and in no time I realized that I was speaking Ukrainian every day, usually for multiple hours a day. As much as my tutors helped me early on, I learned quickly that falling in love is a fool proof way to begin excelling in a second language.

Due to my shower situation we began spending just about every weekend at her place, mostly just going on walks and doing nothing in particular because both of us were too cash strapped to go on any real adventures. With that said, life with her was never lacking, and as I fell deeper and deeper, I entered into a new territory of companionship that I had never tasted in the previous twenty-three years of my life. I soon began putting more of an effort into other aspects of my life, such as looking presentable, getting the wrinkles out of my clothes, washing those clothes consistently, and keeping my apartment tidy for the few times she ever wanted to bite the bullet and forgo a day or two of showering in order to come to my place.

It would be hard to leave her in October of 2020, the final month of my service, but in the midst of a new and beautiful relationship, I had no intention of going anywhere.

....

My first big decision of 2020 was on extension of service. Peace Corps is a twenty-seven month experience, but many volunteers have the option to extend their service up to a year, and ever since moving to Mukachevo I had debated whether or not I wanted to extend. I even remember thinking on my first day at site that if my service was fulfilling enough, I could easily do an extra nine months in this comfortable and croissant-ladened town. Now with Alina by my side, the decision was a no brainer.

Although Alina was the biggest factor, she wasn't the only reason for extending. Over my first year and a half as a volunteer, I was lucky enough to find a heartfelt pleasure in teaching, doing pedagogical workshops and leading summer camps. After a bumpy first full semester at School 16, by the second my teachers and I had gotten into a groove, that kind of groove you get into when you fully assimilate to the company culture and actually feel like you know what you're doing. It's a blissful period where the days go a little smoother and the weeks flow a little faster, and after eventually getting over the mid-service slump, by January I was as confident and competent as I had ever been in Ukraine.

Along with things naturally coming together at work, I even mustered up the gall to ask Maryana for Fridays off. I didn't know how that was going to play, seeing that my eighteen hour a week workload was about half as much as most other teachers, so I proposed teaching an extra two hours a week in order to sweeten the offer.

"Sure Robert," Maryana replied on her balcony, with no pushback whatsoever.

After that painless conversation, one that I may have shied away from a year earlier, I now had a permanent three-day weekend and a four-day work week. Along with the obvious pleasure that comes from sleeping-in three days a week instead of two, I came to realize that the extra two hours at school made my work-week feel way more productive, which was a much needed change from the earlier semesters.

One of the biggest problems Peace Corps volunteers face, aside from the isolation and conditions of living in a second or third world country, is the copious amounts of free time. This may seem like one of the better problems to have, but a sense of worthlessness and a lack of purpose can really begin to eat away at you with that kind of schedule. During my first couple of semesters my schedule would typically look like this: One class at 9:30, a two hour break, a forty minute lunch break, then one or two classes in the afternoon. Rinse and repeat five days a week. I hated waiting in the break-room for multiple hours, followed by only about ten or so minutes of actual teaching in the subsequent lesson. It didn't exactly scratch my do-gooder Peace Corps itch, and the lack of purpose and productivity, along with the isolation, was quite the potent depression cocktail early on.

Many days I'd go home and feel guilty about not doing more, and then I would have eight hours to kill until bedtime.

So along with the extra day of rest, travel, and/or time with Alina, my last semester at school was shaping up to be the most rewarding, with five classes a day instead of the typical two or three.

Yes, this was also going to be my last semester at School 16. While I had the intention of staying in Mukachevo for an extra year, I had set my sights on switching organizations. As much as I enjoyed teaching, in order to extend I had to bring a little something extra to the table. Peace Corps policy stated that we couldn't just extend because we wanted to hang out in Ukraine a little bit longer. Instead, there had to be a project or some other tangible reason why we needed to take another four-hundred dollars a month from the hardworking American taxpayer.

It was a perfect excuse, because while I genuinely enjoyed teaching, it had begun to get a little repetitive. I felt like there wasn't much more room for growth, both professionally and intellectually, so I was fortunate that I had been curating my next move over the past year and a half.

Enter REENA.

"You are so busy at school, it is a pity!" Nadia would often say to me. What a pity indeed. I had missed countless trips to Roma and refugee settlements because of my day job at school. While side projects like REENA were typically encouraged by the admin, it was under the condition that they shouldn't overtake a volunteer's primary assignment. I had a certain pride (and let's be honest, smugness), of working on my primary teaching role, unlike a few other volunteers who had pretty much ditched their main assignments entirely. However, it didn't sting any less when I had to pass on the various opportunities presented by REENA on a Wednesday at ten in the morning.

By the start of 2020, my desire to be working in human rights instead of the plateaued experience of teaching English began to strengthen rapidly. I came to Ukraine not even really knowing what I'd be doing, only knowing that I wanted to work for the Peace Corps, and while I was grateful that I enjoyed teaching, I had never dreamed about working in education. REENA was the next step on the path of achieving some sort of life dream that hadn't been specified yet, and a year and a half into my service, I was ready to make a move.

During the second or third week of January, Nadia and I met in a coffee shop. By then, after countless meetings over the past year and a half, she already knew what drink I wanted.

"We'll have a cappuccino, a latte, and two slices of cheesecake," Nadia said in Ukrainian that I could fully understand at that point.

After a subsequent incomprehensible conversation with the waiter, she turned to me.

"So Robert, how was your vacation?"

"Good, good. Feeling refreshed."

"I bet you were happy to see your family after such a long time."

"Absolutely, I got a great week with them, I got some presents, and I saw some old friends. It was just what I needed."

"And are you ready to get back to School 16?" She asked with a smile.

I already knew where this was going. Nadia would always insinuate that working in a school was lame, and usually I'd just brush it off and try to change the subject. But this time was different.

She continued on, "It must have been a nice break to get away from all those kids for a while. I worked in a school, you know, and I could never go back! Too much yelling, and not just from the students."

"Yeah," I replied, "I agree. It does become a bit too much sometimes. I've had a really great time there, but I actually wanted to talk to you about something."

Here goes nothing.

"I've decided that I'm going to do an extra year in the Peace Corps, and I was wondering if I could be your volunteer for my third year."

Nadia looked at me, and after a second or two, she smiled and slammed her fist on the table, almost spilling my cappuccino.

"This is wonderful news!" She exclaimed, "You've always been so busy at school, so we've never been able to get you on any significant projects. But this is perfect, I already have so many ideas that we can work on together. Right now REENA is working on getting some of the refugees employment documentation. We want to make a grant for funding, we need funding, you know to fund workshops, to show the refugees how to open and run a business. Would that be something you're interested in?"

She didn't need to ask. The idea of helping refugees attain documentation and teaching them how to run a business made my heart race. It was exactly the kind of project I wanted to work on, and it was the exact kind of project that the Peace Corps would need to hear in order to green light my extension. I knew nothing in the slightest about how to run a business, but if I worked hard and got some other volunteers in on the action, this could be a crown jewel of my service. Better yet, it would be the exact type of project that Samuel or Victoria would want to see before hopefully helping me get into the field of human rights.

It was everything I needed, and it fit like a glove.

"I would love to help out," I replied, "I don't know a ton about that stuff, but I'll do whatever I can."

"Oh, that's ok," Nadia said while stirring her latte, "You can start with editing our grant proposal. When is a good time for you this week?"

And just like that, I began working with REENA on the nitty gritty human rights work that I had been waiting for since I began my first English club almost a year and a half earlier. I started, like Nadia proposed, editing a grant proposal or two, having more than enough time in my schedule because of the extra day off from school.

I began walking to REENA one extra time a week and began staying later and later after English clubs. I did my best to brainstorm what this business workshop could be, but I mostly just proofread grant proposals. I was still doing English-related work, but I had little doubt that by the time the workshop rolled around, I would have had enough of a role to feel proud of the impact that we would potentially make with these vulnerable populations.

The one wrench in my plan was the transition to REENA from School 16. Telling my co-teachers that I'd be leaving school but not leaving Mukachevo had the potential to put an awkward damper on the last year of my service. I also didn't want to just outright stop working there, even though the screams from first graders in the hallways had gotten more and more on my nerves as time went on.

Thankfully, I got yet another win. During a call with my extremely accessible country director William, I told him about my intentions of switching over to REENA.

"Oh REENA," he said, "That sounds great, we love REENA. We had a volunteer working there a few years back, but she had to leave early in her service. I think that's a great idea, although you know it wouldn't exactly be TEFL work."

"Yeah, I know. Would that be a problem?"

"Problem? No, you won't need to worry about that. Heck, in the past when we've had volunteers switch sectors, which is what you'll be probably doing because your work will likely be classified as community development, some of the volunteers still wanted to do some work at their schools. You could do that too, like a hybrid schedule, where you'd teach at your school for two days a week, then go to REENA for three, or your school for one day and REENA for four, what have you. You can do it however you want, if that sounds like a good option for you."

"That sounds perfect," I replied, barely believing how easy this was turning out.

"It's something to consider, just let us know and we'll figure it all out. Glad you brought this up Bob. Anyway, how's the self care going?"

After an extended conversation about the importance of meditation, I found myself bouncing off the walls once again in my apartment. As much as I was looking forward to working with REENA, I knew all about the struggles of community development volunteers and how many of them felt underutilized in their work environments. I wasn't blind to the fact that there'd likely be many dull days of grant writing, editing, and waiting around for more work, so a pinch of teaching every Monday or Friday would provide a perfect balance for a third year volunteer like myself. I could still teach my favorite students, work alongside teachers, and feel productive doing the work I was trained to do.

Every single aspect of my life was rolling with an almost unstoppable momentum and they all fed into each other: A satisfying relationship made me more satisfied with work. The packed four day work week without large chunks of dead time made me less depressed and more sure of my purpose. A three day weekend gave me more time to focus on my relationship. More focus on my relationship made my personal life more satisfying, and helped me excel in Ukrainian at the same time. To top it all off, I was finally starting to do some human rights work. It was harmony.

It was all flowing into each other, which felt long overdue after the first year of debilitating culture shock, isolation, issues with communication, loneliness, FOMO, and a feeling of worthlessness from being incompetent at a job I had never done before. It was all coming together. Finally.

Until it suddenly stopped.

Chapter Sixteen

Evacuation

While making a six egg omelette in mid-January, I was listening to some NPR podcast about this new virus that had completely shut down a city in China. The correspondent was stationed outside of Wuhan, and wasn't able to enter because the city was "quarantined." Quarantined. Hmm. I had never heard that word in the news before. She discussed how a new virus had originated in a fish market there, and after a quick rise in cases, the Chinese government decided to completely quarantine the city.

Classic China, I thought. They aren't known for Human Rights and love of liberty, so a strict Chinese lockdown didn't scare me as much as it should have.

After my plethora of time off during winter break, which included various trips to America, the Republic of Georgia, Norway and Lviv, I continued my work at school, soaking in the last few months I would be teaching full time before transitioning to REENA. However, as February rolled around, my focus was drawn more and more to this virus that made it out of China, and started popping up in Italy. A Western European country undergoing quarantine which set off some major red flags, and as soon cases started arising in various European countries, I began fearing the worst.

The weeks leading up to the global lockdown was like a slow moving train crash. Cases began exponentially multiplying, and it seemed like every day a new country was reporting their first Covid infection. As more and more people started to get infected, I naively held out hope that Covid wouldn't make it to Ukraine. Seeing how Ukraine isn't exactly the biggest tourist destination in the world, I thought that maybe the country I had grown to love could sneak out of it unscathed by this unknown virus.

By mid-February, when things started to get serious in some parts of Europe, Ukraine still had zero cases. On top of that no other volunteers were really talking about it, and we hadn't received any word from admin about any quarantine or travel restrictions. This was the same admin that enacted the strict travel policy during the Kerch Strait incident and the month preceding the election, so I thought their lack of notice was a good sign.

However, being the paranoid and worrisome person that I am, I began to freak out that this virus could be coming to Ukraine. And if it came to Ukraine, a second world country lacking optimal infrastructure, the health and safety of volunteers would be put in serious danger. And that could only mean one thing: Evacuation.

Shit.

···

The day before Valentine's day, Alina graduated from university and received her master's in law. There was a big ceremony, and Alina emphasized over the phone that her mom was going to be there.

"Don't worry," she said the day before, "My mom is very sweet. You two are going to sit together, so make sure to look sharp. She speaks mostly Zakarpattian so don't worry if it's a little hard to talk to her. And Robert?"

"Yes Alina," I said after scribbling down some notes.

"Make sure there aren't any stains on your shirt, ok?"

I didn't take that comment as patronizing, because on any given day there was a decent chance there was a stain that I failed to detect.

The morning before the ceremony I ironed my best button down and khakis, and after getting Maria to confirm that there were no stains or unseen wrinkles, I ventured over to Uzhhorod. When I made it to the city center I bought flowers (after being told by every single one of my colleagues to do so), and I arrived at the conference hall a couple hours early. I then wandered around aimlessly, and ended up going to a coffee shop for one of the last times in the foreseeable future.

After two espressos and thirty minutes of Ukrainian practice, I made my way over to the ceremony. As I entered the lobby, there were hoards of people wearing clothes that were a little bit nicer than mine, and holding flowers that blew my bouquet out of the water. I tensed up, but soon calmed down when Alina greeted me.

She looked stunning. Her black heels, which accompanied a black dress, almost brought her up to eye level, and her newly curled hair that brushed the sides of her face left me at a loss of words.

"Wow," I said, forgetting to hand her the flowers.

"Thanks Robert" she replied, taking them out of my hand, "You're early. But that's ok, my mom is too. Are you ready to meet her?"

No.

"Yeah, let's go."

Alina took me to the presentation room, which was a small theater on the second floor. Her mom was one of the only people in the stands at that point. She was fiddling with some paper, and shot a force smile my way when we came up to her. I was happy to see that she was just as nervous as I was.

"Hello," I said, extending my hand, "I'm Robert."

"Robert, Hello! Hannah," her mom said while standing up to hug me. She then said a lot of stuff I didn't understand, and I darted my eyes towards Alina.

"Mom, Robert doesn't speak Zakarpattian. He only knows Ukrainian."

"Oh, ok. That's ok, it's good you know Ukrainian! You don't need to learn Zakarpattian. Here, sit down."

Alina left to prepare for the ceremony, and soon her mom and I began sitting in silence. Then, there was more silence. And more silence... It's hard enough striking up a conversation with your partner's parents for the first time, but with the language barrier it was all but impossible, not that that made it feel any less weird. Thankfully, a couple minutes later two of Alina's friends, Ihor and Stas, showed up and saved the day. I lucked out that some of her closest friends were not only a couple of guys my age, but were also fluent English speakers. After some firm handshakes, Ihor and Stas made sure to sit right behind Hannah and I, and offered to translate so that we could start getting to know each other. I was finally able to have that classic first conversation with a girlfriend's mom, albeit with a translator.

After the ceremony we all took pictures in the lobby, which was littered with people. Later on Alina and her mom took me out to lunch, where I struggled to conceal my uptight disposition. I tried to do my best to not say anything stupid or out of line, while at the same time prayed that I'd be able to make out at least some of what her mom was saying. Because Zakarpattian has some Ukrainian and Russian in it, I wasn't quite sure when her mom was speaking her native dialect or when she was switching to Ukrainian. No matter how hard I tried to parse through her dialect, I was at most getting about ten percent of it, and even with the language barrier in mind I felt like a clown for not being able to understand the most simple of sentences.

It was a classic meeting the parents situation.

Alina ended up doing a fantastic job of translating my Ukrainian to Zakarpattian for well over an hour, and I'm sure she made me sound much more intelligent and elegant than my broken second language ever could. We ended the arduous lunch with volcano cake, and finally around 5:00 pm we drove back to Alina's apartment. We thanked her mom profusely for paying, and after hugs and goodbyes, Alina and I finally ventured it to the front door of her apartment, and took a deep breath for the first time all day.

At that moment, I took out my phone and saw a message from the Zakarpattia Peace Corps group chat: Someone in Mukachevo was suspected of contracting Coronavirus.

I turned to Alina, and I'll never forget how she looked in that moment. After a long day in which she culminated her studies and successfully introduced the person she loves to her mother, she looked content. She looked like someone who had absolutely everything, and I was about to take it all away.

Going against my better judgement, I showed her the message.

"Oh," she said, "Well, it's only a suspected case, not a confirmed case."

"Alina, if things get bad in Ukraine..."

"Evacuation?"

"Yeah."

She paused. "That would make me sad. Very, very sad."

"Me too," I said.

She then took my phone and put it in my breast pocket, "Well, maybe we shouldn't think about it tonight. And maybe even Covid won't get that bad in Ukraine. No one wants to come here, anyway."

I laughed, "Yeah, this might be the one time to be thankful that Ukraine's not like France or Spain."

"Exactly," she said while opening the door, "Let's get things ready. Stas and Ihor will be here soon."

We decided to forget about the impending doom of the world and spent one of our last normal nights together. After Stas and Ihor arrived we cooked dinner, played cards, and I fell asleep at midnight while Alina and the boys stayed up until five in the morning.

A few weeks later, on March 2nd, I was sitting on a bench in the center of Mukachevo, having some time to kill before an English club. People were walking around aimlessly, stepping on the last remnants of snow and seemingly undisturbed by the concerning news of an unknown virus slowly but surely taking over the world. Peace Corps Mongolia had already been evacuated by then, and rumors started to fly that other posts were next. While listening to Youtube Music (because Spotify wasn't yet approved in Ukraine), I got a terrible alert on my phone from our country director. The first case had been confirmed in Ukraine in the western oblast of Chernivtsi.

Ok, I thought, *This is bad. But it's in Chernivtsi. No confirmed cases in Zakarpattia yet. This can still work out.*

My denial turned to panic just a few days later. After reading how a seventy year old woman who had tested positive went to Church in order to (I presume) make peace before her eventual death, my stomach revolted and I barely had enough time to make it to the toilet before throwing up. After dry heaving for a few minutes I went back to my bed and began crying, because right then and there I knew it was all over.

I was going to get evacuated, and I was going to lose everything. My job, my future career in human rights, my home, my girlfriend...my girlfriend. There was nothing I could do. All I could do was wait until the Peace Corps gave the official word that life as I knew it was about to end.

That process began a little more than a week later, on March 12th. It was the third day of English Week round two, and throughout the day I led a scavenger hunt with the middle school and gave out candy to the winners. By the time school let out there were tons of fifth and sixth graders mauling me in the lobby, reaching out their hands and trying to break into the bag where I held the treats. At a certain point I stopped checking to see if they finished the scavenger hunt, and I just gave them as much candy as I had. I was just happy to be there. Like during the Kerch Strait incident, school was the one thing that helped me forget about a potential evacuation. While teaching you can't afford to let your mind wander, or else things break down quickly.

About an hour after making it home, I once again got a terrible message, this time from Mukachevo.net, a website I subscribed to in order to get updates on Covid in Zakarpattia.

All Schools in Ukraine to be Shut Down Immediately.

There it goes.

While some other volunteers began celebrating what they thought would be a temporary vacation, I was in a bit of a different headspace. Within the next few minutes I headed over to the new grocery store by my apartment, and immediately bought as much rice, beans, and pasta I could fit into the shopping cart. Yes, I was one of those hoarder assholes, but I thought I was going to be trapped in Ukraine during the middle of a Covid outbreak. At that point we hadn't received any word on evacuation, instead just a bunch of vague emails telling us to standby.

If I was going to standby and be confined to my apartment, I wanted enough food to last as long as possible.

That's where my head was at: I thought I literally wasn't going to be allowed to leave my apartment for the foreseeable future. And that wasn't too out of line, because at the time, no one knew what was happening, how bad things were going to get, or what a quarantine/national lockdown was going to look like.

That night I got a text from one of my co-teachers, Yana.

"Robert, did you see that the schools are closing?"

"Yes. It's crazy."

"I know. All of the teachers are meeting at the school around 9:00 am tomorrow to discuss what to do next. Are you able to come?"

"Of course, I'll see you there."

The next morning I made a solemn trip to School 16, understanding that it might be my last time seeing all of them for the indefinite future. I stepped into room 27, the biggest room in the school, and already saw most of the teachers already there. It was the first time I was one of the last people to a meeting, and it wasn't even 9:00 am yet. Things were getting serious.

However, you wouldn't have known it from the general disposition of the teachers. The majority of them were laid back, chatting and cracking jokes with one another while waiting for the principal to get things started. It again reminded me of the Kerch Strait incident - A resilient and battle-tested people, those Ukrainians.

Close to 9:02, the principal stood up and started things off. The meeting, of course, was conducted only in Ukrainian, but I'm incredibly grateful that after months of practicing with Alina, my Ukrainian was good enough at that point to where I could understand most of what they were saying.

"First and foremost," the principle said, "Everyone is still going to get paid. You do not need to worry about that, so please do not ask me anymore." A satisfied murmur came over the room.

He soon began discussing the logistics of virtual learning, which I couldn't quite make out, but afterwards he brought up the virus itself.

"So, it looks to be a pretty serious virus, much worse than the flu. In Germany, for example, the death rate is about two percent." He then paused and, strangely enough, started smiling, "So, you know, if the death rate in Germany is two percent, in Ukraine it'll be about twenty."

The room burst out laughing, while the director did his best to not look too satisfied with himself. I would have laughed if the shock from the joke hadn't taken away the rest of my breath. Ukrainian humor is dark... In the subsequent aftershock I looked down and began to doodle in my journal.

For the next half hour or so I zoned out completely. After a long Q/A, the meeting eventually deteriorated into tangents and jokes. After a pretty sick joke that once again had the whole room laughing, the vice-principal turned to me and said, "Evacuatsia?" while making a flying gesture with her hand.

Well, I guess I should talk about that. Might be my only chance.

I stood up, and after the crowd calmed down a bit, in Ukrainian I began the last words I'd ever say to my colleagues.

"Well, I might get evacuated. I don't really know if I will, because no one knows anything. But I think right now it might be safer for me to be in Ukraine than the United States. But I don't know, we will see."

All the eyes in the room were on me, and no one was having a side conversation. This was for sure the last time I would see them.

"However," I continued, "I bought a lot of macaroni and rice, so if there's a lockdown I think I'll be ok." The room once again burst out laughing, and amongst the rambunctious laughter I heard various classic Ukrainian motherly phrases, such as,

"Did you buy some buckwheat? You gotta have buckwheat."

"You're going to need some chicken with that rice!"

"You can cook? Robert if you can't cook just call me and I'll tell you what to do."

I thanked them for the advice and sat back down, happy to have one moment like that with my coworkers. A few minutes later the meeting finished up, I said a few individual goodbyes, and I walked home from School 16 for the last time.

....

A couple days later, after not leaving my apartment since that final meeting, I woke up at 8:00 am for an interview with an online English teaching company. I had to cancel, after reading an email for a month I had been dreading to receive. I've redacted bits of pieces of the email, but you'll get the gist from the following:

Hello PCVs,

It is official. We are working on evacuating 261 PCVs. This will be fast, before Tuesday 12:00am, hopefully from four Ukrainian airports if we can secure the flights...

The last 24 hours have resulted in an unprecedented shutdown of Ukraine, which accelerated in what feels to me like almost no time. Last night's decision by the government of Ukraine to close all airports for at least two weeks starting 00:01 am March 17 is the main reason that resulted in this decision...

This has been a very difficult several days since school quarantine was announced...

Your PC Ukraine staff has been working very hard to coordinate this fast moving departure and will follow up with an email with logistics about from which airport you will travel...

The Admin team is working on flights now and when ready, they will be emailing you your flight information and creating a spreadsheet for us to understand all of your departure information...

I didn't bother reading the rest of it. I was being evacuated. It was all over. Even though I saw it coming, I could barely breathe from the shock. I laid down for a few minutes, but soon started to get REALLY SAD, so I immediately looked for something practical to do. I began to pack up my entire life, just three months after coming back from America with a new wardrobe.

I was given the task to fit all of my possessions into three bags, meaning I would have to throw away a huge chunk of all of the things I had collected during my service. There was no time to waste, so I spent the next two hours packing and trying not to look at any of my PC group chats, which were all going absolutely nuclear. I kept hearing notification after notification of volunteers freaking out, so I turned the sound of my phone off. I didn't want to feel alone during one of the worst moments of my life, but even while going through the motions I knew being around that wasn't going to do me any good.

Keep packing. Don't lie down. Don't think.

I initially didn't want to tell Alina. She was planning on coming over the next day, and at first I thought it would be a good idea to tell her in person. I didn't want to ruin her Saturday by telling her that the guy she was about to move in with actually had to say goodbye, perhaps forever. Oh yeah, we were planning on moving in together. We had already found an apartment and everything, and we were going to make the transition within a week. That was out the door, along with any future we planned together.

Tell her in person. This is something you should tell someone in person. I couldn't bring myself to call her, and anyway I knew that she had a really busy day of preparing face cream from scratch for a new cosmetics business she started.

However, as I slowly started to process the situation, the terror of evacuating brought me to my knees. After a couple hours, no matter how hard I tried, I couldn't simply pack and forget about it anymore. So many of my possessions were on the ground that I couldn't even see the rug in my bedroom, and everything was so disorganized that it almost made me nauseous. It all was too much for me to handle, and during the third hour my packing became slower and less efficient. At one point I began to aimlessly walk around my room, picking things up and then putting them down, paralyzed with the decision of what to keep and what to leave.

That's when I called her.

"Alina."

"What's wrong?"

I had already started crying.

"Robert, what's wrong? Please, Robert, what's going on?"

"Alina," I said, almost inaudibly. "Evacuation. Evacuation is now. We're leaving."

I didn't hear anything on her end for a few seconds.

"When did you find out, Robert?."

"A few hours ago."

"Robert," she said, "Why didn't you tell me earlier?"

"I didn't want to ruin your day."

"Fuck. When do you leave?"

"I don't know."

"Ok, let me think... Ok, Robert, I need to finish one more shipment and then my mom will drive me to your place. It'll be about three hours. Are you going to be ok?"

"Yeah, I'll be ok. Thank you."

"I love you. I'll see you soon."

Three hours. It was noon, and after our phone call I took my first deep breath of the day.

12:00. Three hours.

Time had now entered into the equation.

I looked again at my phone, where my colleagues in the group chat hadn't stopped texting in all caps. I looked at my room, which was covered in partially filled suitcases, clothes, notebooks, silverware and knick knacks. I looked at my kitchen, which was filled with too many packets of rice, pasta and buckwheat.

This was really happening.

I then turned my head to look at the only place that didn't make me feel terrible: Outside. It was a bright and sunny day, one of the most beautiful days of the year.

At that moment I turned off my phone, stopped packing, and put on my running clothes. I had one more chance to see my town, and this was it. On my typical jogging route I would be able to see most of the major landmarks of my service, so I stepped outside for the first time that day ready to begin my final goodbye to Mukachevo. I started by running to my school.

Man, I was lucky it was a beautiful day. After almost a week of rain and grey skies, the evacuation gods had blessed me with fifty degrees and clear blue skies. In a matter of minutes I easily made it to that big yellow building that we called School 16, and luckily I saw about fifteen or so of my students playing basketball. I hopped the fence, and they all turned around and ran up to greet me.

"Mr. Robert!"

"Hi everyone. I have some sad news."

"What is it? Covid?"

"Yeah. I'm being evacuated. I have to leave"

"What? Why?"

"My organization is leaving Ukraine, and I have to go home."

Most of the group of middle schoolers looked down. None of us had anything to say, and as much as I wanted to, I couldn't think of anything that could make the situation better. That's when one of the eighth graders finally looked up and asked, "When will you return?"

I appreciated that he said, "When."

"I don't know, Viktor, but one day I will come back. I don't know when, but I promise you I'll come back to Ukraine."

I was soon engulfed in hugs. Even the boys, who typically tried to put on a masculine front, skipped the handshake and went for an embrace. I wasn't expecting to say goodbye to any of my students, so serendipitously getting to hug at least a few of them made one of the darkest days of my life just a little bit brighter.

Before I continued my jog I told them to wash their hands, cough into the arm and to stop smoking, which they all laughed at because they definitely weren't going to stop smoking. I said my last goodbyes, got every Instagram handle I could, and continued on.

My run soon took me to a path between the river on the left and some residential buildings on the right. Beyond the river in foreground are foothills, and even farther away from the foothills are the legitimate mountains of Zakarpattia. It would have been a shame if I had stayed in my room all day, not even getting a glimpse of those mountains which defined so much of my service to that point. I slowed down to enjoy the most scenic path in Mukachevo one last time, and in the deep distance I saw a snow capped mountain. It was a rare sight in the middle of March, and one I wouldn't have noticed if it were any other one of my aimless walks. I took a mental picture and continued jogging.

The path by the river soon took me to REENA. They usually have pretty tight security, but on that day in particular the front door to the Church was left wide open. I walked in and started looking for people, hoping I would get to say some final goodbyes to Nadia or some of the social workers. Unfortunately it was a ghost town, and I had no idea why. Then it hit me.

It's Saturday, you dummy. I lost track of the days after not working for four days straight, which turned out to be a very common occurrence during the early months of the pandemic.

After snapping back to reality, a wave of depression hit with the realization that I wouldn't get to thank Nadia for everything she had done for me. I decided to do the next best thing and began rummaging around in one of the social worker's offices. After finding a pen and paper, I headed back to the kitchen, the same kitchen where Nadia must have fed me over thirty times, and I wrote my final goodbye.

Hello. I'm being evacuated. I am sad and I am sorry, but I promise that one day I will come back. From Robert.

I finished writing and used one of the magnets to put my note on the fridge, which was fitting after being fed there so many times. I took one last look around,

213

thanked the Church, and dipped out, unsure why yet extremely thankful that REENA's doors were open on a Saturday.

I continued my jog and made it to the center, where I soon found more eighth graders smoking. I had already told this batch earlier in my service to quit tobacco, so this interaction mainly focused on the hugs and goodbyes. A few minutes later I continued my run, and in less than a minute I found another group of kids from School 16.

This process repeated throughout my jog: Every few minutes or so I found a group of my students, who were acting like nothing significant was going on in the world. I told them I was being evacuated, we hugged it out, and then we exchanged Instagrams. I bumped into tenth graders, seventh graders, some of the adults from my English club, and also an eleventh grader, Alex, who had been the most consistent student at my REENA club.

"Alex, I'm so glad I found you," I said in the heart of the city center, "I'm being evacuated, and I have to leave. It's because of Covid."

"Oh, that's a pity, I'm sorry to hear that. Stay safe, and thank you for the club."

"Alex, I'm so grateful you came every week. You've been my favorite student, and I'm so happy we could get to know each other over the year."

"Well you've been my favorite teacher! I've never had a teacher like you. Thank you Mr. Robert, and all I ask is that you try to come to graduation in the summer!"

It seemed she hadn't really realized how bad Covid was going to get.

"Ehhhhhhh I don't know about that, I'll try but we'll have to see. But thanks Alex. Stay safe, and cough into your arm."

"Thanks Mr. Robert, you too!"

Over the course of my run I ran into about thirty different people that I knew. On one of the most beautiful days of the year practically my whole town was out and about, which gave me the perfect opportunity to get at least a partial form of closure. I didn't know how long it would take me to get back to Ukraine, and in the coming days and months those were the type of memories that I needed to hold onto during the incredible amount of misery that soon would arrive.

On the final leg of my jog, I slowed down to a walk, not wanting to confront reality. After a dreamlike jog filled with hugs and goodbyes, I began to process more and more how terrible this evacuation experience was going to be. Leaving Alina, packing, the logistics, and not to mention the actual danger of traveling in the midst of a pandemic. I was getting caught up in what turned out to be one of many minor breakdowns during the evacuation process, but somehow I was able to catch myself, breathe deeply and prevent myself from going into a tailspin. I looked up at the trees, which were practically still, and I tried to appreciate the last time I would ever walk back to my apartment, after mindlessly doing so for the past year without even thinking about it.

For the first time all day, everything was silent.

As I walked back through my apartment gates, I was greeted by Maria and Maryana, who were lounging around on a couple of rocking chairs, calm as a breeze.

"Shame," Maria said after I told her about getting evacuated.

"Yes, it is a shame," Maryana agreed.

I couldn't have said it better.

"When you leave let us know. We will take the keys. Do you need help?"

"I don't think so," I replied. Even with evac on my mind, I did not want them seeing the state of my room. They had seen a lot in that apartment over the past year, but nothing compared to the mess awaiting me after my jog.

I made it back to my apartment, but due to nerves I still wasn't able to pack a goodman thing. Thank god Alina came.

After showering and laying around in a mess I only had myself to blame for, I got a text from Alina to come outside. She was waiting on the sidewalk with her mom, who had driven Alina across the region on a moment's notice.

I immediately began crying at the sight of her.

"Oh Robert," she said to me. She opened the trunk and pulled out a few suitcases. "I brought these to pack your stuff. You can leave whatever you need in the village and pick it up when you come back."

I hugged her, which only led to more crying. I turned to Alina's mom.

"Thank you, Hannah. Thank you so much for bringing her."

"Thank me? There's nothing to thank me for. She's my daughter, and I love her. There is no need to thank me."

I hugged Hannah, and with bags in my hand and tears streaming down my face, Alina and I headed to my apartment, preparing to clean for who knows how long.

Our time packing and cleaning together was terrible. The negative energy that consumed the apartment outweighed any sort of chance for us to appreciate one of our last days together. I was overjoyed that I was able to be with her that last night, but every moment of joy quickly turned into despair, knowing that this was all going to be gone in a less than a day. Every time we hugged I was reminded that I might never get to touch her ever again, and every time I saw her I was reminded of who I was about to lose. We tried our best to only cry one at a time, hoping to avoid whatever would happen if there wasn't someone to calm the other person down.

Most of the time it was me crying and Alina holding me and telling me to breathe. She was much more emotionally stable than I was, and did a great job holding herself together while I had various breakdowns throughout our night together. I'm so thankful she was there for me, not only because of the emotional support, but also because we had a ton of cleaning to do.

We spent a good six hours packing and cleaning that apartment, and after the first couple hours I realized how screwed I would've been if Alina hadn't helped me. Without her I simply wouldn't have had enough time to pack and clean up, and I don't know how other volunteers without helpful and considerate girlfriends got through that part of evac.

"Robert," she said while sweeping up the dust bunnies under my dresser, "How long have these been here."

"The whole time," I said.

"Oh Robert," she laughed," I'll teach you how to clean these when you come back."

There was that word again, "When."

That night, in the middle of cleaning, I received another email from the admin. Alina and I were dying for any sort of information about the evacuation process, and around 8:00 pm we got the news. Alina and I hunched around my phone, looking for some sort of hope or guidance that could help us plan for the future.

First, the email said that I needed to be in Kyiv by Sunday night.

"Tomorrow night??" Alina asked.

I did the math: The train from Zakarpattia takes thirteen hours, so I had to leave pretty much ASAP in order to make it to Kyiv on time. We quickly hopped on the ticket website in order to find the next possible train. There was only one available: 6:30 the next morning, with four seats left.

Fingers shaking, I entered all my info and the ticket. My order thankfully went through and I let out all the air that I had pent up since reading the email, not knowing what would have happened if I didn't get a ticket back on the only train to Kyiv before Sunday night. Yet, after the slight relief, time once again made itself a factor.

10 hours. You have 10 hours until she's gone.

I started crying again, and Alina once again consoled me.

"Everything will be ok, Robert. Everything will be ok."

Not believing her, I grabbed my phone and went back to reading the email. The massive amount of information on our oncoming logistics almost put me to sleep, but through my adrenaline I skimmed through most of the email until I found what I had been looking for: What was going to happen to the Peace Corps?

...When we reopen PC in Ukraine, which we all hope will happen once the virus is under control, you can all request reinstatement and possibly return to post, if medically cleared again. We will stay in touch with you throughout this next stretch of time to ensure that you are apprised of how to do this, if interested...

After that I smiled for the first time since Alina arrived.

"Alina," I said, barely believing what I had just read, "The Peace Corps is coming back. After Covid they're coming back."

"Are you going to return??" she said, tears in her eyes.

I paused for a second. Just one.

"Yes, I'm going to return. I'm coming back. I promise."

At that point, we hadn't openly talked about the massive elephant in the room of whether I would return or not. But there you had it: I'm coming back to Ukraine.

She was the one crying now, "Oh Robert, thank you. Thank you so much, I love you so much. I will wait for you. However long it takes."

"However long it takes," I said, "I'm coming back for you."

That's when we both started crying, thankfully this time due to happiness instead of terror and sadness. We both laid down on the bed, holding each other and doing our best to hold on to this small moment during a day that felt like the world was ending. It isn't over, my life in Ukraine isn't over, my life with her isn't over. We didn't know when we would see each other again (I was initially thinking it would take over a year) but we didn't need to wonder if we would see each other again. Right there, we had one last happy moment to hold on to over the coming months of misery.

After a couple of minutes, unavoidable thoughts of cleaning and packing once again emerged and we got out of bed to finish up. Even with this breakthrough of me returning, the painful cycle of looking in her eyes and crying repeated until we finally gave up cleaning for the night and broke out a bottle of wine.

After only finishing half the bottle we fell asleep. I didn't think I would be able to fall asleep during a night like this, but after a few sips my eyes became heavy, and our collective emotional and physical exhaustion lulled us into sleep.

....

You know that feeling of relief you get when you're having an extremely realistic nightmare, only to wake up and realize it was all a dream? Waking up in Mukachevo on Sunday, March 15th, was the exact opposite: I had a normal dream, only to wake up to my world crumbling around me. Once I realized I was no longer dreaming and yes, all of this was actually happening, I began wailing. I was literally in the fetal position and crying my eyes out. Looking at Alina only made it worse; I couldn't accept that I was holding on to someone I would soon have to let go of indefinitely.

We got up at 3:00 am and spent our final hours together cleaning up the rest of the apartment. The night before I thought we were basically done, but Alina's pristine eye caught a lot of dust, dirt and grime that I definitely would have missed. I couldn't believe I had to leave her.

While she was cleaning I tried making myself useful. I looked over to the kitchen and saw the mountain of pasta, buckwheat and rice that I had been hoarding. I took one of the suitcases that Alina brought over for me and started packing them up for Alina to take back home.

"Robert," she said laughing, "You really don't need to give me all that. I'm going back to be fine."

Like some of my students, I felt that she didn't quite understand the severity of Covid. I was preparing for the worst and thinking about the potential of food supply chains breaking down and Ukraine devolving into total anarchy.

"Alina, take the rice."

She laughed again, "Robert, I'm from a village. It's basically a farm - You know, a farm? Where all the food is? If there is anything Ukrainians are good at, it's avoiding going hungry. We are going to be fine, so just try to worry about yourself. Do you have your ticket?"

219

"On my phone," I said, "What about water? Here, take the water. I only have six liters left but-"

"Robert," she said after kissing me, "We have a well."

"Your village does?"

"No, my family does. The water's free and safe to drink. We'll be fine."

At five in the morning on my last day at site, I thought back to my training village of Hryshkivtsi, and how the sole advantage of living there was that, unlike in most of Ukraine, the tap water was completely fine to drink. The pain fled my stomach, knowing I could leave Ukraine without worrying about Alina's safety.

"Well, take the water anyway."

"If it makes you happy, then no problem."

I continued to sit in my arm chair in the corner while she vacuumed, as I mentally prepared myself for the journey ahead. As much as I protested, the minutes that morning seemed to go by much faster than usual, and before I could believe it her mom arrived at our apartment at 5:30 before the sun had even risen.

Alina and I stepped outside with all of my things and the rice/pasta she was set to take home. I tossed the keys over the gate, like Maria instructed, and left my apartment for the last time.

Her mom drove us to the train station (which was a twenty second drive from my apartment) and Alina and I sat in the car holding hands.

As the sun began to rise, I began to see Zakarpattian volunteers trickling into the station, and I took a moment to thank my lucky stars I lived so close to the station. I sure as hell wasn't pleased about the late notice about getting to Kyiv, but at least the train station was barely a minute away. Many of my colleagues, I later learned, pulled an all nighter and needed their counterparts to drive them over to Mukachevo in the middle of the night.

"Do you want to be with them?" Alina asked me.

"Absolutely not," I replied. I knew in the coming days I would have more than enough time with my colleagues, unlike with Alina, who would be leaving my life indefinitely in forty-five minutes.

Around 6:15, Alina and I begrudgingly walked to the platform. On our way we bumped into Daniel, the guy who gave me his water on the first bus from the airport. He shook Alina's hand and said, "Nice to finally meet you, although I wish it were in a different circumstance, haha." Smooth, Daniel.

Alina and I stood at the platform, hugging each other and trying not to think about the future. Unfortunately, the train came right on time. Alina made sure once again that I had my wallet, passport, and phone. We took a few pictures, and she made sure I didn't forget the sandwiches and chips that she had packed for me.

We hastily walked to my wagon and got to the front of the line, with the idea that I could throw my stuff on the train and then hop off to get one final goodbye before leaving. After I got on and dropped my stuff in my room, I tried making my way back to her. The problem was that this was an unusually small train with super skinny hallways, and I couldn't quite squeeze through the other passengers to get to the exit. I tried pushing through other volunteers, but as the conductor was screaming incomprehensibly at all of us, they weren't able to budge. They kept moving forward as I was pushed deeper into the depths of the train car.

I had no way to hug her again. I had no way to say goodbye.

The train began moving, much sooner than I expected, so I darted to the window to catch one last glimpse of her. The window wouldn't fully open, so all I could do was put a few fingers out the top to give a futile wave. She started talking, but throughout the mayhem I could barely hear anything she said.

The only thing I caught was "Sunshine... sunshine, it's ok. It's ok, my sunshine..."

Within seconds her voice faded away, soon enough she was out of sight. She was gone. I ran to the bathroom and threw up.

Chapter Seventeen

Evacuation Part Two

"It'll only be a couple months," my new sitemate Sarah said in our train car, as we took a final ride through the mountains and foothills of Zakarpattia. As I looked into the distance, trying to appreciate the natural beauty for one last time while also attempting to process the last twenty-four hours, the only response I had was, "Thanks Sarah," when I actually wanted to say, "Yeah fucking right."

Every website I came across said it would take twelve to eighteen months to create a vaccine. No matter how long or how hard I tried looking for a different answer, I couldn't find any solution that would take less than a year. We were going to be in this for the long haul, and the future, one I had planned so meticulously and thoroughly throughout my time in Ukraine, was completely uncertain. The only certainty was the family I was coming back to and my relationship with Alina. Those were the only things I could grasp.

After the initial pain of leaving Alina, about thirty minutes into the train ride I was surprised to find that the whirlwind of emotions from the previous day had died down significantly. As much as I didn't want to leave, the process of evacuating Mukachevo was a storm of shock, distress and anxiety, so a thirteen hour train ride with nothing to do and no where to go was quite welcomed. Additionally, aside from potentially catching Covid, I didn't feel like I was in too much danger. As federal workers I knew that we had the power of the United States Government behind us, so at least we didn't have the stress of organizing a flight back home. Some people out there who may have been on vacation at the time were going to be stuck abroad, but as Peace Corps volunteers we were guaranteed a free ticket back home as soon as possible.

As soon as possible was the key part, because there wasn't much wiggle room to get out of the country. The reason why there was such a rush to make it to Kyiv was because the Ukrainian border would be closing at midnight on Tuesday, March 17th. The plan was to have all volunteers in Kyiv by Sunday the 15th and to fly out the next day. We were cutting it close, but with a plane on Monday at 6:00 pm, we all had faith that we could make it out of Ukraine before Covid got out of control.

Although I was feeling more chilled out, after we got past the mountains the monotonous ride began to bore the crap out of me. I'd rather be bored than terrified, but usually the move is to take the overnight train to Kyiv so that you can sleep through eight hours of it. Taking the train in the middle of the day gave us an entire day of free time, leaving us simply to our thoughts and podcasts after losing our jobs of the past eighteen months. Some other Zakarpattia volunteers gathered in one of the train rooms to chat and tell stories, but I wasn't in any mood for it. I stayed in my bed most of the time, listening to sports podcasts talk about how there weren't any sports anymore.

On three hours of sleep, I didn't rest for one minute on the way to Kyiv.

....

After making it to Kyiv, I wanted to get to my Airbnb as soon as possible, so much so that I left one of my bags on the train. Even after half a day on a train I was still somewhat disoriented, but I was grateful that Daniel caught up and handed me my backpack.

Backpack in hand, I rushed out of the crowded train station, and instead of calling an Uber I took the first cab I could find. You don't have to look too far on the internet to learn that cabs in Kyiv are a complete rip-off, and cost about ten times the amount of an Uber. Yet, my unyielding sense of urgency pushed me to pay a rate for the ridiculous cost in order to leave as fast as possible.

After just a five minute drive we arrived at my Airbnb, which was located on the third floor of some grey geometric soviet looking apartment building. I handed the driver five hundred hryven (twenty dollars) for the ride and got out to prepare for my last night in Ukraine. I made it up to the apartment, which was a total contrast compared to the more brutal aesthetic of the outside. This is rather common in Ukraine: There are tons and tons of Soviet-era apartments that are complete eye sores, but inside more often than not they have gone through a series of renovations and look better than most places you'll find in the States.

My Airbnb was no exception. I was glad to be in a comfortable landing spot, with a room that was close to double the size of my apartment in Mukachevo and heated floors in the bathroom. I quickly called Alina to tell her I made it to Kyiv. Once again, the sound of her voice made me cry, and I could hardly get a sentence out.

"You can cry, Robert. It's ok, you can cry. Everything will be ok, we'll be together soon. However long it takes, remember?"

"I remember," I said, "Thank you."

"You're welcome Robert. I love you. Get some sleep tonight, ok?"

"Ok," I replied, knowing more or less that I was lying to her.

Even amidst all of the heartbreak, terror, and overwhelming loss, I still didn't want to miss out on what was going to be my last chance to hang with my volunteer buddies. I hadn't messaged any of my friends at that point, but I decided that I wasn't going to spend my last night in Ukraine holed up in my airbnb feeling sorry for myself. I wasn't trying to go to a bar or a club at the onset of a pandemic, but if I was going to get on a plane with all these people, I thought it probably wouldn't increase our Covid risk if we hung out together.

I found myself at a kick back with four or five other volunteers, most of whom most weren't in the mood for shenanigans. I heard that there were some other volunteers that were going crazy and doing whatever can be described as the complete opposite of social distancing, but other than that there didn't seem to be too many in a celebratory mood.

I went home around 1:00 am, which would have guaranteed me a full night's sleep, but unlike the night before, I just couldn't get to bed. For the next few hours, I did what anyone does after midnight, which consists of nothing healthy or productive. I spent most of the time doom scrolling through Covid articles and how it was going to ruin everything. I got into a weird and toxic space where I didn't want to read about anything except Covid, and there was no shortage of information, including from the Director of the Peace Corps, Jody Olsen. Close to 5:00 am local time, I saw yet another unimaginable announcement.

Peace Corps announces suspension of Volunteer activities, evacuations due to Covid-19.

At that point only a few countries near Europe and Asia had been evacuated, but right then and there it was official. For the first time in fifty years, there would be no active Peace Corps volunteers. That was just one of many moments which revealed that this virus, this all encompassing virus, was unlike anything anyone alive on earth had ever experienced.

After a few more hours of reading the news and chatting with friends who were awake in the States, I watched the sunrise on the apartment balcony. By then it was 7:00 am, and while walking back into the apartment I caught a glimpse of myself in the mirror. After a night of not sleeping a wink, unsurprisingly I was looking at someone pale, baggy eyed, and drained of energy.

Then, a terrible thought came to my mind.

"You know what you look like?" I said to myself in the mirror, "You look like you're sick. You look like you have Covid."

Cue the panicking. If you have Covid, you can't get out of here. I wish that this was an irrational thought due to sleep deprivation and stress, but unfortunately that possibility wasn't completely off the table. Emails from PC said that there would be fever checks at the airport, and when we asked what would happen if a volunteer had a fever, they told us that they weren't exactly sure. The admin didn't say as much, but it wasn't too hard to jump to the conclusion that if someone had a fever, it wouldn't be possible for them to get on the flight. They would be trapped in the country, while the rest of their colleagues flew safely home.

And there I was at seven in the morning after pulling an all-nighter.

You NEED to get to sleep, I thought. I jumped onto the bed and tried forcing myself to sleep, but my heavy eyes and sporadic nervous system weren't cooperating. After about an hour of falling in and out of a dream, my alarm went off, signaling that I had to pack up and check out. I felt and looked like crap, and I found myself once again in a terrible and completely avoidable situation.

···

I left for the airport about six hours before our flight. I had nothing else to do, and due to the minimal sleep I wasn't really feeling like doing anything else but sulking in the airport. In the Uber on the way there, my driver decided to strike up some conversation.

"Airport's closing tonight, did you know?" he said nonchalantly.

"Yeah, pretty weird," I replied, "I'm actually getting on one of the last flights."

"Yeah? Where are you from?"

"America," I said, not knowing when I'd ever answer that question again.

"America!" He said with excitement. "Let me show you something."

He reached for his phone, and pulled up a video while trying to keep his eyes on the road.

"Watch this."

The other day I heard about how Americans were panic buying, and that toilet paper, hand sanitizer and other goods were nearly impossible to find. Some people were even getting in fights over the last available rolls at Target and Walmart. I proceeded to watch this exemplified in a meme video, where a roll of toilet paper had been photoshopped over a rugby ball, and players with American flags over their head were tackling each other and chasing after it. The caption was something along the lines of America right now. What was the world coming to? What was America coming to?

I did my best to give a fake laugh, but after looking at the driver's disappointed expression, I don't think I convinced him. He pulled his phone away and tried changing the subject.

By the end of the forty minute car ride, he had some kind words while helping me get my bags.

"Don't worry, man," he said, "She will wait. Alina will wait for you!"

"Thanks Danya. Good luck and stay safe."

"Stay safe my friend. I will see you again."

We shook hands and said goodbye. That turned out to be one of the last hands I shook for a long time.

I arrived to a sight of about fifty other volunteers who all had the same idea I did. By that time our flight had already been delayed two hours, but it made no sense to keep bumming around Kyiv with our entire lives packed up in suitcases. I found a seat in the airport lobby far from most of my cohort and chilled out for a while, doing my best to avoid any and all small talk. I didn't want to sit alone, solely because that would signal to some fellow kind hearted volunteers that I needed help, so I made sure to sit near a couple of people who were buried in their phones or staring off into the distance. Other than the fact that all of our lives were being upended at the same time, I didn't think there was much to talk about.

Over the next few hours, more and more volunteers trickled into the empty grey airport, greeted by an itinerary of flights which were all followed by the word "cancelled" written in big red letters. At that moment Danya's words dawned on me, "The airport is closing tonight." Just saying that out-loud, "The airport is closing," sent a chill down my spine. It once again reminded me how Covid was turning the world upside-down. The NBA was cancelled, the airports were shutting down, the stock market was crashing, all of the Peace Corps was evacuated for the first time in it's fifty year history... Life was we knew it was changing in an instant, and in a matter of days, I would be back in America. And then what?

I had spent the past year and a half building up my life in Ukraine, and in a matter of days it would be all gone. My life was being torn down, and in a day or two I would be in my room, staring at my ceiling.

Or so I thought.

By 6:00 pm, most of Peace Corps Ukraine was in the airport, besides one guy who said screw it and decided to stay in Ukraine as a private citizen. We were all spread out through this uninspiring metal post-Soviet space, hoping desperately that we would be back in the States before any one of us caught Covid. Two hundred and fifty Americans tied at the hip and traveling together? Talk about a super spreader.

On top of that only a couple people were wearing masks, and no one bothered to maintain any distance between one another. Our group, along with the rest of the United States, was a little slow to follow the recommended Covid guidelines, and after packing up our entire lives on short notice, the majority of us weren't in the mood to isolate ourselves and stay away from our friends, all of whom we would soon have to indefinitely say goodbye to.

However, as the hours passed, we still hadn't gotten any info on our flight. It began to darken outside, and soon we were merely hours away from the border closing. Cue the nerves and panicking from various volunteers.

"Aren't we supposed to board two hours before the plane?"

"If it's a charter do we even have to go through security?"

"Why was the first flight delayed?"

"Are we going to get our temperature checked?"

"How are we going to get two hundred and fifty people on a flight before midnight?"

Most of the questions were greeted by PC admin with "When we are updated on the situation, you all will be the first to know." I genuinely believed that they themselves had no idea what was going on, but the uncertainty just led to more people pacing, conspiring in groups, and drinking. At that point tons of people were already drunk from overpriced airport beer, but I didn't mind that at all because they were much more tolerable compared to the sober volunteers who were filling the air with anxious and nervous energy. Overall I was happy with my decision to stay the hell away from everyone else, and spent most of the time talking to Alina.

"Robert, why haven't you flown out yet?"

"I don't know. None of us know. We think that the American and Ukrainian governments are negotiating as we speak."

"Shit, Our government is terrible! You might be there for a while, I'm afraid. But tell me Robert, how are you feeling? Are you ok? Are you hungry?"

Thank god I had her as an outlet. Alina constantly reminded me that I would be ok, that we would see each other again, and that she was safe at home with enough food and water to survive a zombie apocalypse. For a twenty-two year old who had every right to shut down and panic, she once again stepped up for me when I needed her most. She not only calmed me down, but helped me avoid a rapidly deteriorating mental health situation amongst our group, which only got worse and worse as time went on.

Things continued to worsen around 9:30 pm, which was a few hours after our delayed flight was supposed to leave. By then it was completely dark outside, and besides our group, the only folks in the airport were and the people who worked there.

Then, all at once, our entire cohort got a text from our safety and security manager.

"Flight delayed. Take off at 11:30 pm. Be ready".

11:30pm, just half an hour before the borders closed.

At this moment, the conspiratorial volunteers began to believe that a flight wasn't coming for us.

"It's not happening," my friend John said after coming to check on me, "It's just not happening."

I didn't believe it, because I thought that those types of ideas were popping up simply due to panic and anxiety. I took the highroad and trusted that the big daddy federal government would swoop in and bring us to safety.

We continued to sulk in the airport, with no official word on what to do next besides just wait. So we waited, and waited, and waited. Soon midnight approached, and we hadn't even started boarding. It was becoming more and more clear that the delays from earlier in the day were foreshadowing a harrowing situation.

So here's the scene: A group of two hundred and fifty people, all whom had just lost their jobs and had to evacuate from their homes of one to three years without saying goodbye, are trapped in an airport. After two delayed flights, many of them are anxious, some of them are crying, and a noticeable amount of them are wasted. This was the set up when we got the news many of us had been dreading.

Right before midnight, Victoria, the Director of Training and number two in Peace Corps Ukraine, gathered us together in the middle of the lobby and finally revealed what many of us had expected:

"It pains me to announce that our flight has been cancelled, and there is no flight coming for us tonight. Stand by for more information."

Chapter Eighteen

Evacuation Part Three

There were a variety of reactions. The people who had been drinking over the past six hours valiantly seemed to take it in stride, while the sober straddlers like myself either cried, lashed out, or shut down entirely. I was too tired to spend any energy on tears or anxiety, which was a small blessing in disguise when I gauged the reactions of some of my colleagues. Despite being indefinitely trapped in a second world country during a worldwide pandemic, somewhat thankfully the only thing I could think of was sleep.

Where will we sleep? Not in the airport, right?

"No, of course not," Victoria said after a flurry of questions, "We are currently looking for places for you all to rest. As you all may know, many hotels have shut down due to the city-wide lockdown, so we're going to have to wait for a while until we find accommodation. You all will be the first ones to know when we find something.

"Additionally, our flight is being rescheduled for tomorrow. But, and listen closely everyone, you need to keep your phone on while you go to bed. We may only get one chance at this, and if we get word in the middle of the night that our plane is coming, we're going to call each and every one of you. Keep that volume on high."

At that point I felt for the admin, who were in the nearly impossible situation of finding accommodation for two hundred and fifty people in the midst of a global lockdown. Many other volunteers, who were crossing their arms and shooting frustrated questions at the admin, seemed to be missing the volunteer spirit, but during such a shit-show I'm not going to blame anyone for how they reacted. We all just wanted to get the hell out of there, but that was far from happening.

After another hour of volunteers either drinking, crying, complaining, or staring into the distance like me, we received the welcomed news that the admin had managed to book us every possible room at the airport hotel, which was one of the only hotels still operating in Kyiv. En masse, we walked over, wishing this nightmare would end but realizing that it had only just begun.

"Don't get too comfortable," another one of the administrators told us at the hotel, "This hotel is shutting down tomorrow in the afternoon. If our flight gets cancelled again, we'll need to find another place to stay."

I couldn't care less. It was 2:00 in the morning, I was on an hour of sleep, and to cap it all off, I was in the back of the goddamn check-in line.

I started muttering under my breath. The muttering quickly got louder, although I wasn't talking to anyone in particular. I could feel a scream coming up from my stomach, ready to announce that I was through with this entire process and wanted everyone to know about it. All the energy I had saved in the airport was used up, yet my tired eyes and still operating body once again weren't cooperating. I was ready to lose it.

A few moments before breaking down, one of my buds John noticed my chagrin, and let me cut him in line.

Thank you John.

Right before 2:30 I entered my hotel room and took a glance at the small bed and the even smaller living space. It looked like a paradise. My stiff twin bed couldn't have felt more comfortable, and I had no issues with the rock-like pillow I found under my head. I turned my phone volume all the way up, and unlike the majority of the other volunteers, I said a small prayer that I wouldn't be woken up in the middle of the night and that we wouldn't be flying in the next seven hours.

To the pain of many volunteers but to my absolute pleasure, I woke up at 10:00 am with no updates on the flight. I hated the uncertainty of our situation, but if I was going to get through whatever catastrophe would be waiting for us the next day, I needed enough sleep to do it.

Ironically enough, after getting a good night of rest, I finally had enough energy to begin processing and subsequently freaking out about my current dilemma. After transitioning out of survival mode the night before, intrusive thoughts started to roll through, and I began to accurately assess how bad of a situation I was in.

The border is closed. We need to get out of here. Every minute here increases the chance of getting this virus. We need to get out of here.

In the middle of my first downward mental spiral of the day, Alina called me.

"Any updates?" She asked.

"Not yet. We don't know anything."

"Dang. How are you feeling?"

"I'm feeling better than yesterday."

"That's good. I love you. Call me when you have some updates, ok?"

"Ok. Love you too."

Sticking with my strategy in the airport, I stayed as far away as I could from other volunteers. I found a few packets of instant coffee on the desk, along with a couple of small water bottles. After mixing the coffee in the lukewarm water, I chugged it, and soon started to feel a little bit better about things.

After making sure to pocket the rest of the instant coffee, I checked my phone around 11:00 am. Still no update. At that point I decided to give up any sense of control that I thought I had and succumbed to the fact that worrying about this situation would only make my life worse. At the same time, unfortunately any form of letting go was stifled by those words from the admin the night before. *Don't get too comfortable...hotel shutting down tomorrow...YOU ARE SCREWED, BOB!*

He didn't say that last part, but he may as well have. We either had to find a flight during a time when no one was allowed to go in or out of Ukraine, or find a new hotel that could accommodate hundreds of people with no notice.

I can't take any more movement. Not after the past two days.

Meditation and deep breathing was no match for my covid-anxiety, and almost as quickly as I started the deep-breathing exercises, I let go of letting go and began to panic again. Thankfully I was saved again, this time from a knock on the door, where John was waiting with a clipboard in his hand.

"Hey man," he said while leaning on the doorframe, "Victoria said for everyone to meet in the lobby."

"Oh yeah? For what?"

"Not sure. Just don't forget your key. You get any sleep?"

"Yeah, I did. Thanks for letting me cut you in line."

"Don't sweat it bud. I got a bigger room anyway."

With a wink he left and went on knocking on more doors down the hallway. I guess he was the messenger for whatever atom-bomb Victoria was about to drop on us.

I made my way to the lobby, where a group of volunteers had already gathered. Everyone was dealing with this uncertain and terrifying situation in their own way, but even while sympathizing I still intended on avoiding ninety-five percent of the Americans I was stuck with. I wasn't necessarily trying to avoid them due to Covid. It was just... let's just say that there wasn't a lot of positive energy going on.

When enough volunteers gathered in the lobby, Victoria dropped the hammer.

"Hi everyone, I just want to update you all on the situation. Our flight that was supposed to leave tonight has also been cancelled, and we currently do not have a flight on the way. We are working with the Ukrainian Embassy and negotiating a way to get you all safely back home as soon as possible."

Daaaang.

"This hotel, as you all know, is closing today. We are looking for another hotel in Kyiv where we will transport everyone. We are still waiting for the go ahead, but we are going to need everyone to stay alert, keep those phones on, and to be ready to go when we-"

At that point I left. I went back to my room, laid down on the bed, and that's when anxiety took over once again, this time to all new heights.

You're never getting out of here. You're going to get Covid. Everyone is isolating in America right now, but you're traveling in a massive group of two-hundred people. You were just in an airport. You were just on a train. You were just in a lobby with all of them. You're going to get Covid, and you're going to die.

It felt like a good time to call Alina.

"Robert, what is going on?"

"Our flight was cancelled again," I said lifelessly, "We don't know when we are going to leave, and our hotel is closing."

"I fucking hate our government."

"I don't know if it's your government's-

"No Robert, it's our government. Our government is such a joke I just hate those guys."

After a quick tirade against her government that I couldn't understand, she said the words that in that very moment I so desperately needed to hear.

"Robert, you're going to be ok. You know you're going to be ok, right? You have no idea how strong your immune system is. I've never seen someone as healthy as you, I mean you haven't gotten sick all winter. I've gotten sick like five times, and you were around me and didn't get sick. You go outside without a hat on all the time, and you run in the rain. You are very strong, and I've been reading that younger people who get covid are asymptomatic, asymptomatic, that means without symptoms. You're going to be fine. Just listen to your football podcast, ok?"

Thank god I understand Ukrainian, because no American in the group of volunteers was level headed enough to calm me down.

"Ok. Thank you. I love you."

"I love you too. Try not to think too much. Listen to that podcast - It'll make things better. Call me if there's another update, ok?"

What an incredible person, who months later revealed that at the time she was just as scared as I was. I'll remember that moment as one of the most important conversations I had in my life. Thank you, Alina.

I proceeded to do what she said and turned on my football podcast. I was shocked to hear that DeAndre Hopkins had been traded to the Cardinals, and not even for a first round pick. Stefon Diggs had also been traded, which would have been a huge story if not for the DeAndre Hopkins trade.

Now this Diggs trade is just an afterthought. I wonder if he will work well in Buffalo...

As I listened to some football jabber, the fight or flight panic response that had been firing on and off for the past couple of days simmered down, and for that hour the world felt completely normal. By the time the podcast concluded I was completely at ease, and once again understood that I would probably be fine and I would definitely make it home. We just didn't know when.

The answer didn't come for a while. For the next three hours I continued to wait in my room, listening to more podcasts about more things that weren't important.

Later that day I heard another knock on my door. It wasn't John this time.

"We're having another meeting outside of the hotel," Not John said.

I left my room again, this time having showered, and went outside to learn the game plan. By the time I got outside pretty much the entire cohort was already there, this time spread out a little more than we were in the airport. I think at that point more and more volunteers were trying to stay a little further away from each other, finally coming around to the idea of not wanting to create a Covid outbreak before our flight home.

A few seconds after I found a metal bench without a backrest, Victoria hit us with the news.

"We still don't have any word on the flight, but we have found accommodation!"

Everyone cheered. It was our first victory since the process began.

"We are going to be staying at the Stert Hotel in Kyiv tonight. They are making an exception and opening for us and us alone. We will be there indefinitely until we get word on what to do next." Our group was looking for any sort of stability, so while many of us were bummed that our flight was still suspended, I was thankful just because we had a place to sleep that night.

"Also," Victoria said, "This is where I usually stay in Kyiv, and this is where the ambassadors stay as well. I think you all are going to enjoy it."

Finally, the federal government coming in clutch.

For the second time in as many days, we grouped up and journeyed to our next hotel, hoping desperately it would be our last.

Once we arrived, the idea of being stranded in Kyiv in the middle of a pandemic didn't seem like such a bad time. The Peace Corps booked us what had to be the most expensive hotel in Ukraine, and I was excited to learn that I would have a queen-sized bed all to myself on the twelfth floor. After a long bus ride I made it up to my room, got settled in, and finally started to relax. One of the walls was a huge window, which gave me a great view of the beige and subpar Kyiv skyline. I became engulfed in my incredibly comfortable bed, and right then and there I decided I wouldn't do anything else to risk my health or emotional state like I had done after staying up all night. I made a point to do everything I could to put myself in the best position possible to make it out of Ukraine without many complications.

That inclination subsided later that night, when my friend Sophia invited me over to drink. After quickly rationalizing this decision by telling myself that I might never see these people again, I made my way over to Sophia's, where a few people had gathered.

That night, while switching between some old school rap and EDM, we got the notification we had been waiting for for the past two days: Our plane was finally coming. We would touch down in Jordan before taking off for the States.

"FINALLY!" I cheered, and took a celebratory sip of my drink.

"I don't know about this one," one of the fellow degenerates said, "I'll believe it when I see it."

Well, I was believing it. I was way more overjoyed than my colleagues, because being naive, I still trusted any of the information that was being given in such an uncertain time. I texted my mom and dad, saying that I was finally on my way home. They were also overjoyed, and my dad, who was celebrating his 60th birthday, said it was the best birthday present he could've asked for.

Unsurprisingly, my judgement turned out to be foolish, because less than two hours later we got an email saying that our flight was cancelled after the Jordanian government bailed at the last minute. We were devastated, no one more than myself, as I had to once again tell my parents that we weren't leaving just yet. Would we ever make it out of there?

This exact situation repeated itself over the next couple of days, minus the drinking. Night after night, we got the same email that a plane was finally coming. Night after night, I went against my better judgement and told my parents. And, without fail, night after night we would later get another email telling us that our flight was cancelled.

All in all, we spent four nights in the hotel. I drank with my friends twice, and proceeded to regret it each morning, wondering if I had screwed up my immune defenses against a virus that had already killed thousands of people around the world. To be fair, only drinking twice was one of the tamer reactions compared to my more party-friendly peers: On our fifth day of purgatory, as I walked to a grocery store I saw a group of about five or six of my friends hanging out in a public plaza, surrounded by fifths of vodka. They were loud and stumbling around, basically announcing to the whole world that yes, we are publicly wasted. While I thought it was a bit dumb to be publicly drunk in the middle of a hard lockdown, I couldn't judge, seeing as I was the one who blacked out during orientation and tossed all my valuables around the Irpin Conference Hall.

A little while later I heard that the group had almost been arrested. Getting arrested in Ukraine during the first week of lockdown was nightmare material, and would've been even worse because that was the day we finally got a flight home.

Yes, a plane finally came. We didn't spend the rest of our lives rotting in Kyiv, although by the fifth day it sure as hell felt like it. I for one hadn't given up hope, but had stopped believing anything I was told about our departure. Ironically enough, when we finally got the actual email of our departure, I read it and didn't give it a second thought.

I'll believe it when we're on the bus.

However, I started to really believe we'd make it out of there after a subsequent email from our safety and security director struck a slightly more confident tone:

LET'S GO!!

Our aircraft is in the air, let's start moving!!

Over the span of an hour, hundreds of us came down to the lobby, where we saw about five or six buses. It was around 10:00 pm, so we were surely going to be staying up for a while, but at that point I just didn't care. None of us cared. All we cared about was that we were finally getting the hell out of Ukraine.

Thus started the most appreciated yet depressing bus ride any of us had ever been on. There we were, taking a look at Kyiv for the last time, not knowing if we would ever make it back. It was hard to think of anything that could have made the bus ride any worse.

Then came the bus driver. While driving a group of Americans to the airport in the middle of a world wide lockdown, he had the bright idea to GIVE A TOUR OF KYIV. He began talking over the loudspeaker and started to give a tour of a city that we were hastily leaving, and one that some of us for sure would never see again.

"And on your left you'll see Podil, one of the most popular places in Kyiv. It is so beautiful, a must see in my eyes. If you go there you'll be able to find really great coffee shops, delicious hot wine, and a free tour the city."

It soon became clear he was one of those "funny tour guide" types, cracking jokes to the toughest audience imaginable. I initially felt bad for the guy, but his lack of situational awareness stifled any and all sympathy. I mean, even if he didn't know we were being evacuated, why would he be giving a tour while driving to the airport? After looking around and noticing the general disdain of my colleagues, I spoke up because I couldn't concentrate on my podcast.

"Excuse me," I yelled from the back, "A lot of us are having the worst day of our lives. Could you stop giving us a tour?"

"What?"

"STOP TALKING, WE ARE TIRED."

"Oh, ok," the guide weakly replied. At that moment I felt bad, but all of us were completely spent. We were ready to get all this over with, but even after a week of purgatory our trip hadn't even really gotten started. While arriving at the airport, we realized it was only just beginning.

For the second time in a week, two hundred and fifty of us packed ourselves in the lobby of the Kyiv airport. There were a few other people besides volunteers there, so unlike our hotel I doubt the airport stayed open just for us. However, after the U.S. Embassy negotiated with the Ukrainian Embassy for five days to find a way to get us back home, that wasn't out of the realm of possibility.

We got in three separate lines in order to get our boarding passes. For the 40th time I checked to make sure that I had my passport, and after assuring myself once again, I started another podcast.

After forty-five minutes the podcast ended, and I hadn't moved an inch. I started another one. After another forty minutes, we still hadn't moved. What was going on?

"Hello everyone," the woman at the check in desk announced, "Our machines aren't working, and we have called in IT to come take a look. It is going to cause a delay, but we are working on it as quickly as possible."

Amazing. I put on another podcast. After a few futile attempts from the IT department, the people at the check in desk had no other choice but to print out 300 blank boarding passes and write them from scratch. Unbelievable - after standing inline for two hours, this was bound to at least take another sixty minutes.

I left my bags in the middle of the line and took a seat as far away from the other volunteers as I could. By now it was about 2:00 am, and being around yet another group of sleep deprived and sulking volunteers in the airport became extremely trying. I bought a coffee and listened to another podcast, and after a while one of my Zakarpattian volunteer friends, Jamiece, came up to me. She had the look of a tired shock on her face.

"What's the matter?" I asked her.

"We just got an email," she said while staring at nothing in particular, "The Peace Corps just COS'd (closure of service) all of us. Our service is over. We are Returned Peace Corps Volunteers now."

My mind went back to our country director's email during my last night in Mukachevo, when he said that we were all coming back.

"Um, didn't we get an email last week saying the exact opposite?"

"Yeah," she replied, "But now it's changed. We're done with the Peace Corps.

After reading that email the week before, I committed to staying with Alina and returning with PC. Now we were getting COS'd? What would that mean for me and Alina?

Luckily, I was once again too tired and emotionally exhausted to react to the news. We had a long trip ahead of us, and I was subconsciously saving up as much energy as I could to get through it all.

I got my hand written boarding pass around 2:45 in the morning. Our flight would be connecting in Madrid, which at the time was home to one of the biggest outbreaks of Covid in the world. Did that stop our massive group from congregating extremely close together? Absolutely not. At least by that point we were wearing masks, but still, if someone had Covid in our group, many many more people were going to get it.

However, I tried not to think about that. I simply tried to focus on getting home and laying down in my bed, a bed that I went from dreading to begging for within the course of a week.

After getting my boarding pass, I took my stuff and headed towards security, where PC admin was waiting for us to say goodbye.

"We can't go any farther than here," Victoria said as I headed to security, "But thank you for your service and for everything you've done."

"Thank you Victoria, goodbye."

I haven't seen any of them since. I was too tired to properly thank them, so I'll do it here: Thank you all for getting us out of there. Thank you all for finding us hotels and for working day and night to find us a flight home. Thank you for being great leaders during my entire PC experience. Thank you for everything.

I made it through the quickest airport security of my life, and by 3:00 am I was finally at the final checkpoint. All I could see were various volunteers, who like me were sprawled out on benches ready to go to sleep. The empty terminal was almost completely quiet, and the posters with Eastern European flight attendants advertising holiday getaways felt straight out of an apocalyptic novel.

I found a set of chairs to lay down on, and one last time opened my bag to make sure I hadn't forgotten anything, especially Flipper, a stuffed animal I had bought for Alina a few months earlier.

"Take him with you," she said while packing in Mukachevo, "I think he'd appreciate seeing America."

I rummaged around my backpack, and thankfully Flipper hadn't run away. I tried falling asleep, but my hard metal bed wasn't doing me any favors. I spent an hour laying there with my jacket over my eyes, too tired to think about anything, until I heard a boarding call for Spain. I got up, grabbed my stuff, and before I left Ukraine indefinitely, I made sure I got a picture I could send to Alina, showing her that I was ok and everything had gone on according to plan. She would wake up in a few hours to the news.

We were finally making it out.

We made it to Spain, then waited (again) for a few hours for our flight back to America. The only significant thing to come from our time there was that we learned we would have our temperature checked before getting on the flight. While boarding once more, everyone got checked before finally walking down the hallway to America. Thank you Rachel, for that ibuprofen, because without it I may have stressed my way into a fever. Luckily I got on the flight, and was finally on my way back home just one week after packing up everything and leaving Mukachevo.

An hour into the flight my buddy Lucas found out that the charter was serving alcohol. Over the next two hours, our group of volunteers proceeded to drink every drop of beer and wine that plane had to offer. At a certain point Lucas went to get more beer, but there was literally none left when he asked for more. Frankly, I'm surprised our cabin, which consisted of hoards of young adults who had developed unhealthy drinking habits over two years of isolation, didn't finish off the booze sooner, and in hindsight I'm even more surprised that we only started drinking after a couple hours had passed. At one point, things started to get a little rowdy, which was followed by the pilot putting the fasten seatbelt sign on due to "turbulence." There wasn't a lick of turbulence.

After touching down and getting our bags, we all took a shuttle to the DC airport, and many of us began drinking in the hotel lobby. The flight attendants, who were also staying in the airport, passed us by while walking to their rooms and couldn't believe what they were seeing.

"Seriously, more alcohol?" One of them said in a beautiful Spanish accent. After what we had been through? You bet.

The next day I got up at 6:00 am. A van took me and a few other volunteers back to the airport, where I had a flight back to Nashville at nine in the morning. Compared to what our COS celebration would have been, my final send off was saying goodbye to a few tired and traumatized volunteers in an airport lobby, none of whom I knew that well. That was my send off after eighteen months of service in the Peace Corps.

After the week I just had, it was hard to care too much. At that point I was just trying to get home.

After my flight home was delayed by two hours, I finally touched down in the Nashville airport eight days after leaving Alina in Mukachevo, still not quite able to believe what had really just happened.

Chapter Nineteen

Not in the Swing of Things

It's March 2020, and I am not in a groove. In an instant, everything that I built up over the past year and a half had crumbled around me.

So many returning Peace Corps volunteers are greeted by celebrating friends and family, but during this twisted reunion I didn't even have the luxury of hugging my loved ones. When my father picked me up at the Nashville airport we gave each other elbow bumps and headed home with the windows down. We drove through a mostly deserted Nashville, drifting through downtown without seeing as much as a single business open, besides some grocery stores. I didn't know what to expect coming back from my stint in Ukraine, but this was far from what I imagined my post-Peace Corps homecoming would be.

We drove up to my stepmother's house in suburban Nashville where I would be staying in a room I had never slept in before. I was quarantining in my stepsisters' room because my brother was recovering from surgery at my mom's house. I came to this decision in the second hotel in Kyiv, and deciding to quarantine at my stepmother's was just the first of hundreds of carefully (and not so carefully) calculated Covid decisions that we all had to make over the course of the pandemic.

As for my stepsister, she was going through a Covid nightmare of her own in Spain. She was living there and also teaching English, but without the federal government to swoop in and airmail her home, she was stuck in Madrid during one of the biggest surges to date. While I laid in her bed, ready to be taken care of by the adults in the room, she was teaching English in her cramped Madrid apartment and not allowed to go outside. Yet another situation that my dad and stepmom had absolutely no control over. They just had to wait.

I also had to wait. As I stepped into my stepsister's room, my two-week quarantine had officially begun. At that point, after being in multiple hotels, airports and flights with hundreds of people who weren't socially distanced, I was almost certain that I had Covid. While I felt perfectly fine, I assumed there was no possible way that I could've gone through the week I just had and not be infected. All I could do now was wait two weeks and hope to not wake up to a cough or fever. I tried not to think about it too much, and did my best to be grateful that I was back home after multiple cancelled flights.

After a week of moving from hotel to hotel and airport to airport, laying down in that bed was finally a long-term moment of stillness and stability. I finally had the space and time to think about what the hell just happened to me and some of my closest friends, and all I could think about was how much I lost. After a year and a half of building up a life in a foreign country, and going through mountains of work just to feel confident and comfortable with the language and my duties at school, it was all gone within a week. I learned the cruel lesson that no matter how long it takes to create something, it can be destroyed within minutes. I had gone from an impeccable situation, filled with fulfilling work, a loving girlfriend, and endless future opportunities to being holed up in a strange room with no professional prospects, all while beginning a long-distance relationship in the midst of the deadliest pandemic in over one hundred years.

I soon began to cry. My father brought me pizza and a diet coke. I felt a little better.

Relatively speaking it was a decent spot to be in, compared to some of the suffering that many other people were going through all over the world. Not to mention that I'm sure there were countless volunteers who didn't have such a safety net to fly back to, some of whom sold their cars and even their houses before heading off to service. I was extraordinarily grateful for my family being there for me at the time when I needed them most, and I tried to not let them forget it.

After doing the mandatory "Well, it's not all bad" thought exercise, I went right back into the darkness. Compared to where I was just a month before, as I watched my girlfriend receive her master's degree before Valentine's day, my current situation of staring at the blank white ceiling thousands of miles away was nothing short of a nightmare. I found no shortage of sources to catalyze a sense of misery and depression during my first few nights and weeks back in Nashville. Whether it was being lovesick, fearing getting sick, missing my students, or losing future opportunities in the field of international human rights, I was never short of a sense of loss.

The only sense of joy in my life came from my daily phone calls with Alina. She, like me, was back at her parents' house, but unlike me she had more than enough to do. Before getting her master's in law she realized that she hated law, and had begun freelancing as a social media marketer for a few different department stores in Ukraine and Russia. While many of her classmates got burned by graduating one month before a worldwide lockdown, Alina was clever enough to have online work already lined up before graduation. Her work continued on as normal, and the only big change in her life was that her boyfriend was thousands of miles away and she wouldn't be hanging out with him anymore.

While she was much busier than I was, her flexible schedule and my complete lack of anything at all gave us the opportunity to talk multiple times a day.

"However long it takes," Alina would always say to me at some point during our hour-long conversations, "I will wait for you. However long it takes."

"Of course, of course. However long it takes. How's the food situation?" I would blurt this question out every other day or so. I still wasn't sure how the food supply chain in Ukraine was going to be affected by Covid, but after seeing pictures on Facebook about the empty shelves at Walmarts in the United States, I was fearing for the worse in a much less developed country. I thought back, trying to make sure if I gave Alina all of the pasta and buckwheat I had stored up before getting evacuated, but even that would only last them a week. During the first few weeks of lockdown my anxiety for her general safety and well being was extremely high.

She always laughed at this question, and repeated what she told me in Mukachevo.

"Robert," she would say, "I live on a farm. Farms have a lot of food. We also have chickens, although they are quite stupid. Just don't worry, Robert. We are going to be just fine."

She was my only sense of hope, of something to look forward to, during the darkest days of my lifetime. Throughout quarantine and the subsequent months back in the States, we managed to talk every single day, whether it was a few minutes or a few hours. I didn't know if I would ever return to the Peace Corps, or to REENA, or to any of my students, but I believed that as long as Alina and I stayed together, there would be a way for me to return to the only current source of happiness in my life at the time.

When I wasn't thinking about Alina, my mind often drifted back to other parts of Ukraine, and all that I had left there. I missed my students, most of whom I didn't get a chance to say goodbye to. It pained me that I didn't have one last day with all of them, to explain what was happening and why I was leaving. In their eyes, one day I was there, giving them candy for completing all the tasks of a pho-to-scavenger hunt, and the next day I was gone. It hurt to think I'd never be working in that school again, and any sort of closure would be postponed at best but would most likely be impossible.

Sometimes I thought about Mukachevo, and how lucky I had been to spend so much time in such a nice town. I especially missed the mountains in the back-drop whenever I needed to get some groceries, and walking through the cobble-stone center on my usual route to go second hand shopping. I yearned to go back to my simple routine, as I'm sure everyone else in the world did too. We were all going through a similar experience of reminiscing the times when we could go wherever we wanted and do whatever we wanted without needing to think too much about life and death.

I also missed the "against the grain" lifestyle I had come to love after a year and a half in Ukraine. For my first six months I was overwhelmed by it all, not understanding the language, customs, or even how to use public transportation or ask for a cup of coffee. However after nineteen months, I finally felt like I was winning Peace Corps. I was speaking Ukrainian on a regular basis, crushing it at my school, and was busy with friends or Alina every weekend. Things had really come together, and just a few months later would've been a final summer with my veteran and grizzled cohort, with nothing to do but celebrate and squeeze every last experience that Ukraine had to offer.

Oh yeah, I lost a ton of friends. We were supposed to have a COS (closure of service) conference in July, about a month or two before the non-extending volunteers were supposed to finish their service. COS is a week-long conference where volunteers essentially do a victory lap, and celebrate getting through the toughest job they'll ever love. Instead, my final memories with my fellow volunteers were a week-long evacuation process, which ended with us saying goodbye in the DC hotel lobby at six in the morning before one of the hotel vans took us to the airport. That was our COS conference.

To be fair, in a sense everyone had lost a bunch of friends. We were all holed up in our homes, waiting the first two weeks to see if any Covid symptoms bubbled to the surface, and then afterwards waiting indefinitely for something different than our current reality. A vaccine wouldn't be coming for at least the next year, if at all. It's easy to forget that the possibility of a vaccine not being possible was in the forefront of our minds during this time. Thankfully they came around (and at a rapid pace at that), but in the months leading up to their approval there was a heavy uncertainty about this potential silver bullet, which was the only way of making our lives go back to normal.

Normal. How normal everything had been on March 8th, International Women's Day, a national holiday in Ukraine. I woke up at Alina's apartment, fixed us breakfast, then walked past droves of people through the city center to meet some of my Zakarpattian volunteer friends. It was a bright spring day, unusually warm for early March in Ukraine, as hoards of people were slowly strolling along the riverside. How normal everything was, and how long it would be for us to ever capture that again.

Other than going through these bittersweet memories, I had absolutely nothing to do. The first week of this wasn't a problem at all, because I was busy putting the pieces of the past few weeks together and trying my best to let everything sink in in order to fully grasp what happened. However, by the end of my quarantine I started to get a little antsy. I was lucky to be cleared of Covid, although there weren't enough tests to 100% confirm that, but as I returned to my mom's house, I was more than ready to have something/anything to do in order to keep my mind off of evacuation.

I began to look online for a job to hold me over until I could finally make it back to Ukraine. I didn't have much luck. The unemployment rate had ballooned to almost fifteen percent, and my specific qualifications of "I can teach English, I'm intermediate at Ukrainian, and I don't know how long I'm actually going to be staying in America," were less than enticing to the one or two employers that I actually got in contact with. I also didn't want to find a part time job in a grocery store or something like that, out of fear of giving my family Covid.

After realizing this conundrum during my second week of quarantine, I felt trapped, frustrated, and defeated. That's when my dad said the obvious.

"Bob, why don't you go back to online teaching?"

I groaned. "I really don't like teaching online. It just feels like a joke."

"Just give it a try. It's probably your only option."

"I just wish there was something different."

"Well," he said, "It might be better for you than doing nothing, especially if you're waiting for the Peace Corps to come back."

He was right, but that didn't make me like Cambly any better.

I started with Cambly, a low-effort online English teaching company, in September of 2019. I heard about Cambly from a fellow volunteer who, like me, was a degenerate and usually low on funds due to a few too many trips to Lviv. September was about a month into my relationship, and I quickly realized that having a girlfriend on a crummy Peace Corps salary is a good way to not have a girlfriend. I sent in an application to start working with Cambly, and within days I was approved.

With Cambly the deal is that you sign up for hours, and during your allotted hour you wait around for people to call you. You are basically on call, and if someone sees your profile and thinks you're interesting, they give you a ring. And then you talk with a stranger for however long they want to. The call can be five minutes or over an hour, and the pay is seventeen cents a minute. Cambly is advertised for students who want to practice their conversation skills with a native English teacher, so there is absolutely no prep or anything of that nature. I just had to wait around for someone to call me and then talk to them.

Cambly was, in the strongest possible manner, purely a BS side gig that gave me just enough money so I didn't have to ask my mom to pay for my dates. I really hated the process of waiting on pins and needles for the Pavlovian Cambly ringtone, only to talk to someone who might not know any English in the slightest, but before Covid it was a means to an end.

Now it was the end in itself. What used to be my side gig of all side gigs by March 2020 turned into my only real option as long as I intended on making it back to Ukraine. This side hustle afterthought paying ten dollars and twenty cents per hour of talk time had now become my primary and only form of income.

So much for an internship with the U.N.

The cherry on top was that I had to use a fake name. Cambly recommended using an alias, so that students couldn't, I don't know, find you on social media? I tried Bob and Robert anyway but they were already taken, so I ended up choosing "Brendon."

Every time I had a lesson, I started off a new teacher-student relationship with a lie.

"Hello, I am Brendon."

"Hello, I am Sergio. How are you, Brendon?"

Then, another lie.

251

"I am good."

My name is Brendon and I am good - these were my two most consistent lies of 2020.

With Cambly as my only available option, throughout my time back home I was desperate for any sort of update from the Peace Corps. I had every intention of returning to Ukraine, and I would often remind myself what our our country director said in that email on my last day in Mukachevo:

"Everyone has the option to return if they want to, we will make sure of that."

Reading that email and getting the possibility to return was the last joyful moment I shared with Alina, and it was my last piece of hope of being able to return to the life I worked so hard to obtain.

In the first couple of weeks after evacuation there were numerous Peace Corps Ukraine-sponsored zoom meetings, all of which I attended in order to get any sort of information on our possible return. So many of us initially thought that Covid was only going to last a few months, and while I was less optimistic than my sitemate about our return date, I was hoping that we would be able to make it back by the time we had flattened the curve and squashed Covid by the summer.

I woke up from that pipe dream in early April, not even a month after evacuation. We received an email on April 9th from Jody Olsen, the Peace Corps director, with news I should have known but didn't want to believe.

Since the pandemic is in its early stages in much of the world, there is a lack of specific information to adequately predict when it will be safe for Volunteers to return to the field. Under current conditions, in which health and safety circumstances change daily, we currently assess it is unlikely that we would be able to place Volunteers in the countries of service before September 30, 2020. However, we will continue to reevaluate the situation on a country-by-country basis, with the aim of returning Volunteers to service as quickly as possible.

"September 2020," I said to myself, "Six months from now." I knew that it would take a long time to get back, but after getting an actual number, my heart sank.

Six more months of waiting for the Peace Corps to come back. Six months of long distance. Six months away from Alina, without a job, living at my mom's house.

Just when I thought that I'd turned a corner, this email sent me into the shadow realm. I knew that it would take a while to get back, but seeing that the earliest possible return date would be longer than my entire relationship with Alina, the hopelessness, loneliness and despair immediately returned to the pit of my stomach. I was close to an all time low, and staring into the barrel of six more months minimum of joblessness and long distance glued me to my bed for the next few days.

The piles of government cash helped. One of the benefits of doing Peace Corps, aside from the character building that they talk about in the movies, is that for every month served, PC puts around $325 into a savings account that we can only access after completion of service. I had earned close to $6000 by the time evacuation rolled around, but PC did us all a solid by paying us the full two year readjustment allowance.

Additionally, all volunteers earned a $1500 evacuation stipend, basically saying, "Hey, sorry about that whole potentially life threatening week-long evacuation... here's some cash." Within my first two weeks of returning I had $11,000 dollars in my bank account, which was the most money I had ever seen in my bank account in my life. The only cost was getting evacuated!

Additionally, while PC volunteers typically are not eligible for unemployment, a provision was put in the CARES act to make an exception during Covid. I applied in May for benefits, however, I didn't put too much hope into the process. I had heard horror stories of people calling the unemployment office fifty plus times before getting through to them. I still made sure to file every week, and sure enough four months after I first filed I received a lump sum close to $8,000 in my bank account. Overall, the cost of evacuation was about $19,000 dollars, and while no amount of money could bring me back to the life I still spent hours every week daydreaming about, money is money, and the piles of government cash boosted morale.

And then, for the next three months, I pretty much did the same thing everyday. I'd wake up, call Alina, and talk to her for about an hour. After hearing about her day, I would start mine, which consisted of a combination of working out, reading the news, journaling, doing a few hours on Cambly, watching youtube, going on a walk, and then finally getting bored. By then it was usually only 4 or 5 o'clock, and I still had another six or seven hours to kill. There's only so many hobbies, both productive and unproductive, that someone can do before they just run out of stuff to do. I would then spend the next few hours browsing the internet, drinking with my mom after work, and playing video games.

The loss of purpose and sense of worthlessness that I managed to get past by my second year in Ukraine had roared back stronger than ever. There was all the pressure in the world to start a new side hustle or to learn a new skill, seeing as most of us would never have this much time for the rest of our lives, but the collective trauma of waking up everyday to a gargantuan and slow moving nightmare wasn't exactly the best atmosphere for cultivating new passions. I started writing this book in February of 2020, thinking it would be a fun idea to jot down some fun and educational stories about Ukraine and my Peace Corps experience, but after getting evacuated I could barely think about my Ukraine experience without tearing up, let alone write about it.

I didn't feel any spark, creatively or otherwise, but at that moment in time, any sort of spark or excitement for life seemed like nothing but a luxury during such a dark and terrible period in the world. I was satisfied enough to find any sort of routine while waiting to return to Ukraine, so I wasn't exactly kicking myself for not taking advantage of all of my free time that I would never get back again.

Before this period I had never experienced long term depression before. Even during the hardest days of isolation in the Peace Corps, there was always something that made me excited and joyful about the future. There was always something that motivated me to work hard or at least get out of bed the next morning.

However, as the days blended together, and I was confined in the same cramped room every morning, afternoon, and evening, it was hard to see the point of doing anything. Even with Alina supporting me and helping me get through these emotions, I still felt like I lost something in March that I didn't know I'd ever get back. I lost some sort of excitement, a spark, or pointless optimism. Whatever it was, I always had it before Covid, even during my saddest moments and my biggest failures, but now it was nowhere to be found. I was in uncharted waters, and slowly being eaten away from the inside.

Thank god the borders reopened.

On June 15th, exactly three months after I left Alina at the Mukachevo train station, I got the news that instantly brought back all of those feelings I thought might never return. Joanna, another volunteer from my cohort who was in the exact same lovestruck situation I was in, messaged me right after a pretty decent Cambly lesson with a Japanese woman who was preparing for a job interview.

"Yo!!!" she wrote after sending me an article, "Check this out!"

Cabinet of Ministers Allows Foreigners to Enter Ukraine.

I couldn't believe it. The border was opening in June? What kind of sense did that make? We were still in the middle of the apocalypse, right? I put the over under at getting back to Ukraine by March of 2021, but in the thick of Covid hell, here was Ukraine opening back up for anyone who wanted to swing by.

While laying in my bed that June morning, staring at the same white walls that I had been confined to for the previous three months, I felt a confusion mixture of elation and bewilderment. I had no idea why Ukraine was allowing foreigners to enter the country during a pandemic, especially considering its lack of medical infrastructure, but after a few minutes I deduced it was due to of economic concerns. Ukraine, one of the poorest countries in Europe, may have been desperate for any sort of revenue that would come from an influx of tourists. Sure the United States could whip up a three trillion dollar rescue plan in a matter of weeks, but Ukraine and so many countries throughout the world didn't have that luxury.

I counted myself incredibly lucky, and I only felt slightly guilty that my luck came due to poor economic conditions. I was even more lucky that Ukraine was able to open up at all, because the vast majority of Europe was under a hard lockdown and it was virtually impossible for foreigners to enter the EU.

Throughout the course of 2020 and 2021, the EU had extremely strict border policies and almost all Americans were banned from entering EU countries. I remember reading a few articles about couples who were apart for the better part of a year because one of the partners was visiting their home outside of the EU in March 2020 and now couldn't return. If Ukraine had been in the EU, similarly I wouldn't have had any chance at all of seeing Alina for foreseeable future. Getting back to Ukraine would have been a hopeless endeavor, and I would have either needed to wait for an unguaranteed vaccine in order to get back to her, or break up and move on with my life.

However, as you might expect, Ukraine is light years away from EU membership, so I was never faced with that horrible decision. Ukraine had the ability to make its own rules about who could cross their border, and in June gave the full green light to all foreigners.

I began to laugh at the irony of the situation.

Ukrainians have wanted to be in the EU for decades, but a whole host of problems, many of which mainly stem from the massive amount of corruption, are holding the country back from these coveted closer economic and social ties with the west. I felt that a portion of my work in the Peace Corps, through educational reform and working with the future leaders of Ukraine, was to push the country closer and closer to becoming the open and democratic state that many of its citizens dream about. That was basically the Peace Corps' entire mission, whether it was through country wide pedagogical workshops, the entire Youth Development Sector, the HIV awareness work, the refugee assistance - all of it was one way or another trying to get Ukraine closer and closer to adopting western and democratic values, and subsequently EU membership!

However, after a year and a half of working to forward these values, in a twisted way I was now over the moon that Ukraine wasn't in the European Union. The same problems holding Ukraine back were the reason I could return, just a few months after the world shut down.

Thank god for rampant corruption in Ukraine? At that point I was taking any victory that I could get, and right then and there I got my first real victory since getting evacuated.

For the first time in a long time, I was genuinely excited about something. While I still planned on returning with the Peace Corps, the math was simple: Go to Ukraine for three months, the longest amount of time an American can travel there without a visa, and then wait and see what happens with the Peace Corps. If they return on September 30th, like Jody Olsen's email said, I'll just return right back after visiting. If the return gets delayed again, then I'll be happy as hell I got three months with Alina after leaving her in such a hectic and somber fashion. Additionally, with the piles of government money, deflated travel fares and low cost of living in Ukraine, it would be far from financially burdensome.

I quickly made up my mind and ran down to my mom's room.

"Mom," I practically shouted, "I'm going back to Ukraine!"

"What? How?"

"The borders are open. I'm going back to Ukraine!"

"Well," she said after a sigh, "Let's find you a flight."

I couldn't wait to tell Alina the news. It would have to wait until the next day, because she was eight hours ahead of me and already fast asleep. All I could do was wait, but this time, waiting felt much sweeter.

While laying in my bed at the start of the fourth month of quarantine, about fifteen pounds heavier, a whole lot worse at Ukrainian, and with no serious professional prospects, I felt a sense of levity and hope for the first time since getting the email about reinstatement on my last night with Alina in Mukachevo.

But this time it wasn't due to some sort of future promise for a date to be known later. This was finally something tangible.

Finally, some certainty. Some direction. Some hope. That's what I had been missing all this time, and after one piece of news, it all came roaring back.

Chapter Twenty

Crawling Back

It is March 13, 2021. Three hundred and sixty-four days ago I got the evacuation email. Almost a year later I am back in Ukraine indefinitely. What a ride it has been.

I hardly knew it at the time (although with more life experience maybe I would have been able to), but due to evacuation I was faced with a choice: Stick with my love interest or my meticulously planned out career path. The Peace Corps still hasn't returned, and there's still no official date for when it'll come back. It's also looking like PC will be structured completely differently, and most sites will have to be stationed close to Kyiv, meaning I'd have no chance of getting placed back in Zakarpattia. With this realization, I either had to return to Alina without the Peace Corps and give up my dream of working in international relations, or break up and move on.

Life rarely hands you such a dichotomy, and although I couldn't see it through all the panic and wreckage, that was the simple choice that I had to face. I chose Alina.

It was hard forgoing the plethora of entry level federal jobs that would have provided me stability and purpose (not to mention an enticing 401k and pension plan), but whenever I began to strongly consider going down that path, the thought of breaking up always put those ideas at a full stop.

Even with that said I often second guessed myself, wondering if returning to my six month long relationship in a second world country instead of walking into a comfy and intellectually stimulating government job would be the biggest mistake I ever made. I saw my beautiful PC friends start working in the Foreign Service, the Korean Embassy, the Social Security Administration, Eurasian think tanks in DC, and USAID, just to name a few. It was hard to see these updates across my various social media feeds and not feel insecure about my hollow LinkedIn profile. I spent a lot of nights in my room, thinking about how unemployable I'd be if things didn't work out with Alina and I had to eventually move back to the States.

However, whenever those thoughts came up, I remembered how Alina calmed me down when I was in the airport hotel room, after learning that no plane was coming and thinking I was going to die. I remembered when she came to Mukachevo with no notice and helped me pack and clean up my apartment while I was having a nervous breakdown, all while staying strong during the worst nights of my life. I remembered how she was the only bright part of my day during those early days of lockdown and helped me get through the emotions and traumatic flashbacks of evacuation.

In the end, simply going back and ruminating on those moments made the decision an easy one. Those memories helped my insecure twenty-four year old brain make it past the toxic "I'm ruining my life" thoughts, all of which boiled down to caring way too much about how others thought of me. In a sense I wanted to take back control of my life and to not let Covid destroy the greatest thing and greatest person that ever happened to me. This decision saved me from being broken, and if that meant I wouldn't get to travel the world helping refugees and stateless people with a name brand international aid agency on my LinkedIn profile, so be it.

When the pandemic hit, all of the carefully constructed plans I had spent years developing were ripped up in a matter of days. In a young and impressionable mind, such a major event has an incredible impact, even on someone who had already made the post-college step into adulthood. Compared to my pre-Covid mindset, I no longer think of how decisions will impact my financial and personal stability thirty years down the road. If I did, right now I would be working for the first federal job that gave me an offer. Instead, with a new frame of mind I was able to fight against all of my doubts and insecurities and make a move I would never have considered before March 2020.

So now, I am back. I crawled and climbed and flew back.

I am currently living in Ukraine without the safety net of the Peace Corps. I've returned albeit unfortunately without the companionship of other volunteers, aka the only people who can relate to exactly what I'm going through. However in a post-Covid world, you have to count your blessings. I'm just exactly where I should be, and at this point in time that's all I can ask for.

I live in Uzhhorod with Alina. The first time I saw her after coming back in July of 2020 was in the same place I left her - at the train station. The only difference was that I was now crying from happiness, and that she was now wearing a black mask, although it could barely hide the smile underneath. We worked with some lawyers during the summer to assist with the visa process, and now after a long list of documentation and hoops to jump through, we are finally living together, a full year after we had initially planned.

Ironically enough, I couldn't have made this move confidently without online English teaching. After initially viewing it before Covid as a way to make a little extra cash for some late night adventures, it has snowballed into my current career. Over the past year I've gone from only teaching a few hours a day on Cambly to having numerous private students who I work with on a weekly-basis. When I joined the Peace Corps, teaching English was barely even an afterthought, as I was mostly excited to be a part of a respected brand in international relations. Now almost three years later, the Peace Corps is in the rearview mirror, and teaching is not only my full time job, but is also the only thing that enabled me to move to the opposite side of the world and fulfill my dreams. The irony is not lost on me.

Alina and I work at home during the day, and like most other parts of the world we are still under quarantine. I'm using Ukrainian everyday, I still get to see those mountains when we go on walks together, and most importantly I still get to be with the most important person in my life. We are finally together, which is something I doubted I could say a year ago at this time.

So, it's official. I've returned. After numerous train rides, plane rides, two-week quarantines and a few too many Covid scares, I am back where I'm supposed to be. It's not the same, and it'll never be the same, but I'm just grateful that after a year I was able to somewhat build back my life again. It's a process that we've all been going through during this tragedy, just in a variety of different ways, and I hope that whenever this pandemic finally simmers down we'll all have been able to rebuild our lives to a point to where we no longer long for the past and what was, but instead are comfortable enough with what is, and can finally lead happy and fulfilling lives again. That's been my goal, at least. And I think I'm already there.

Made in the USA
Las Vegas, NV
15 March 2022

45699797R00144